Beyond Bad Apples

Beyond Bad Apples

Teacher Education for Police-Free Schools

HANNAH CARSON BAGGETT

HARVARD EDUCATION PRESS
CAMBRIDGE, MASSACHUSETTS

Paperback ISBN 9798895570395

Library of Congress Cataloging-in-Publication Data

Names: Baggett, Hannah Carson, author.
Title: Beyond bad apples : teacher education for police-free schools / Hannah Carson Baggett.
Description: Cambridge, Massachusetts : Harvard Education Press, [2026] | Includes bibliographical references and index. | Summary: "In Beyond Bad Apples, Hannah Carson Baggett provides pre-service educators with an abolitionist introduction to SROs, pushing them to move beyond classifying School Resource Offices (SROs) as individual actors--some of whom may be "good" and promote public safety, while others may be "bad apples" or "villains" who abuse their power--and instead draw their attention to the systemic issues and policies that have put police in schools in the first place, and consider how they can best advocate for students who may come into contact with SROs"--Provided by publisher.
Identifiers: LCCN 2025030204 | ISBN 9798895570395 (paperback)
Subjects: LCSH: School police--United States. | Law enforcement--United States--History. | School discipline--United States. | Police brutality--United States. | Police abolition movement--United States. | Teachers--Training of--United States.
Classification: LCC LB2866 .B34 2026
LC record available at https://lccn.loc.gov/2025030204

Published by Harvard Education Press,
an imprint of the Harvard Education Publishing Group

Harvard Education Press
8 Story Street
Cambridge, MA 02138

Cover Design: Dave Kessler Design

The typefaces in this book are Adobe Garamond Pro and Myriad Pro.

Contents

Foreword

We Must Be in "Right Relation" with Each Other in Order to Be Safe: Abolition and the Practice of Doing Things Differently

We live in a moment where many of us find ourselves tired and exhausted. Genocidal extermination campaigns in Palestine, Sudan, and Congo, and the ongoing conflict in Haiti dominate the headlines and send many of us into a tailspin of worry and despair. Domestically, it becomes difficult to imagine what might happen when a narcissistic, tyrannical sexual predator wins a presidential election without a plan beyond his own hatred for any entity that opposes him. I can say for sure that I have found myself in moments where everything feels like it's on fire while the mess continues to grow. Unfortunately, it's felt that way for quite some time.

Even though the moment feels troubling, there is something inside that reminds me of the necessity of working to change our conditions. The weight of the world makes things seem daunting and unattainable, but an alternative perspective challenges me to revisit my despair. Here in the United States, I often find myself murmuring out loud, "What did I expect from a land founded on white supremacy, enslavement, genocide, wrongful land appropriation, and settler colonialism?" From this myriad of reasons, this statement, while still troubling, brings a calming energy. As much as it is recognition, the sentiment also operates as a directive, pushing me to remain a student of history. Although we've been here before, each time of tumult feels a bit different. Each moment sits on your skin differently. Despite the discomfort, I am thankful for a community that recognizes similar feelings, while pushing each other to continue to work. Like the ancestor comrades who worked before me to abolish enslavement, it is a recognition that the current moment is unacceptable. Herein lie the premise of abolition: if we find the current carceral state as unacceptable, then we must work with others to change our conditions, eventually replacing the things that are unacceptable. Police, as power's mechanism of coercion and containment, rationalize the absurdity agreed by the rulers to be acceptable.

Some might read these first two paragraphs and say out loud to themselves "What does this have to do with education?" My answer is "Everything." "Schooling," as the system of rewards and compliance for regurgitating the rules of white supremacy, has been challenged in perpetuity. If we live in a nation-state that has become so protectionist of itself that it is willing to ban critique and recognition of factual evidence, then my earlier point is affirmed: the vestiges of white supremacy, enslavement, genocide, wrongful land appropriation, and settler colonialism remain intact. As communities push for education (the process of supporting and creating questions aimed at changing our condition while working with others), an embrace of abolition becomes inevitable.

In the same vein, "progress" is relative to the extent that people can work to improve the conditions of the marginalized—not the people who would be fine if nothing changed, but the people who have been perpetually contained and isolated by the carceral state. If we shift our focus to start our work with this group of people, the opportunity increases to develop new perspectives and approaches rooted in humanization and critical consciousness. It would reverse prioritizing the "expertise" of those with fancy degrees and would center the fact that the people who bear the brunt of the current moment are often the ones who are closest to the solutions that we need. It would be a project rooted in being in right relation with ourselves and the people we are in community with.

It's important for me to be clear here: I do not use the term "right relation" to signify more wrongfully appropriated language from the Indigenous people of Turtle Island (i.e., the upper Western Hemisphere). Instead, I understand it as a set of instructions that require us to reconceptualize safety as the process of recognizing who we are in relationship with when our communities are faced with adversity. You are in right relation with the people you know and are responsible to. If this is happening inside a school, the premise of any interaction in the building is based on the relationship that you are engaged in. It is never with one person. Instead, every individual is connected to someone that you are "in relationship" with. It stands in contrast to what we often see in many teacher education programs across the country that give us the empty rhetoric of needing to be in relationship with students and families. Even though very few people in colleges of education know how to do it—let alone can teach how to do it—preservice and practicing teachers across the country are left to figure it out on their own. This is particularly disturbing when it is one of the toughest times to be a K–20 educator in the last eighty years.

I write this from Chicago, the place of my birth and a deeply contested city. Against the narrative of crime and despondent youth, a collective of young people permanently removed police from K–12 public schools. This group of young people got tired of the rhetoric that they didn't care, and they began the process of asking their peers if police made them feel safe in school. When they organized themselves and began to survey their peers, one of the resounding responses was that police did not make them feel safe. On the contrary, they said that police made them feel more threatened and fearful. Instead of police, the youth stated that they wanted counselors, psychologists, academic support, and after-school programming in place of police. As they pushed back against city council members, the Chicago Police Department, and other groups of adults, a group of supporters emerged, backing the young people's declaration that cops did not make them feel safe. When it came to a vote by the Board of Education, the mayor's office thought that they could create a work-around by allowing individual schools to decide whether they would keep police. The plan backfired completely, with the majority of Chicago Public Schools voting to remove police from their buildings.

In closing, I am impressed with Hannah Baggett's efforts to engage in the abolitionist project of taking a principled stance on the end of police in schools. Because abolition is a constructive project born from the will to live differently, I am in solidarity with her efforts as we move forward in an uncertain world.

David Stovall, PhD
Professor of Black Studies and Criminology, Law, and Justice
University of Illinois, Chicago
January 3, 2025

INTRODUCTION

Are there "bad apple" officers in schools? Of course . . . and they should absolutely be held accountable.

—Abby, preservice teacher in secondary education

This perspective, shared by a preservice teacher whose family members are in law enforcement, reflects a mainstream narrative about school police, as well as a broader narrative about policing. It affirms the inherent "goodness" of policing, but it also leaves room for the possibility that there are individual police officers who are responsible for harm and wrongdoing. Abby's perspective takes policing for granted, emphasizing that it is just another profession that may, from time to time, need occasional tweaking and reform to make sure that it functions properly and any individuals in its ranks who engage in wrongdoing are held accountable. I used to think this way, too. Growing up as a white girl in North and South Carolina in the 1980s and 1990s, I did not see police stationed at school, except for Drug Abuse Resistance Education (D.A.R.E.) officers who came to warn us of the dangers of drugs and alcohol. But I had friends who were skateboarders, and we often posted up in mall parking lots to skate and hang out. Police, almost always white men back then, often showed up at these spaces. They harassed and sometimes joked with the teenagers skating, but often eyed us young girls as if they were imagining what we might look like in a few years' time. I was not at all confident that if something bad were happening to me, I could call the police to come to my aid. But I also still assumed that police were necessary, and the officers who used to harass my friends and me were simply "bad apples" who felt like they could get away with hassling teenagers who were just hanging out.

Years later, in the 2000s, when I was a high school teacher in a predominantly Black and Latinx high school in North Carolina, I was around police all the time. A School Resource Officer (SRO) was regularly stationed at the end of my hallway next to my classroom before and after school and during class changes. I watched him yell incessantly at kids: "Pull up your pants!" "Take off your hat!" "Go to class!" These commands reflected the tremendous power that school police held over students. At the school where I taught, police in the hallways made many students uneasy at best and antagonized them at worst. They often escalated issues like verbal arguments among teenagers to the point of pepper-spraying hallways full of students and even handcuffing a few, to be dealt with in the front office and perhaps even at the police station. And this was happening in high schools across the country. Research shows that in the 2000s, when I began teaching high school, the number of police was ballooning—there were around 20,000 officers in schools in 2003.[1] And, like at the school where I taught, police in schools across the country were treating students as potential criminals, as they continue to do today.[2]

One morning, as I was greeting students at the door of my classroom, the SRO posted on the hall told me the skirt I was wearing made my "legs look good."[3] I flashed back to my days as a teenager. I was no longer that young girl in the mall parking lot. I had already begun to realize that the officers at the school where I was teaching were not supporting the students, by virtue of how they instigated conflict with students in the hallways. I had also reflected that, had my teenage skater friends and I years earlier been more readily marked as kids of Color, or perhaps more visibly queer or trans, or perceived as immigrant kids, the police would have likely treated us much differently in the mall parking lot and at school, perhaps arresting us . . . or worse. But now, I too had experienced explicit police harassment as an adult.

This experience crystallized for me that police in schools are sources of harm—not just for students, but for teachers as well. It helped me realize that the comforting claim that policing keeps us safe is a trap. It forced me to interrogate all the ways that I had been socialized to believe that officers are good actors in a system of policing designed to complement and uphold a healthy, well-functioning society. And it forced me to not only reckon with the ways that police were inflicting harm on the students who I was so invested in supporting, but also to learn about the stories of millions of Black, Brown, and Indigenous folks, queer and trans folks, immigrants, and folks with disabilities who have been sounding the alarm about police violence throughout the twentieth century. In short, this experience was a catalyst for my journey to police abolition.

It's been twenty years since I first started teaching in public schools. Teachers today face so many of the same pressures I faced as a new teacher—pressures around standardized testing; restricted, scripted curricula, and even banned books; and policies that dictate punishment for students. In the last six years, though, discourse and action around policing and abolition have entered the mainstream in ways that they had not before. The year 2020 brought not only disruption due to COVID-19, but an increased awareness of racial injustice and police violence. In the years since, students around the country have successfully organized to defund and remove police from their schools and classrooms, the result of decades of organizing in some communities.[4] These students, in addition to the adults who support them, have given us the imagination and tools to build a better way of doing school—without police and policing. Indeed, abolition is not just about "getting rid of"; it is a way of imagining how to build school communities that center relationships and care above all else. This book draws on, honors, and mobilizes their work, as well as the work of so many folks doing the work of abolition in communities across the country, to prepare and educate teachers to do school differently. Isn't it time for us to imagine a different way to be accountable to one another and with students, so we can be safe from the harm that comes with policing and punishment?

"BAD APPLES" THINKING ABOUT POLICE IN SCHOOLS

Police are a ubiquitous presence in many public schools across the United States, stationed outside school entrances, in hallways and cafeterias, and at after-school events like football games, track meets, and fundraisers.[5] Some are in plain clothes, while others are in full uniform, complete with guns, tasers, pepper spray, and handcuffs on their belts. And some even have police K-9s at their side—dogs trained to sniff out guns, bombs, and drugs. Police are also routinely in and out of classrooms, engaging in instruction with K–12 students. They read books to elementary school children, teach about police roles and responsibilities, engage in "bite" demonstrations with K-9s, and encourage students to become law enforcement officers when they grow up. They engage in programming with high school students, teaching about laws and the benefits of policing, simulating traffic stops, and instructing students how to comply with officers if they are pulled over while driving. And they run drug education programs, mentoring campaigns, and even extracurricular events like youth camps with cops.

School police, also known in some school communities as SROs or SSOs, have a long history in US public schools.[6] There is also a long and distinct history in this country of policing both teenagers and adults, especially Black and Brown people, queer and trans folks, immigrants, and women.[7] Police have also been at the center of some of the highest-profile events in public schools over the last two decades. For example, in South Carolina in 2015, a Black student named Shakara was using her cell phone in class. Her teacher told her to put it away, and when Shakara did not follow her directions, the teacher asked her to leave the classroom. When Shakara did not leave, the teacher called the assistant principal to the classroom. Eventually, school police were called to the classroom as well; the officer, a white man, escalated the situation, eventually throwing Shakara from her desk to the classroom floor. Her classmates recorded the incident, and it went viral online. The officer was ultimately fired, with media outlets and his supervisor painting him as a "bad apple."[8] The sheriff who fired him stated that the officer's treatment of the student made him want to "throw up."[9] At the same school, years later, an SRO sexually harassed and assaulted students for years with no repercussions. When the *Washington Post* published a national story about his behavior, he finally lost his job.[10] In a very different type of incident in Oxford, Michigan, in 2021, a school police officer confronted a fifteen-year-old who had just shot eleven people at his school, leading to the student's arrest. The officer was lauded for his bravery, reinforcing support for the policies and funding that put him on the "school beat" in the first place—ostensibly to protect students from shootings. The president of the National Association for School Resource Officers (NASRO) said at the time that "there's no doubt in my mind that that saves lives, and who knows how many lives it saved in Oxford."[11]

These portraits of individual school police as either heroes or villains support and mirror mainstream rhetoric about police: that policing is a public good, police keep us safe, and more police means more safety; when things go wrong, the "bad apples" are simply individual officers who didn't do their jobs or who have gone rogue. But what these narratives about "good" and "bad apple" officers obscure is the inherent violence and harm that come with the institution of policing, which we will learn about in the coming chapters, especially as it is practiced in schools with youth. In other words, focusing on the "bad apples" misses the orchard for the trees. This kind of individualized thinking is a trap that diverts our attention from the routine, everyday harm that police presence inflicts on the psyches, hearts, and bodies of young people who show up to public schools each day. It's also the trap I fell into for many years, including during some of my time as a public school teacher. As a teacher, I realized I was an active participant in a carceral system with a long and complicated history. Navigating out of this carceral trap required me to enact a shift away from this individualized "bad apples" perspective and toward a more collective, critical analysis of policing—and ultimately toward imagining police-free schools.

Yet individualized, "bad apples" thinking is deeply rooted, and it shows up even in the context of some of the most horrific school tragedies. For example, after the 2022 school shooting in Uvalde, Texas, the school district police chief there was heavily criticized and even indicted for his failure to issue directives that many believe could have prevented the deaths of children at Robb Elementary.[12] Other officers in Uvalde were also charged, with one parent noting, "They are going to finally bring someone to justice. We feel there should be more facing charges."[13] The anger and pain of communities who experience the tragedies of school shootings cannot be overstated. But this parent's statement reinforces the "bad apples" theory of policing, in that it presumes that holding individual officers to account can deliver justice for those harmed. A focus on the actions of a few officers also implies that different, or maybe even more, police on the scene would have prevented the shooting, a common misperception that does not bear out in research. And demanding justice in the form of "charges" and punishment for individual officers is rooted in the same carceral logics that justify police in schools in the first place, which we will learn about in later chapters.

School shootings are often thought of as the big driver of the placement of police in schools. As the executive director of NASRO stated in early 2024, "It's not the way I want to gain business, but some of the busiest years we've had training-wise are 18 months after a school massacre. I can tell you that 2019 was the biggest year in our association's history by far—and that's coming right off the Marjory Stoneman Douglas massacre."[14] Yet police have been in schools for much longer than we might think, which we will learn more about in chapter 1. For example, police presence in US public schools first appeared in the 1910s and 1920s and continued into the 1950s and 1960s as a response to perceptions about rising "juvenile delinquency" and to quell student activism during school desegregation.[15] Police in schools increased with the onset of the War on Drugs in the 1980s and ballooned with the implementation of zero-tolerance policies about drugs, weapons, and fighting in the 1990s and 2000s.[16]

Today, police are present in schools via multiple contexts and pathways. Some school districts contract with local police departments and sheriff's offices to employ SROs, where regular police officers undergo some training to work in schools in both legal and educational ways.[17] In other places, schools might employ school "security" officers, who may be off-duty or retired police, or even employees of a private security company.[18] And in still other places, school districts may have their own forces, with more traditional policing organizational structures and hierarchies located on school grounds, like the school system where Robb Elementary is situated in Uvalde, Texas.[19] While these efforts are conducted in the name of student safety, this vast network of policing across school districts is part of a carceral system of surveillance, punishment, and removal of students from schools—and learning opportunities—as we will learn throughout this book. Simultaneously, community coalitions comprised of students, parents, and teachers recognize the harmful effects of policing in schools and are working to resist the placement and expansion of school policing, even succeeding in the removal of school police in some school systems.[20] Put bluntly, not all community members want cops in their schools. Students and community members all over the country, like those in Oakland, Chicago, Atlanta, and smaller, more rural communities around the United States, have been fighting for decades to reimagine schools without police, providing blueprints for systemic and local change.[21] Their work signifies a radical break from the tradition of policing.

GUIDING FRAMEWORKS: ABOLITION, CARCERALITY, AND POLICE-FREE SCHOOLS

These community coalitions, premised on resistance to school police, are often rooted in a broader *abolitionist* movement, which also has its own long and distinct history. *Abolition* is often associated with the period of enslavement in the United States. Abolitionists then fought to end slavery and slave labor, arguing that the economic system built on exploiting labor by racialized Others, including Black Africans, Indigenous people, and even Chinese workers during Reconstruction, was inhumane and cruel. Today, there are abolitionist movements around ending imprisonment and incarceration, the death penalty, and policing as we know them. Abolitionist perspectives guiding the "police-free schools" movement push us to interrogate the harms that come with policing and to commit to working toward school communities that do not rely on policing. Police abolitionists argue that, regardless of their titles and responsibilities, school police do not keep students safe from school shootings, violence, or harm. Instead, the police themselves are actually the cause of harm, as in Shakara's case. And in the case of Tauris Sledge, who was slammed into gym bleachers when an SRO at his Tennessee school grabbed him by the hair and backpack.[22] And in the case of Omauri Stephens, who school police body-slammed in a hallway after he attempted to check on a friend who had been involved in a fight earlier at his Georgia high school.[23] And in the case of the many students across the country who experience harassment, surveillance, arrests, and assaults at the hands of school police every day.

As abolitionists Mariame Kaba and Andrea Ritchie note, "Billions have been spent to police schools instead of supporting students, and there has been a dramatic increase in school-based police violence—including sexual violence—and youth criminalization through student arrests, suspensions, and expulsions."[24] In fact, in 2023, districts across the country spent a combined $2.6 billion on SROs and $12 billion on school security guards—indeed, schools spent more on security guards than on any other role except teachers.[25] At the end of the 2019–2020 school year, there were approximately 23,400 sworn SROs in schools, 69 percent of who said they had responded to an incident in a classroom within the past thirty days.[26] It's no surprise that rates of suspension have increased in recent decades, rising from 1.7 million in 1974 to 3.1 million in 2000.[27] After the COVID-19 pivot, suspension rates continued to rise in some places—by as much as 27 percent in New York City Public Schools, for example.[28] Some studies have found evidence that SROs increase the use of exclusionary discipline and removal of students from school compared to schools without them.[29] Citing numbers about school suspensions and expulsions in their communities, organizers like those in the Black Organizing Project have worked to educate school communities about the harmful effects of police in schools, asking teachers to pledge *not* to call police, Immigrations and Customs Enforcement (ICE), or the US Department of Homeland Security on children in their care.[30] And, to raise awareness about the physical violence that comes with school police, abolitionist organizations like the Advancement Project have even begun tracking police assaults on students in public schools, as with its #AssaultAt map.[31] They found that school police "disproportionately assault" Black students; since 2011, more than 80 percent of students assaulted by school police have been Black.[32] These are just a few examples of how communities are gathering data and working toward police-free schools around the United States.

POLICING IN A CARCERAL SOCIETY

Abolitionist perspectives teach us that policing operates as part of a *carceral society*, meaning that here in the United States, we choose to invest in criminalization, punishment, and incarceration instead of support, repair, and transformation. The United States accounts for only 5 percent of the world's population but 20 percent of its incarcerated population; put another way, we imprison more people than any country in the world.[33] We invest in incarceration even more than public education, with scholars noting that "since the mid-80s, jail and prison spending increased at three times the rate of elementary and secondary education."[34] Policing is connected to incarceration because it produces criminals. In other words, who and what police choose to focus on, and what they determine to be "criminal" behavior, lead to arrests, charges, and in some cases sentences for punishment in jails and prisons (incarceration). We justify policing, punishment, and ultimately incarceration by drawing on ideas about legality, criminality, and "good" and "bad" people. This false binary of good and evil is deeply rooted; it is part of how we are often socialized or raised to think about police, people, and behaviors, and it is difficult to unlearn. For example, we are socialized to believe that the presence of police in schools (a good) helps keep out school shooters and other folks who might do kids harm (an evil). But police themselves often engage in harmful, sometimes criminal behavior with kids. And, importantly, ideas about what and who constitute a "bad" person or a "criminal," both in school and out, have long been structured around raced, classed, gendered, sexualized, and abled identities. For example, early systems of policing, both in the Northeast and the South, were predicated on ideas about a criminal or delinquent underclass consisting of poor white folks, enslaved and free Black folks, and new immigrants—a class who, it was thought, needed to be surveilled and controlled.[35] In other words, policing was part of how the very fabric of US society came to be.

Abolitionists interrogate the presumption of criminality as we ascribe it to particular behaviors (and people), and thus as deserving of control by police.

Instead, abolitionists acknowledge that criminalization, policing, and prisons are part of a system that pits us against one another in competition for resources that are intentionally made scarce.[36] Due to this scarcity, we become hyperfocused on property and space and become suspicious of one another in the name of "security."[37] Informal and formal legal doctrines criminalize homelessness, trespassing, vagrancy, and theft, even of simple goods that some families need for basic survival, like baby formula.[38] In this worldview, the police play an integral role, representing a "thin blue line" that supposedly protects "good" people from "bad" people, and the thinking goes, that prevents society (including schools) from descending into lawlessness and chaos.[39] Police round up supposed "criminals," and those criminals then may be punished via incarceration. This "thin blue line," however—as we have seen throughout history, and as many abolitionists have argued—is much more about protecting the interests and property of those in power than it is about keeping us safe.

Policing and prisons are also a profitable industry, part of what some scholars have called the "Prison Industrial Complex (PIC)." As Critical Resistance, an organization devoted to prison and police abolition, explains, the PIC describes the "overlapping interests of government and industry that use surveillance, policing, and imprisonment as solutions to economic, social and political problems."[40] According to scholar and abolitionist Erica Meiners, the PIC is "the multifaceted structure in the United States that encompasses the expanding economic and political contexts of the corrections industry: the political and lobbying power of the corrections officers union; the framing of prisons and jails as growth industry in the context of deindustrialization; the production, marketing, and sales of technology and security required to maintain and expand the state of incarceration," which include police and police in schools.[41] The PIC is deeply embedded into our world, from schools to the ways that we think about each other—as "good," "bad," "innocent," and "criminal"—and policing plays a major role in how these ideas and stereotypes are upheld in our minds and communities.

Policing, including policing in schools, also comprises a billion-dollar industry.[42] For example, over the last seven years, my home state of North Carolina has dedicated approximately $100 million to school police.[43] In Alabama, the state where I live and teach now, there are robust police programs in many school districts, including police-youth outreach and sophisticated social media campaigns to document these efforts.[44] Meanwhile, in Alabama and across the country, police generate millions of dollars in fines and fees off school community members under the pretext of traffic violations or stop-and-frisk policies, sometimes to the tune of half of municipal budgets.[45] And truancy officers, often working in close concert with police, refer parents and guardians to "truancy court," where they may be fined thousands of dollars when their children are absent from school. This "truancy trap" is just one example of how school systems and criminal justice systems are not just linked but are part and parcel of our carceral society.[46]

In this carceral society, policing continues to be presented as a solution to many issues that could be addressed in other ways. For example, instead of increased regulations on adult drivers in the 1920s and 1930s, we deputized children to police their peers and escort them safely across the street.[47] In the 1950s and 1960s, we sent police into schools to arrest Black students and community members who were advocating for change instead of expanding resources to those who had previously been denied educational services.[48] More recently, rather than expand community mental health and social work programs in schools in the midst of stressors such as COVID-19 and increasing family poverty, we relied on school police in moments of crisis, often with disastrous consequences.[49] And even more recently, rather than further regulating the sale of vapes, we have imbued police with the power to crack down on teen vaping, even investing in new tech surveillance in schools to detect vapes, and going so far as to take teens to "vape court" when they are caught at school.[50] Outside of schools, instead of increasing funding for community recreation centers and local libraries in rural and poor urban areas, we increasingly rely on police to provide services like athletic leagues, mentoring programs, and summer camps for youth. In 2019, for example, spending on police was $123 billion nationwide, while library spending was $13.3 billion.[51] This investment, both financially and socially, means that police are so pervasive in so many communities that they seem like an inevitable part of our everyday lives, especially for youth.

Police in schools operate as part of wider systems of surveillance and security, including metal detectors, drug-sniffing dogs, and closely monitored cameras. Many community members in public education, whether policymakers, teachers, students learning to become teachers, or parents, take for granted the presence of these police and security measures. Again, police, we've been led to believe, keep us safe. But research tells us that school-based policing actually has not reduced school crime and violence.[52] Instead, schools with police routinely report more students to law enforcement, and school police now often handle student behavior that would once have been addressed by teachers and administrators. This policing contributes to the criminalization of student behavior, all while purporting to uphold "law and order" and keep students safe.[53]

Police surveil, criminalize, and arrest Black and Brown students, students in poverty, students with disabilities, queer and trans students, immigrant students, and students who embody multiple identities across these groups.[54] For example, data from the Office for Civil Rights (OCR) from the 2015–2016 and 2017–2018 school years indicate that "Native Hawaiian/Pacific Islander, Black, and American Indian/Alaska Native students were arrested at rates that were two to three times higher than White students"; when these identities overlapped with disability status, arrest rates at school were even higher.[55] When police arrest students for things that happen at school, they contribute to student "pushout" and removal from schools that affect student trajectories to adulthood.[56] Police arrests at school perpetuate a legacy of targeting and marginalizing these specific groups of students in public schools, formalizing disenfranchisement across generations. To be clear, these data patterns do not mean that arrests should be more balanced across populations; the solution is not to mete out punishment or to arrest groups of students more equally. Instead, these data patterns are a call to action that we should move toward police-free schools. These patterns tell us, just as the voices of youth organizers and teacher activists across the country do, that police do not create a safe learning environment in which all children thrive. Police instead normalize the surveillance, suspicion, and unequal treatment of others, reinstantiating this legacy of harm.

ABOLITION

This book is written from an *abolitionist* perspective. Contemporary abolitionists acknowledge that police do not keep everyone safe, instead underscoring that they are the root of harm, danger, and violence in many communities, including schools. Abolitionist scholars and organizers situate policing as part of a surveillance and carceral state that criminalizes, punishes, and incarcerates those deemed "dangerous," "threatening," and/or pushed to economic margins.[57] As previously mentioned, these labels—about who is dangerous and who poses a threat—are bound up with stereotypes about race, class, gender, sexuality, ability, immigrant status, and other identity dimensions. Abolition, as a framework for understanding and a tool for organizing, pushes us to imagine and work toward a world without policing and without prisons. According to education lawyer and former middle school teacher Derecka Purnell, abolition is "a bigger idea than firing cops and closing prisons; it includes eliminating the reasons people think they need cops and prisons in the first place."[58] That means *unlearning* some of what we've been taught about "good" and "bad" people, behaviors that have been deemed "criminal" and "illegal," and how we use punishment as a means to try to hold people accountable for their actions. And sometimes, people do not commit any actions at all. Police harass and assault people simply on the basis of being, producing criminality in the process. Abolitionist perspectives also teach us that we must also abolish the "cop inside our heads," who pushes us to regard one another with suspicion and positions surveillance and policing as the solutions to keeping us safe—both inside and outside public school classrooms.[59]

This unlearning also must happen regarding how we view and treat students and the behaviors that we expect from them in K–12 classrooms and schools. In my previous book, we documented the school discipline landscape in Alabama, the state where we live and teach. We pushed readers to unlearn their taken-for-granted assumptions about students by arguing that many of the behaviors that educators interpret as "defiance," "disobedience," or "disorderly conduct" might actually be students' resistance to culturally irrelevant curricula, oppressive learning conditions, and teachers who have not worked to build relationships with them. We explained how educators' interpretations of student behavior are laden with racialized stereotypes—ideas that equate Blackness with criminality and whiteness with innocence—in addition to stereotypes about gender, sexuality, socioeconomic status, and ability. These processes, which we referred to as the "grammar" of school discipline, mean that educators and administrators suspend, expel, and refer to law enforcement Black and Brown students, queer and trans students, students with disabilities, and poor students at higher rates in schools not just in Alabama, but across the country. Decades of research have documented what many in educational and legal contexts have called the "school-to-prison pipeline."[60]

But many scholars have argued that the "pipeline" metaphor—where students are "piped" from school to jail—does not adequately explain how schools are already prisonlike environments for kids. The pipeline metaphor acknowledges how certain practices might more readily move students from schools to prison, but it glosses over the ways that both the physical school environment and our ideas about disciplining students are already carceral. Scholars and activists like Erica Meiners and David Stovall have instead pointed out that schools and prisons operate more as a "nexus."[61] This school-prison nexus, according to Meiners, "captures the historic, systemic, and multifaceted nature of the intersections of education and incarceration."[62] For example, the physical setup/layout of many schools may be stark, with blank, concrete walls, just like in prisons. Hallways might also have extensive surveillance and camera systems, monitored by either school personnel or school police. In classrooms, windows might be set high or covered so that people cannot see in or out. Metal detectors might greet students at the front of the school. And, of course, police or security guards might be stationed throughout the school or at the front of the school to search students and/or check in visitors.

Other aspects of schooling beyond the physical space resemble prison, like the carceral ways that we approach discipline. Teachers might have extensive sets of rules predicated on control and order, sometimes at the expense of learning. Those routines and rules are often derived from particular sets of norms—namely, those rooted in white, middle class, cishetero communities.[63] And, we favor punishing students in an attempt to hold them accountable, just as prisons do, instead of offering support and possibilities for transformation. We remove students from their classrooms, teachers, and peers to other sometimes solitary spaces, more commonly called "in school suspension (ISS)." Or we further remove students from the general population of the school, sending them home for "out of school suspension (OSS)," or even to other schools known as "alternative schools." We also sometimes refer students who engage in so-called misbehavior to school police, which can result in formal charges and/or court appearances for students and their families, or even incarceration. These practices undermine the very ethos of what teaching and learning should be; they fundamentally betray principles of relationships, care, and safety.

ABOLITION AND TEACHER EDUCATION

What we also know about disciplinary incidents in schools is that teachers are often the first point of contact; sometimes it is even the teacher who calls school police to the classroom in response to some perceived student misbehavior or wrongdoing.[64] That means that students are not just getting in trouble for things that happen in the hallways and bathrooms, like fights or vaping, but that their teachers are calling police to their classrooms about sometimes vague, subjective reasons like "defiance of authority," "disobedience," and even for situations involving cell phones, like Shakara in South Carolina. Yet, even as we prompt future teachers to reflect on their own experiences as learners in schools as they focus on content area standards, technology standards, early childhood and adolescent development and learning, or classroom management, we seldom prompt them to think about the roles of discipline, surveillance, and policing in the day-to-day routine of schooling. Rarely do future teachers experience sustained instruction about the history, role, and consequences of police in schools, or clarification about the relationships between and among teachers, administrators, police, and school discipline policies and practices. This is despite persistent rhetoric in the public sphere about how the presence of school police contributes to the school-to-prison pipeline and high-profile news stories about school police violence toward students. Put simply, we do not often teach future teachers about what might happen when they call the police on kids, or ask them to envision what they might do instead.

Many students who are learning to become teachers in the United States have also experienced school shootings, lockdowns and active shooter drills, and the constant presence of police in their schools, perhaps even reinforcing beliefs about the necessity of police. Yet they also may have witnessed or even participated in discourse and activism about the possibility of #policefreeschools—abolitionist imaginings heightened in the wake of the police murders of George Floyd, Breonna Taylor, and so many other Black lives and the protests and activism of summer 2020. But again, most teacher preparation programs have not substantively integrated curricular and instructional activities about school police, nor have they introduced abolitionist perspectives that push us to reframe how we think about accountability and safety.[65] Moreover, decades of research tell us that teachers tend to teach how we were taught, also known as the "apprenticeship of observation."[66] Thus, future teachers who themselves may not have had negative interactions with police at schools may be likely to rely on them without questioning the effects or consequences for their students.

Given the heightened scrutiny that both teachers and school police face in our current sociopolitical context, preparing teachers to work in schools where police are stationed, and to disrupt the work of school police, is an urgent need. Preparing teachers to disrupt policing in the school-prison nexus *is* the work of teacher education. Teacher education spaces can serve as contexts in which educators and school communities can work toward abolition and to push against ideas about the necessity of police and policing, including the ways that we are trained to police students in our classrooms. This means explicitly acknowledging the repercussions of policing in schools, including its past and present as a violent institution. It also means prompting educators to think differently about student discipline—moving away from deficit thinking about students and families and toward reflection about student behavior in classrooms, emphasizing repair and transformation when harm occurs. We must create professional development for both preservice and practicing teachers who are skeptical of or even uncomfortable with police in schools, giving them space to do the necessary unlearning around policing and teaching them how to advocate for students who are in contact with school police. We must even teach about the possibility of police-free schools—an abolitionist project that redefines how we think about safety and accountability—and how students and communities around the country have organized to reimagine them.

Abolitionist perspectives further push educators to unlearn ideas that situate students and families as problems in need of correction and to instead be accountable for the harm that punishment causes to those students and families. Therefore, the work of abolition is also self-work. It urges us to think more critically about our own views, comforts and discomforts, attitudes, and relationships with those in our communities. It prompts us to interrogate how carceral logics creep into our daily practices despite our best intentions. It forces us to come to terms with how we, as educators, are preparing and shaping the lives of generations of students, and how we position ourselves as members of communities in and out of school. And, as abolitionist artist Olly Costello reminds us, "We are having to unlearn generations of teachings that taught us how to dehumanize and encouraged us to prioritize punishments."[67] Therefore, this unlearning does not happen all at once, nor do we ever totally arrive at an end point. Instead, this unlearning is an ongoing, lifelong process as we build community and relationships with one another to affect change in our local contexts.

And that's just what the folks who have been fighting for police-free schools for decades have been doing: students, teachers, and community members have been building relationships with one another, educating, and ultimately making demands to power structures about the possibilities of safe schools without police and policing infrastructures.

WHO AM I?

I am writing this book from a particular standpoint. I am a career educator, and I've taught lots of different students: elementary school, high school, undergraduate students learning to become teachers, and graduate students seeking master's and doctoral degrees. I've also taught lots of different content areas: French, English as a second language, classes about theories that explain how injustice and inequity come to be, and classes that teach people how to conduct research in the hopes of transforming educational systems. Currently, I am an associate professor in a college of education at a large research university in Alabama. Many students in my classes are public school teachers and administrators.

In addition to my university teaching, I've taught high school classes at alternative schools in my community as part of my faculty outreach program. Working with students in alternative schools pushed my learning and unlearning in specific ways: issues I had once framed as related to "race, racism, and social justice" developed into a critical consciousness about issues of racial capitalism, policing, the PIC, and the school-prison nexus. The relationships I built with students and coworkers during and as a result of that work pushed me toward abolitionist frameworks and practices because the stories alternative students told were about experiences with carceral schooling: irrelevant curricula and instruction, surveillance and deficit thinking from teachers and administrators, and contact with police and justice systems. My journey to abolition, therefore, not only draws on my own experiences with police but is also student-centered, as is the police-free schools movement, guided by a strong ethical framework and rooted in relationships.

Working with alternative school students, in addition to my prior research about school discipline, has taught me that teachers play a critical role in disciplinary processes and in police-youth interactions in school; as previously mentioned, it is often the teacher who calls police to a classroom for some perceived student wrongdoing or violation of school rules. Yet the preservice and practicing teachers and administrators with who I work now report rarely, if ever experiencing any instruction or conversation about police in schools, including how to interact with police or to interrogate their presence. Instead, police presence is largely taken for granted and unchallenged: positioned as an overall, universal good, holding the line against criminal conduct, thwarting disruption, and keeping schools safe. Thus, this project reflects my desire to leverage teacher education spaces as sites for unlearning what we so often take for granted—about how the problem of "a few bad apples" among police is a fundamentally poor framing, about the harm that comes from relying on ideas about students as "troublemakers" and in need of punishment, and about how carceral classrooms undermine our goals to teach kids. In this way, teacher education spaces become places where we imagine the possibility of and work toward safe schools without police.

This book is therefore intended for teacher educators, future teachers, and even teachers already in the classroom. It is intended to function as a type of intervention: it provides a foundation for understanding how police came to be in public schools; it pushes readers to trouble the taken-for-grantedness of school police by learning from preservice teachers who have grappled with police in their own schools, past and present; and it prompts imagination about what police-free schools can look like. More specifically, this book aims to close gaps in both practice and scholarship by presenting what we already know about the work and the consequences of police in schools and by reporting on curricular interventions to prepare teachers to work in policed schools. Data include field notes from my work with preservice teachers at several large universities across the United States, written reflections from these preservice teachers as well as practicing teachers, informal and formal interviews with both preservice and practicing educators, and reflections on my experience teaching both public school students and teachers. Preservice teachers who are featured in the book attended teacher preparation programs at universities in the Midwest, Northeast, and South. They span a range of teaching interests, including different content areas and grade levels. The K–12 students' and teachers' voices that I have included also represent diverse subject interests and fields. From English classrooms to science labs, kindergarten teachers to high school social studies teachers, new preservice teachers to seasoned teacher educators, they are people who I have worked alongside over the years. My hope is that readers may see themselves reflected in the vignettes presented across the chapters, recognizing how they too might begin the process of unlearning.

OVERVIEW OF THE BOOK

So, what do police actually do in schools? Who do they really keep safe? At what cost? This book explores these questions both broadly and in the context of teacher education, where we might prompt those learning to become teachers to move beyond the characterization of individual police in schools as "good" or "bad apples" and instead focus on the systemic issues, policies, and politics that put and keep police in schools. This book also leads us beyond characterizing individual teachers and students as "good" or "bad," instead focusing on the ways that teacher education can operate as a space to unlearn our taken-for-granted assumptions about punishment, accountability, and safety as we disrupt status quo schooling. And it pushes us beyond thinking about people more broadly as "good" or "bad"—ideas that both prop up policing and keep us from imagining life without them.

Chapter 1 gives a more in-depth accounting of the history of school police, especially as we might think of it in the larger project of policing in the United States, as well as how power structures have criminalized student behavior like activism. In chapter 2, we learn about the state of things in schools now, including the harm that comes with policing, and efforts to resist. In chapter 3, we learn more about how we are socialized to equate policing with safety, as well as how that socialization shows up in preservice teachers' thinking about the roles and responsibilities of police in schools. Chapter 4 further creates dissonance around the taken-for-grantedness of policing in schools; we read about preservice teachers' reactions to numeric data that detail the troubling patterns in school discipline practices, including school-based practitioners referring students to police. This chapter also presents counterstories from preservice teachers who witnessed police violence in schools, or even experienced it themselves. Chapter 5, coauthored with a high school teacher, details how school-based practitioners like administrators and teachers engage in "soft policing" of students in classrooms; in this chapter, we learn how to move away from these disciplinary practices and toward abolitionist accountability. Chapter 6, coauthored with teacher educators, presents our reflections and stories from public school classrooms as we chronicle our journey to police abolition and teaching from abolitionist perspectives. Finally, chapter 7, coauthored with a youth justice scholar, teaches us how we might reimagine "safe" schools, drawing on the imaginations of preservice teachers to do so.

This reimagining is also featured throughout the book in the form of artwork. Between each chapter is a piece of art that honors the ideas and visions shared by preservice teachers when I asked them to describe what a "safe" school looks and feels like. Their words and ideas are explored in detail in chapter 7.

To anchor each chapter, I alternate between and among the perspectives and voices of preservice teachers, practicing teachers, and K–12 students to demonstrate the ubiquity and impact of school police. Each chapter ends with Abolitionist Activities, which prompt the reader to explore the nuances of police presence in schools both nationally and locally, recognizing that teachers are charged with supporting youth in their school communities and beyond. As abolitionists and educators Sheeva Sabati, Farima Pour-Khorshid, Erica Meiners, and Chrissy Hernandez argue, "teacher educators have the immense responsibility of cultivating teachers who understand their freedom as being bound up with that of their students."[68] This book challenges us, as educators, to grapple with the fact that policing constrains that freedom, and to instead imagine schools, and a world, without it.

CHAPTER 1

A History of Police in Public Schools and the Criminalization of Students

The only thing we really talk about is behavior management. . . . I don't even know the class that could talk about police in schools.

—Elizabeth, future elementary/special education teacher

Preservice teachers like Elizabeth rarely experience instruction to prepare them for working in schools with police, in whatever form they may show up. Nor is it common for preservice teachers to learn about the history that has led police to be such a fixture of the US educational system. This chapter contextualizes the place of police in schools, outlining when and how policing and schooling became so connected. It also provides historical context for abolitionist perspectives that police in schools have never protected students, even though we are told that's what they are placed there to do. We will learn why abolitionists argue that policing, even though we are taught that it keeps us safe, is actually a violent institution. The chapter ends with Abolitionist Activities that support learning about policing histories, which push us to rethink our support of their placement and the role that policing plays in shaping students' futures.

HISTORICAL OVERVIEW OF POLICING IN THE UNITED STATES: WHAT WE DON'T LEARN IN SCHOOL

Many scholars and historians begin with a tracing of police in schools that starts in the 1990s. For example, the shooting at Columbine High School in Colorado in 1999 is often marked as a turning point that rapidly accelerated the placement of police in schools.[1] Columbine was really the first major school shooting of my lifetime, and the deadliest shooting at a school until the 2018 shooting at Marjory Stoneman Douglas High School in Parkland, Florida. I was in college at the time that Columbine happened, and it felt like a huge shift occurred in how we talked about lots of things: school violence, access to guns, bullying, even what students wore to school.[2] And of course, it shifted conversations about safety and school police. Now, school shootings feel so commonplace for so many young people, with events unfolding in almost real time on social media and students forced to routinely engage in lockdown and active-shooter drills to prepare for what is made to seem inevitable.[3] And, these concerns about keeping students "safe" from shootings continue to fund the placement of police in schools and drive reform efforts around school policing.[4]

But police have been in schools for much longer than we often read about or learn about, even though there have not always been this *many* police officers in schools, engaging in this *much* programming with youth. Scholars have argued, for example, that policing and learning have always been intertwined; some scholars have urged us to go back as far as the policing of enslaved Africans' attempts to learn to read and write, and the policing and removal of Indigenous children to boarding schools.[5] Despite the presence of police in schools for over a century, and all the police-youth programming and instruction happening across the country, what teachers rarely learn about is the history of policing in our country: a history of violence that is painful for so many people, and as abolitionists teach us, violence that continues today. This is the history that is documented in this chapter. It helps us to understand the ubiquity of police in schools today and how we've come to accept carceral coercion and punishment as a necessary, rational approach to creating ideal environments for learning.

Origins of policing

Abolitionists and critical scholars of policing believe that the institution of policing has never been a positive, or even a neutral force in the United States. As scholars of policing David Correia and Tyler Wall explain, "The police are a political idea, a public institution, and a product of sociohistorical forces."[6] Many historians begin by tracing the institution of policing to the "rise of the state and the movement away from kinship-based communities."[7] In the original colonies, the first informal police were watchmen, mirroring some aspects of early policing in England.[8] These men were supposed to warn their largely homogenous communities of some perceived threat or danger from people they considered to be outsiders; at the time, this included Indigenous people and other nearby settlers. For example, as early as the 1630s in Boston, men took watch in their neighborhoods, and later in New York and Philadelphia. Many watchmen volunteered in order to evade military service, and they drank and slept on the job. Others had been "voluntold" to join the watch as punishment for some community transgression.[9] More formally designated constables might have also been assigned to watch over the night watchmen, depending on the area, creating some of the first informal policing hierarchies.[10]

Although popular depictions locate the origin of formal policing systems to the Northeast in the 1830s, policing existed both formally and informally in the South and up and down the Eastern Seaboard since the beginning of the trans-Atlantic slave trade.[11] Indeed, a closer look at the history of policing in the South reveals how policing has not only always been about protecting economic interests, but how it has also always been rooted in white supremacy and anti-Blackness. With their genesis as slave catchers, police have long captured, brutalized, and murdered Black people, particularly youth.[12] The first documented slave patrols in the South began in the early 1700s in the Carolinas, although it is believed they existed even earlier, designed to enforce "slave codes" that defined enslaved people as property rather than people.[13] Sociologist Marlese Durr explains that "paddy rollers" in the South were patrols of folks who were to "search slave lodges, keep slaves off roadways, and break up slave-organized meetings," practices that have been contextualized by scholars as precursors to modern-day "stop-and-frisk" policing.[14] These patrols transitioned into formalized police forces by at least the 1830s, much like what was happening in the Northeast, to protect the economic interests of slaveholders and the associated businesses of owning Black people as property. For example, in Charleston, the police department employed one hundred officers whose responsibilities included surveillance of Black movement, "checking documents, enforcing slave codes, guarding against slave revolts, and catching runaway slaves," and even surveilling free Black folks in the South.[15]

A closer look at the history of police in the Northeast also reveals how policing has always been about protecting power and elite financial interests, like land, property (including enslaved people), resources, and means of production. In the early colonies, "Indian constables" were appointed by colonial power structures to police Indigenous people as white colonizers forcibly removed them.[16] In other places, police departments were created under the guise of "protecting" white settler residents from Native folks. This supposed need for "protection" was rooted in anti-Indigenous sentiment that came with settler colonialism and the erasure and removal of Native people from their lands.[17] Later, anti-Indigenous sentiment mixed with white settlers' fear of Mexicans across the border, leading to the formation and rise of both federally and locally sanctioned groups tasked with colonial policing, like the Texas Rangers in the 1830s.[18] The Texas Rangers were notorious among Mexican and Indigenous peoples for their brutal treatment, which continued well into the 1960s and 1970s.[19]

As industry, factory work, and urbanization rapidly developed and increased in the 1800s with the rise of the slavery economy, some white and recent immigrant workers began to recognize their own exploitation. As early as the 1830s, for example, the divide between economic elites and workers was increasing rapidly; workers faced long, grueling hours, unsafe working conditions, and absurdly low pay. What have often been characterized as worker "riots" in history books were actually some of the first strikes by early labor movements.[20] And as workers began to push back on poor working conditions, economic elites arranged "systems of control" in the form of private police forces. As history scholar Gary Potter explains, "The modern police force not only provided an organized, centralized body of men (and they were all male) legally authorized to use force to maintain order, it also provided the illusion that this order was being maintained under the rule of law, not at the whim of those with economic power."[21] And in the mid-1800s, Connecticut, New York, and other colonies enacted laws to criminalize and control slaves. The US Congress even eventually enacted fugitive slave laws, which further concretized policing activities up and down the East Coast.[22] Historian Adam Malka underscores how "ordinary white people" were also bound up with more formal systems of policing, writing that in Baltimore, for example, "during the antebellum years was a police system that legitimated ordinary white men's violence, rendering it so normal as to make it nearly invisible. . . . From the perspective of the state, most free

Black people were criminals. From the perspective of free Black Baltimoreans, ordinary white people were the state."[23]

After the Civil War, the enslaved workforce in the South that was the foundation of the cotton, steel, iron, and export economies, both there and in the Northeast, ruptured. To keep the profit machines running, both leaders of industry and politicians relied on racist laws that permitted and encouraged local police, militias, and citizens to target and convict freed Black folks of crimes and then imprison them. This system was known as *convict leasing*, or "slavery by another name."[24] States in the South could lease Black prisoners to railroads, steel mills, plantations, and other private entities, thus giving both regular folks and police incentives to accuse and arrest Black people, forcing them into the convict leasing system.[25] Even Black folks who were found "innocent" of whatever dubious crimes they'd been accused of were often unable to pay court and municipal fines and fees, securing their place in the convict leasing system and ensuring labor and profits for economic elites.[26] Police were also responsible for enforcing Jim Crow laws that criminalized Black people and enforced segregation, both in the former Confederate states and elsewhere. These practices continued alongside similar surveillance and policing measures of Black folks by groups like the Ku Klux Klan (KKK) and other local militia and lynch mobs.[27] KKK members were also part of formal police departments, where they enjoyed both the power and protection that came with being police, as members of white nationalist groups continue to do today.[28] With this critical context in mind, abolitionist perspectives maintain that the institution of policing was in part developed to ensure and enforce societal hierarchies, even with violence, and to protect those who were responsible for that violence.

By the turn of the nineteenth century, most major urban areas had instituted their own public police forces that were responsible for many public services, like helping to provide housing and even serving poor people in soup kitchens. They were simultaneously responsible, however, for punishing poor people who did not have permanent housing under vagrancy laws, in addition to regulating the movement of both Indigenous and Black people across the country.[29] Corruption during this time was rampant and led to a decline in public perception of the efficacy and utility of police, even igniting fears that police had too much power.[30] As industrialization continued to grow and spread westward, working conditions were still poor, and workers pushed back and demanded better labor policies. With those demands came a police response, at the direction of those in power. Perhaps one of the most documented and infamous clashes between police and workers who were organizing and striking for better working conditions was the Haymarket Riot in Chicago in 1886. This clash resulted in countless deaths of protestors, in addition to police.[31]

As police corruption became more widespread and public concern about the potential of "delinquency" grew, reformers began to push for changes in not just policing, but for social institutions to shape modern US life in different ways. Often known as "progressives," reformers in the 1800s and early 1900s began to push for more centralized bureaucracy to govern everyday life. The temperance and prohibition movements, for example, part of progressive efforts aimed at curbing the sale and distribution of alcohol, proved a particularly contentious space for police. Many police themselves were not prohibitionists; in fact, they both regularly drank alcohol and profited from the sale of it. Some were even bootleggers, but they were also responsible for enforcing laws around the sale and trafficking of alcohol.[32]

The Progressive Era also ushered in more formal criminal and juvenile justice systems, as well as the formalized education system that we now know as public schooling.[33] Although public and private schools existed prior to the twentieth century, a formal system of education, including policing and surveillance of what happened in schools, was part of reformers' plans to encourage assimilation to dominant norms and to quell the potential of so-called delinquency.[34] The progressive movement also crystallized (mis)perceptions about crime and poverty as being due to immigration, poor parenting, and lack of moral education rather than as a result of a fundamentally unequal social system rooted in ideas about profit and property as more important than people. Public education, rather than family units and churches, became a primary site of socialization into "American" ways of life.[35] These ways of life, predicated on ideas about capitalism, individual liberty, and property ownership, were ideas that were also rooted in white supremacy, patriarchy, anti-Indigenous sentiment, and anti-Blackness—only some people were afforded the rights to liberty and property. As abolitionists argue, police served as the institution through which and by which those rights for some were protected at the expense of the criminalization of others, including students.

JUSTIFICATION FOR SCHOOL POLICE: DELINQUENCY

Policing youth has always been linked to perceptions about "juvenile delinquency," concerns that began even before the inception of compulsory education. For example, as previously mentioned, anti-literacy laws prohibited enslaved Black folks in the South, often youth, from learning to read and write, lest they become educated enough to coordinate escapes or rebel against slaveowners and the ruling class.[36] Reading and writing were thus positioned as delinquent behaviors, even among young children. Before the advent of compulsory schooling, free and enslaved children were often forced to work in factories, fields, and mills, supervised and surveilled by adults who often subjected them to horrible working conditions.[37] As new child labor laws went into effect, and with the rise of compulsory schooling toward the end of the 1800s and into the early 1900s, new laws and codes about truancy and absenteeism from school were also adopted to concretize the importance of school attendance.[38] These labor reforms and their linkages to attendance and behavior requirements in schools meant that children could be surveilled to ensure that they showed up to their classrooms. It was, and still is, widely believed that without experiencing a standardized system of formal education in the United States, students, especially poor, Black, Indigenous, and immigrant students, would be delinquent—meaning that they supposedly had an increased likelihood of committing crimes and engaging in otherwise undesirable behavior if they did not attend school.[39]

Concerns about delinquency, therefore, came to shape the institutions of both education and policing. For example, some of the first noted examples of formal police relationships with public schools occurred in the 1910s and 1920s in California. There, Coordinating Councils met to strategize about how public schooling, still fairly new as an institution, might function as a site of control of what many perceived to be "delinquent youth."[40] The police chief of Berkeley at the time, August Vollmer, introduced ideas and concerns about juvenile delinquency, citing that, in his view, teachers witnessed a majority of delinquent behavior among youth since youth were in school most of the day. The councils agreed that educators and police should share information so "maladjusted" youth could be met, according to Chief Vollmer, with "swift and certain punishment."[41] Teachers increased surveillance of students and filed reports with police; consequences included the placement of students into "special classes" and the deployment of police to the homes of students who were deemed to exhibit signs of "delinquent behavior," such as "truancy, sex, having certain mental abnormalities, reticence, having told lies . . . [or] theft."[42] Or, in the case of one family in Berkeley that the council "believed to have more children than they could support," the council "ma[de] a plea to the juvenile court judge that he break up the home . . . declaring five of the younger children wards of the court." Superintendent Virgil Dickson, also a member of the council, argued that this type of surveillance and discipline was necessary because, as he put it, "education is dangerous if it increases your earning power without reference to your habits of choice and your interests."[43]

By the 1930s and 1940s, concerns about youth delinquency, and consequently the policing and surveillance of youth in school, were widespread. Similar police-school partnerships began to appear across the country. For example, as cars became more popular, police in New York and other large urban centers began to partner with schools and automobile clubs to create "school safety patrols" to protect students from traffic.[44] These partnerships not only led to police presence in and around schools, but pushed students to surveil one another for "delinquent behavior" both in schools and in the community.[45] In Indiana, the Indianapolis school system hired an "Independent Investigator" to patrol its grounds for juvenile "delinquency," which grew into the formalized Indianapolis Public School Police.[46] In the late 1940s, the Los Angeles Police Department (LAPD) began to patrol public schools in the name of "property protection" and in response to concerns about "delinquent youth" in desegregating neighborhoods.[47] In 1948, the Los Angeles School Police Department was formalized; it is widely regarded as the first school police force in the country.[48] By taking these wider contextual factors into account, abolitionists argue that concerns about delinquency have always been rooted in racist, gendered, and classist stereotypes, especially as the nation moved toward desegregation and as prolabor and antiwar sentiment grew.[49]

Police-youth programming also ramped up outside of schools over the course of the twentieth century. Police, becoming "youth conscious" in their efforts to supposedly thwart future delinquency in adulthood, engaged in more interventions in public spaces and children's activities.[50] According to historian Tamara Myers, "The pursuit of incipient delinquency or pre-delinquents helped make crime prevention look like social service work, as police officers monitored youths' social venues and spaces, and offered them enticements to join police-directed recreational activities."[51] Youth joined Police Athletic Leagues (PALs), for example, and other social and sports clubs by the hundreds of thousands between the 1930s and the 1960s. Abolitionist perspectives teach us, however, that these campaigns were rooted in efforts to offset negative perceptions of police caused by decades of organizational corruption and the violence and chaos that police were inflicting on Black, immigrant, and working-class communities.[52] Police wielded their power, breaking strikes, rounding up suspected union members who were organizing for better labor conditions, and beating, torturing, and arresting community members who were advocating for better living conditions.[53] In short, police violently suppressed movements throughout the early and mid-twentieth century into what would become the US Civil Rights Movement.[54]

Although we often locate the struggle for equal rights during this movement to Black folks and issues of race and racism, the fight for civil rights included a broad coalition of people and was also about labor rights, economics, and US imperialism. Black folks, poor folks, women, queer folks, trans folks, and disabled folks all marched and participated in direct actions around the country to highlight the injustices that come with not just white supremacy and racism, but also with a capitalist system that stratifies people into "haves" and "have-nots."[55] The ways that police protected and propped up the "haves" became even more readily apparent during this time. Activists, many of whom were students, highlighted these intersections between policing and protection of white, wealthy power structures. For example, the Student Nonviolent Coordinating Committee (SNCC), one of many such groups across the country, organized direct actions like Freedom Rides to highlight segregated travel and transportation, sit-ins at white-owned restaurants that prohibited Black patrons from dining, and voter registration drives for Black folks who had previously been denied voting rights.[56] And with the Civil Rights Movement came some of the most brutal episodes of police violence in modern US history; violence directed at Black folks, of course, but also at this broad coalition of people (again, many of whom were students) who were asserting their rights to live freely and without persecution.[57] We turn now to how this struggle for rights and more just living conditions, as well as the role of police in it, played out in public schooling in this country.

JUSTIFICATION FOR SCHOOL POLICE: THWARTING ACTIVISM

As schools began to desegregate post–*Brown v. Board of Education*, concerns about "delinquent" young people provided an avenue to criminalize Black and Latinx youth and youth activism.[58] School desegregation in the 1950s and 1960s meant that some of the first Black students in predominantly white schools were sometimes escorted there by police under the promise of keeping them "safe," like the Little Rock Nine, the first Black students to enter Central High School in Little Rock, Arkansas.[59] In other places, however, police blocked Black students from entering desegregating schools, mirroring incidents from a century earlier in which police had removed Black students from still-segregated schools.[60] Post-*Brown*, in places like New York, committees began suggesting that police be placed in all schools where they were not already. These committees cited concerns about delinquent "undesirables" that might be in schools after desegregation—coded language rooted in anti-Black racism and anti-immigrant sentiment.[61] In the 1950s, school officials in Flint, Michigan, formally instituted a police force, often considered the first School Resource Officer (SRO) program, which scholars have noted was in response to perceptions about Black activism in the state, including in nearby Detroit.[62]

Outside of schools, police were brutally beating and siccing dogs on civil rights activists, many of whom were students, as they staged sit-ins, protests, and boycotts for equal rights across the country.[63] Police also routinely crossed picket lines and harassed or assaulted workers who were striking for better working conditions and better pay.[64] This highly visible police violence during the 1950s and 1960s, in addition to the long-standing role of police officers as "strikebreakers" in labor organizing movements, meant that many families viewed police as working against the interests of regular, everyday folks who were fighting for labor rights and racial and gender justice. Instead of keeping people safe, police were often seen as protecting the status quo and the interests of the white, wealthy elite.[65] To offset these negative perceptions of police, urban officials began to develop "Officer Friendly" campaigns alongside other police-youth programming like the aforementioned PALs. Originating in Chicago in the 1950s, Officer Friendly programming included an instructional intervention in schools, complete with a curriculum, workbooks, and take-home activities.[66] Programs subsequently popped up in urban areas across the country, where policymakers and officials hoped to socialize children and families into trusting police, despite the fact that many families were still experiencing police violence in their neighborhoods and schools.[67]

As student and community activism for equal educational rights in schools gained even more steam in the 1960s, school officials framed their activities as delinquent, leading to a spate of new school policies and consequences for Black students in particular.[68] Simultaneously, in large school districts around the country, families and activists were pushing for the reorganization of disciplinary codes and policies in efforts to make student discipline more centralized and less bound to educator discretion.[69] Relying solely on educator discretion in matters of student discipline, community members argued, meant increased likelihood of racist treatment, especially in matters of student activism. These efforts at times were met with harsh treatment for those student activists deemed delinquent and further concretized teacher judgments of what constituted delinquency. For example, in the South, school districts implemented new policies that surveilled and punished Black students in newly desegregating schools. This meant that school officials could target Black students for activities like handing out protest flyers, or any interpretation of behavior that they might deem "disruptive."[70] More broadly, though, these new policies and practices connected desegregation-era concerns among white folks to existing fears about juvenile delinquency, effectively criminalizing Black youth in new ways.[71] In Boston, for example, the intersection of policing, politics, and anti-Black calls for "law and order" concretized punitive consequences for Black students in desegregating schools, where educators relied increasingly on suspensions to "suppress Black student dissent."[72] As historian Matt Kautz explains, "The black student protest of 1968, as well as subsequent ones, demonstrated how the growing intimacy between police and schools strengthened this circuitous relationship in which schools' criminalization of students reinforced police power and police reinforced schools' disciplinary power."[73] Likewise, in the Midwest, policymakers and school community members responded to Black activism broadly, and Black Power protests in particular, by placing more police in schools.[74] And in New York, parent and student organizing for community-controlled schools and the abolition of suspensions and policing programs in schools was met by increasingly punitive measures. Students faced police violence, brutality, harassment, and even serious charges for any action deemed to be criminal, including simply being Black in a newly desegregated space. As historian Noah Remnick reports about one school in New York in the 1960s, "Student organizers observed an unmistakable pattern of hostility and intimidation by their teachers, who made a point of singling them out for uniform violations and other infractions that, though minor, often ended in suspensions"; one student noted that "as soon as they get the cops behind them, they show how racist they are."[75] After a series of violent incidents, some students stopped attending the school altogether, with one student asserting, "No use going to that school. That's a prison. Cops, cops all over the place, just waitin' to bust you."[76] Meanwhile, across the country, in Los Angeles, both Black and Chicano students often met police resistance as they organized for higher-quality education, changes in their school disciplinary dress codes, the cessation of corporal punishment, and an increase in racial and ethnic diversity of authority figures in their schools.[77]

By the late 1960s, cities and states across the country had passed legislation granting educational authorities the opportunity to hire school security, all largely as a response to Civil Rights Movement activities in schools. In 1967, "disturbing a school" became a crime in many states.[78] In 1969, Atlanta City Schools and the state of Kansas introduced school security officers and/or police officers.[79] To further contextualize the climate of policing during this time, this was also the year of the famous Stonewall Rebellion in New York City, led largely by queer and trans folks of Color who pushed back against the police harassment and violence that they'd been experiencing in their communities. This event both crystallized and spawned queer student organizing across the country, often met with police surveillance and violence.[80] As historian Heather Ann Thompson explains, "Even though America's school-aged children had since time immemorial engaged in fights, been disrespectful to teachers, skipped classes, bullied one another, and engaged in acts of vandalism as well as other inappropriate behaviors . . . school systems began employing security staffs in order to deal with such student conduct far more aggressively and punitively."[81] Thus, white-led efforts to punish Black and Brown folks' activism for civil rights, in addition to Officer Friendly campaigns, meant that both police placement and police engagement in schools were well entrenched by the end of the 1970s. Simultaneously, Black students and families across the country continued to organize for abolition of police in schools and encouraged policymakers and politicians to rethink punitive policies for Black students in particular that were increasing post-*Brown*.[82] Public schools were therefore contested sites of police violence and folks' continued resistance to it, as they continued to be throughout the twentieth century.[83]

JUSTIFICATION FOR SCHOOL POLICE: DRUGS, SUPERPREDATORS, AND ZERO-TOLERANCE

Historians have chronicled the ways that the 1970s and 1980s were characterized by a punitive turn in social welfare policies; in schools, this manifested by broadening criminalization of student behavior.[84] This time period continued and extended how white power structures had criminalized Black and Brown students throughout the Civil Rights Movement, in addition to the ways that police showed up in everyday schooling practices. As the War on Drugs ramped up in the 1980s, Officer Friendly campaigns in schools continued, but police-youth programming began to expand and take on new forms. For example, the Drug Awareness and Resistance Education (D.A.R.E.) program, created by a police chief in Los Angeles, began in 1983 and had been adopted in schools around the country by the mid-1990s.[85] This programming not only introduced police to K–12 students as legal enforcers around "drug use," it also solidified the place of police as educators alongside regular teachers, teaching an estimated 25 million students by 1995.[86] Police regularly entered classrooms and/or held school assemblies to warn students about the ills of drug use, while also encouraging students to report family and friends for using drugs.[87] But as historian Max Felker-Kantor argues, "Using police officers to deliver the D.A.R.E. curriculum and its messages of personal responsibility, self-esteem, and support for law-and-order ignored the ways the 'drug crisis' stemmed from material conditions and structural inequality."[88] The D.A.R.E. curriculum ignored the lopsided impacts of antidrug legislation and of the criminalization of drug use on poor communities, Black and Brown communities, and queer and trans communities.[89] Localizing drug use to individuals, moral failings, and personal responsibility was also part of catalyzing a focus on misbehavior that would become even more salient in the 1990s during the era of "zero-tolerance" policies.

In the 1990s, scholars began using new rhetoric invoking racist stereotypes to stoke public fears about Black children, labeling them "superpredators" and going so far as to claim that there were "radically impulsive . . . elementary school youngsters who pack guns instead of lunches."[90] According to scholar of policing Alex Vitale, the "superpredator myth . . . generated a huge amount of press coverage, editorials and legislative action."[91] Politicians and policymakers latched onto this mythology, concerned about what they saw as "gang" activity, especially in big urban areas like Los Angeles and New York, perceptions that were highly racialized and connected to the War on Drugs. As a result, new laws were introduced that made incarcerating youth easier, at younger ages. Simultaneously, the Gun Free Schools Act was passed, and zero-tolerance policies were instituted in many schools. These policies meant that when teachers and school leaders found drugs, weapons, or alcohol in students' possession, or even when they caught students fighting, they automatically suspended or expelled them.[92] In other words, they had zero tolerance for certain behaviors, which were outlined in newly revised student codes of conduct in public schools across the country. This period was marked by increasingly severe consequences for students. The categorization of student behavioral incidents, as well as the consequences for those incidents, mimicked the language used in criminal justice landscapes. What teachers and administrators might have once referred to as "talking back" might now be interpreted and recorded in an office disciplinary referral as "disorderly conduct" or "defiance of authority." Many of these incidents were, and continue to be, subject to the discretion of teachers and administrators, increasing the dangers of this context of increased criminalization and punishment for students.[93] Incidents were also categorized in different classes; for example, disorderly conduct might be classified as a "Class 1 offense," while fighting might be a "Class 2 offense," with the gravity of consequences increasing with each progressive class, again resembling language from the criminal justice landscape.

Along with the passage of these more stringent school discipline policies, federal agencies began granting huge sums of money to public schools to employ police in the late 1990s and early 2000s.[94] Educators who may have once handled issues largely in-house now could outsource students who they perceived to be "misbehaving" to the nearest police officer in the school. Simultaneously, police mentoring programs were increasingly implemented in schools, like the Teen and Police Service (TAPS) program. As education scholar Bettina Love describes, in this mentoring program, "officers are assigned to youth and paid to mentor them. . . . In Texas, students are given one high school academic credit for completing the eleven-week program."[95]

All these moves in public education were associated with the fear of rising school crime and threats, but researchers have shown that these fears were actually unfounded.[96] Instead, abolitionist perspectives underscore that the placement of police in schools during this time—much as police had been deployed in the past to create and maintain racial and economic hierarchies—was propelled by stereotypes about Black and Brown youth, immigrant youth, queer and trans youth, and poor youth.[97] The scaling-up of the number of police, in addition to expanding police-youth programming, meant that schools began to feel less and less safe for many students—and also potentially introduced them to juvenile and criminal justice systems.[98] And all these shifts in the landscape of public schools were well underway before the shooting at Columbine happened in 1999.

After Columbine, schools continued to expand the "get tough" shifts in punitive, exclusionary discipline and police presence started in the 1990s, aided by federal grants related to the Community Oriented Policing Services (COPS) Act, with devastating consequences.[99] Many administrators, teachers, and even parents agreed with these "zero tolerance" and "get tough" policies, at least until research began to show just how racially disproportionate these practices were. By the mid-2000s, many researchers, teachers, and parents had begun to sound alarm bells: discipline data showed that teachers and administrators were suspending and expelling many, many more Black and Brown students than white students, even though zero-tolerance policies were supposed to be applied equally across student racial groups.[100] This awareness resulted in a doubling-down among policymakers and school practitioners under the pretense of student "safety," as well as community resistance to the criminalization of students, which continues today. For example, some school communities have been successful in rolling back zero-tolerance policies, while others maintain them.[101]

JUSTIFICATION FOR SCHOOL POLICE: "SAFETY"

Decades of research now tell us that school-based practitioners suspend, expel, and refer Black and Brown students, queer and trans students, low-income students, immigrant students, and students with disabilities to alternative schools at much higher rates, removing them from their teachers and peers.[102] Decades of research also indicate that school systems with high numbers of police, or even their own police forces, suspend and expel higher numbers of Black and Brown students, queer and trans students, low-income students, immigrant students, and students with disabilities.[103] We'll explore these trends in more detail in chapter 2. In addition, school systems that employ police often report many more students, and specifically Black and Brown students, to law enforcement for infractions that once would have been handled by teachers and administrators.[104] This results not only in lost instructional time but also increased burdens on students' families, who must attend court dates and pay fines. Attorneys and advocates at the American Civil Liberties Union (ACLU) have even argued that police in schools target Black, Brown, and Indigenous students, as well as students with disabilities.[105] And yet, after each school shooting over the last two decades, we have seen drastic expansion of school police funding and programming in the name of keeping students "safe."[106] After the Sandy Hook school shooting, for example, President Obama's administration expanded the COPS program to the tune of $125 million in grants to fund additional SROs across the country.[107]

Abolitionists often ask: Who are we really keeping safe? As education scholar Lynn Addington notes, the disastrous consequences of school policing for Black students, and Black girls in particular, are particularly tragic given that most school shooters are white boys and men.[108] But in some places, policymakers are listening to activist demands to keep *all* students safe and in school. For example, in California, because of the ongoing activism of students and families, policymakers have scaled back suspensions for "defiance."[109] And in still other places, like Chicago, school boards have rescinded contracts with police departments after decades of student and community activism to have police removed from their schools.[110] But in places like the state of Alabama, where I live and teach, or in my home state of North Carolina, school policing is still as popular as ever, with police serving as "mentors" and "role models," running youth camps and hosting football games, as well as encouraging students to become law enforcement officers when they grow up, despite the testimonies of students who are skeptical of their presence and those who experience police violence.[111] This is what we call normalization of school police, or "copaganda."

Abolitionist perspectives underscore how we are socialized to believe that police keep us safe from an early age. This shows up in the media that we consume, whether it be social media, streaming sites, or local television news stations and newspapers. For example, many communities have local television channels and newspapers that report on local "criminals," or Facebook groups that track local crime and post pictures and alerts when police apprehend those "criminals." Usually, no context about the crime or the perpetrator is given; we learn simply that someone has acted unlawfully and the police have arrested them and charged them. This type of decontextualized reporting furthers ideas about "heroes" and "villains," "good guys" and "bad guys," centering on the supposed necessity of police to keep people safe. Messaging about police as do-gooders and helpers also permeates the entertainment that we consume. Shows for children, like *Paw Patrol*, present friendly images of police, as do more adult-oriented shows like *CSI*, *Miami Vice*, and *Law & Order: SVU*. Many of these shows present police as heroes who solve crimes and protect victims. Even shows like HBO's *The Wire*, which critique some aspects of policing, stay true to the fundamental idea that police are there to keep people safe and to bust the "bad guys."

Narratives about policing as an inevitable, overwhelmingly beneficial presence in our lives are *copaganda*—propaganda that spreads friendly, positive messaging about police and policework.[112] Copaganda works to offset the overwhelming evidence that police are not a positive presence in our lives. This positive messaging about how police protect us and keep us safe happens at the same time as Black and Brown families are having "the talk" with their children about what to do if and when police stop them on the street, in their cars, at school, or in the library, or when police come into their homes.[113]

As previously stated, this copaganda shows up in schools, too. For example, police officers read books about the benefits of policing to students in their classrooms, enroll students in mentoring programs for so-called at-risk youth, and engage students in K-9 bite demonstrations with dogs, all designed to promote trust in policing as an institution, just as Officer Friendly programming and PALs for youth were designed to do.[114] These programs, like D.A.R.E., also reinforce the idea that there are law-abiding citizens who deserve protection from the police, and then there are "bad guys" who commit crimes and thus deserve to be arrested and locked up as punishment. Police also teach students about laws and the consequences of breaking them, instructing them implicitly how not to become a "bad guy."[115] This socialization and this worldview mean that when police violence occurs, we almost automatically assume that those people must have done *something* to deserve that treatment—that the police are there to protect us, the "good" people, from *those* people, the "bad" ones. After all, how could these same nice police officers who are reading books to kids also be responsible for body-slamming and pepper-spraying students in hallways, or shooting and killing people in the streets?

Extensive copaganda campaigns, whether they be in schools or in popular media, also mean that when we learn about police violence, it's often easier to dismiss that violence as occurring at the hands of a "bad apple" police officer, rather than grappling with the institution of policing as inherently violent. Indeed, sometimes media reports about police violence even use language about "bad apple" officers; we often see these reports juxtaposed with more positive stories about officers who might be, for example, giving out ice cream to children at a playground, reading books to kids in a classroom, or taking kids along for "shop with a cop" campaigns.[116] But if we dig a bit deeper into ideas about criminality and delinquency, especially as they are contextualized by the presence of police in schools, we have to reconsider this binary worldview around "good/evil," "good apples/bad apples," and "good guys/bad guys." This is especially important in our work with youth in schools, where ideas about students as potential delinquents and criminals are deeply rooted and intertwined with the history of public education, racial segregation, and activism. Moreover, thinking about certain students as potential criminals undermines our commitments as educators to student learning and our belief that all students deserve to learn and be in school. Importantly, ideas about students as delinquents and criminals, and thus deserving of policing and punishment, undermine a belief in the fundamental potential of each child to thrive; these ideas presuppose that some students will fall short in life.

So how do we grapple with these historical and contemporary uses of police in schools, and their effects on teaching and teachers' perspectives, with an eye toward removing them? As historian Noah Remnick argues, "While the rise of school policing and student discipline is a development of national importance, education is always a local story."[117] Abolitionists believe that we must start by coming to understand what's happening in our local contexts, and eventually our spheres of influence, imagining what safety might look like in our own communities without relying on police. And even though policing and public schools have always been intertwined, we haven't always had this much police. As abolitionists and activists Mariame Kaba and Andrea Ritchie ask, "What makes us think we always have to?"[118] The following Abolitionist Activities include questions that support this exploration.

ABOLITIONIST ACTIVITIES: POLICING HISTORIES

Consider your own schooling experience and local context:

- What is the history of the school police/SRO program in the school system that you attended?
- When were police first placed in schools there, and for what purposes?
- What parallels does this placement have with histories of activism in the area?
- How do these questions apply to the school system where you currently teach, or plan to teach?

Launch the inquiry:

- Start the exploration exercise at state-level and/or school system websites, in addition to those of local police departments and sheriff's offices, to obtain information about school police.
- Local news sites for journalism about school police programs are also often good sources.
- Informal oral history interviews could be conducted with veteran teachers, administrators, and/or community leaders who have worked in and/or attended schools in the area that you are exploring. What do they remember about school police programs in their communities?
- What kinds of copaganda campaigns, including social media presence and police-youth programs in and out of schools, exist in the school communities that you attended? What about where you hope to teach?
- Finally, consider some questions for reflection: What are your own framings or justifications for police in schools? Where do they come from?

In chapter 2, we learn more about the current landscape of police in schools, including the effects on students.

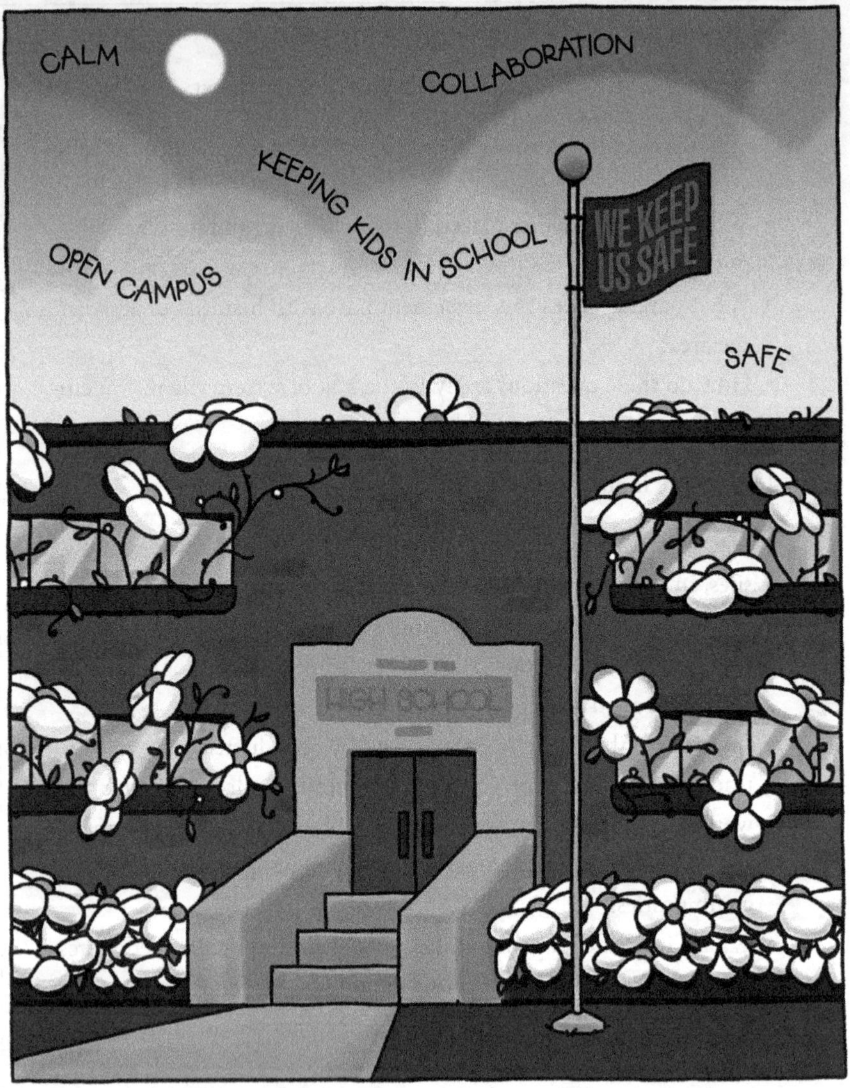
CALM
COLLABORATION
KEEPING KIDS IN SCHOOL
OPEN CAMPUS
WE KEEP US SAFE
SAFE
HIGH SCHOOL

CHAPTER 2

The State of Things

Yeah, the cops at school used to mess with us all the time, just like the one officer who pulls up to the corner where we link up after school. They're always asking us for IDs and saying stuff like, "What kinda trouble are y'all gonna cause today?"

—Deon, high school student

This conversation with Deon happened back in 2018 in the class that I was teaching at an alternative school in Alabama. Students in the class were recounting their experiences with the School Resource Officers (SROs) at the high school that they attended before they were sent to the alternative school, drawing connections to how cops there treated them like the cops in their neighborhood did. I've written a lot about my experiences teaching alternative school students, how adults had characterized them as "bad kids," as troublemakers, and even as unteachable, despite their joy, brilliance, and resistance to unjust learning conditions. In Deon's case, that resistance got him in trouble with his teachers, administrators, and school police, prompting his removal to an alternative school setting. His contact with police, like that of his classmates, was routine; it happened at their home high school, in their neighborhoods, and at the alternative school, where they were sometimes searched by school police on their way into school.

In chapter 1, we read about how police were deployed into public schools at different time points since the turn of the twentieth century: to satisfy concerns about juvenile "delinquency," to quell student and community activism, and ostensibly to protect students from gun violence in schools. In this chapter, we will learn more about the landscape of police in schools today, including how many Black students like Deon, as well as other students of Color, students with disabilities, and queer and trans students, experience police contact in schools all the time. And we will also learn about the various efforts happening across the country to prevent police violence against students and to remove police from schools altogether. The chapter ends with Abolitionist Activities that support learning more about police harm, as well as community resistance to policing.

POLICE IN SCHOOLS, BY THE NUMBERS

According to the latest reports from the National Center for Education Statistics, an estimated 51.4 percent of schools had at least one law enforcement officer with a firearm during the 2019–2020 school year.[1] The US Department of Justice reported that there were approximately 23,400 sworn SROs at the end of the 2019–2020 school year, although researchers have estimated that number to be closer to 40,000, and maybe more, especially when accounting for all the different types of security personnel in school.[2] It is unclear how many school police are in schools today because of lag times between data collection and reporting, because some schools in rural areas share police between and among schools, and because there is really no annual federal mechanism for tracking all the various types of police placement in schools. Yet the National Association of School Resource Officers (NASRO) has touted school policing as the "fastest growing area of law enforcement."[3]

Police in schools in the United States are supported by a patchwork model of funding from federal, state, and local resources. In some places, like in Chicago Public Schools, students and community organizers have succeeded in decreasing both the number of SROs and funding for school police after decades of activism.[4] But numbers have likely increased in other places, given political rhetoric about school shootings and increased federal funding opportunities like Community Oriented Policing Services (COPS) and School Violence Prevention Program grants that public school districts compete for each year.[5] Funding for school police is astronomical, to the tune of billions of dollars each year.[6] Funding for school police, of course, means less funding for other types of school resources; for example, Texas spends the most money on school security per student, yet is among one of the lowest spenders on school social workers.[7] Nationally, during the 2015–2016 school year, over one million students attended a school with a sworn law enforcement officer but no counselor.[8] My home state of North Carolina ranks consistently among the lowest in funding for public schools, and yet it has one of the highest numbers of police placement in schools in the United States.[9] And in Alabama, where I live and teach now, lawmakers in 2024 requested over a $50 million increase from the previous year for funding for "school security," in addition to monies that afford local law enforcement and district attorney offices more leeway to get involved in student truancy cases.[10] Truancy, absenteeism, and student mental health are viewed as some of the biggest issues plaguing school systems in the wake of COVID-19, and yet it is unlikely that budgets aimed at funding school security measures and law enforcement officers will support students and their families. Instead, so much funding for so many police in so many schools means the continued criminalization of students, which we learn about next.

Criminalization of school discipline

School police are charged to adopt multiple roles, such as law enforcement representative, mentor, and even educator, solidifying how they offer legal and carceral socialization for youth.[11] Despite claims of being mentors and role models, however, school police routinely surveil and harass students, stopping them in the hallways, in cafeterias, and on the school grounds outside, especially around issues of perceived non-compliance with school policy. Police interact with students about perceived dress code violations, ask students for bathroom passes, and even attempt to prohibit student cell phone use.[12] In the 2020–2021 school year, schools reported over 61,000 referrals to law enforcement, 14 percent of which resulted in an arrest.[13] The American Civil Liberties Union (ACLU) highlights the example of a thirteen-year-old Texas boy who used a fake $2 bill to pay for his school lunch; he was charged with felony forgery and faced the threat of prison time.[14] School systems that employ police often report many more students to law enforcement.[15] Punishments tend to be more severe in schools where police are stationed, part of what some scholars have argued has contributed to the criminalization of school discipline over the years.[16]

Further, research consistently shows that school police arrest more Black students than white students.[17] For example, in 2015–2016, Black students comprised 15 percent of all students in public schools, but comprised

31 percent of the students police arrested at school.[18] Although these statistics are almost a decade old now, data indicate that school police continue to be in contact with Black and Brown youth by virtue of arrests, and teachers and administrators continue to refer Black and Brown students to police at rates much higher than their white peers.[19] Research shows that school practitioners refer Black students to law enforcement at sometimes twice the rate as white students.[20] And the rates of police arrests of students with disabilities are also much higher; for Black students and students of Color with disabilities, sometimes even up to five or six times higher than students without disabilities.[21] It's important to remember that these numbers represent actual children in public schools. In 2018, for example, an SRO in Texas pinned down and handcuffed a child with autism.[22] In 2019, SROs in Colorado arrested an eleven-year-old Hispanic student with autism and left him in the back of a patrol car for hours.[23] In 2020, school police officers in Honolulu arrested a ten-year-old Black student with disabilities and drove her to the police station, where no charges were filed.[24] In 2024, SROs in Texas arrested a ten-year-old student with autism, even though her father, a former police officer himself, was on his way to the school to de-escalate the situation.[25] And even during the academic year where many schools transitioned to remote learning during COVID-19, school practitioners were referring lots of students to law enforcement—including over 3,500 elementary students.[26] Police have also been documented restraining and handcuffing students as young as five and six years old.[27] While media attention often focuses on elementary school students and young children in an effort to illustrate just how egregious these arrests are, school police continue to arrest middle school and high school students around the country as well.[28]

Teachers and even administrators now look to police to handle incidents that were once handled by regular school personnel.[29] During the 2019–2020 school year, for example, 69 percent of SROs reported having responded to a classroom incident in the prior thirty days before they were surveyed.[30] What we can interpret from this percentage is that it is teachers who are often calling police to their classrooms. Stories from students back this up, in addition to my own experiences as a public school teacher, which we will learn more about in chapter 6. Police presence in school buildings means that they have become part of the fabric of school discipline.

POLICE ASSAULTS ON STUDENTS

When police interact with students, things can quickly go awry, like officers escalating issues when students do not understand or do not comply with their orders, as in many of the incidents noted in the previous section. When police escalate their orders to comply, they often become physical with students. There are countless viral videos on social media, as well as in more formal news outlets, that document police escalating issues with students about cell phones, dress codes, and perceived student misbehavior—incidents that sometimes result in officers who physically assault students.[31] Of course, we have already learned about Shakara in South Carolina: an officer dragged from her desk over a cell phone. There are countless other stories of police assaults against students, both those recorded by bystanders with phones and those that are unrecorded. According to the Advancement Project and the Alliance for Educational Justice, from 2011–2023, there were 372 documented police assaults of students at school.[32] The #AssaultAt map details all the places around the country where police assaults have occurred, resulting in minor injuries to some students and, in one case, permanent brain damage.[33] Police also have sexually assaulted students; sexual assault comprised more than 13 percent of all documented assaults. Another recent report from the In Our Names Network and Interrupting Criminalization details the ways that police surveil, arrest, and sexually assault Black young women, girls, and trans and gender nonconforming students.[34] They argue that "schools are an often-overlooked site of police sexual violence," and detail stories from students who share how police and school security personnel sexualize and harass them, commenting on their clothes, bodies, and appearance and touching them inappropriately.[35] And indeed, a recent news story in the *Washington Post* exposes how a school police officer in South Carolina, at the same school where an SRO assaulted Shakara, sexually assaulted and abused students for years before he was ultimately fired.[36]

THE POLICE-FREE SCHOOLS MOVEMENT

Not all students are arrested or assaulted by police, to be sure. But police presence, while often justified under the guise of "safety" and "care" for students, may actually make some students feel less safe at school.[37] This might be especially true if students have experienced police violence or harassment outside of school, like Deon and his friends did in their neighborhoods. Whether in school or out of school, research indicates that "children and youth report feeling helpless and dehumanized when the police stop, harass, verbally abuse, or physically abuse them or other people."[38] Some Black high school students have described police in school who build relationships with them, only to "then turn around and ask to search your backpack or smell your hands as if I carry drugs," or with the underlying motive to question students about "who's who" in schools and neighborhoods regarding criminal incidents.[39]

It is tempting to attribute this criminalization and these arrests and assaults to "bad apples" or to argue that officers just haven't had enough training.[40] And, abolitionist perspectives push us to acknowledge that individual police officers are not inherently "bad people." Many police officers even state that they are interested in working in schools with intentions to "give back," build relationships, and be role models for students.[41] Yet the patterns of harm outlined in this chapter are what communities around the country point to when they organize to defund and remove police from schools. Further, many police who escalate issues with and assault students are SROs who have been trained by a national organization, underscoring how reforms around training are not the answer. Therefore, instead of working to keep students safe from police violence at school, we must work toward keeping students safe at school without the presence of police.

We must also resist positioning students who have been harassed, arrested, or assaulted by police at school as *only* victims because many of these students and their communities are also the leaders of movements to remove police from schools.[42] While the defund and abolitionist movements are often painted as "fringe" perspectives, communities in places all over the United States have come together and agreed that police have no place in schools. According to a report by the Chicago Justice Project, "60% of the country's top 30 cities saw some change around school policing following the summer of 2020."[43] These efforts extend to other areas of the country as well: in my home state of North Carolina, for example, students in Charlotte-Mecklenburg Schools created the Charlotte Liberation Party to protest police in schools; in Durham, student activist Aissa Dearing organized a march to call for the removal of police in Durham Public Schools, writing an open letter to the Board of Education, and arguing, "Of course I'm terrified of a school shooting. . . . I mean, I grew up practicing lockdowns at school. And school resource officers honestly don't make me feel any safer."[44] In Columbus, Ohio, students returned to schools after the pivot in 2020 to police-free hallways after organizing by students in the CPD Out of CCS movement.[45] And communities in Des Moines, Iowa, removed some types of police from schools and have implemented restorative practices to keep students safe.[46] There are even former police officers, like Evan Douglas in the Washington, DC, area, who are advocating for police-free schools.[47] And these are just a few examples of movements around the country.

Yet some school systems who initially removed police have now reinstated them under the pretense of school safety.[48] It is therefore important to underscore that the police-free schools movement, while it gained more national attention during and after the racial justice movement of summer 2020, has existed for decades. The work continues, despite pendulum swings in nationwide attention on both this movement and in nationwide efforts to expand school policing. For example, students and teachers in Chicago Public Schools have been organizing to remove police as part of and alongside organizations like the Brighton Park Neighborhood Council and the Healthy Schools Campaign.[49] The Black Organizing Project in Oakland, California, has been working for years toward police-free schools by, for example, educating teachers about the effects of harsh school punishments, including the violence that comes when teachers call police or immigration officials on students at school, asking teachers to commit *not* to call police on their kids.[50] In Milwaukee, teachers and school board members have been fighting for years to decrease both police and invasive school security measures like metal detectors and X-ray scanners in their schools.[51] And there are many, many other "victories" by student, teacher, and parent activists towards police-free schools happening all the time across the country, both documented and happening out of the spotlight altogether.[52]

However, contrasted to the experiences of Deon, my former student at the alternative school, and the students across the country who have experienced negative and even violent interactions with school police, another reality exists for students in public schools: a reality where students go about their daily lives, unbothered and in some ways even invisible to school police. Despite the placement of so many police in so many schools, many students, including many white students, have never had an individual encounter with school police, have come to take police presence for granted, or even view police as sources of safety.[53] These perspectives—that policing in schools is natural and police keep us safe, despite so much evidence to the contrary—are the norm for many of the preservice and practicing teachers with whom I've worked over the years. When I first started working with preservice teachers for this particular project, many recalled few interactions with school police when they were students, or recalled police officers fondly—one might even characterize these students as "pro-police." They remembered police in their schools as being "all smiles" with students, creating "positive relationships" with students, and that they "would enjoy coming to school and even love interacting with all of the students." In chapter 3, we'll learn more about how preservice teachers remember police in their schools, including the police-youth programming in their K–12 experiences that aims to shape these positive feelings of policing.

ABOLITIONIST ACTIVITIES: POLICE HARM AND RESISTANCE TO SCHOOL POLICING

- Explore the #AssaultAt map compiled by the Advancement Project and the Alliance for Educational Justice.[54] While this map documents some of the most egregious police assaults on students, it also gives a clear picture of the harm that police cause across the country.
- Read the report put forth by the In Our Names Network and Interrupting Criminalization, describing how police routinely make schools less safe for Black girls, trans, and gender nonconforming youth.[55]
- Explore local news media in your area and in the areas where you plan to teach. What instances of police violence do you find, in or out of school?
- Finally, explore local news media in your area and the area where you plan to teach, with a specific focus on resistance to police in schools. What teacher and/or student coalitions exist in the area? What students have spoken out against police in their schools? What statements have been made in opposition to school policing at school board meetings?

A MORE OPEN DRESS CODE
AUTHENTICITY
ACCEPTANCE OF DIFFERENCES
BETTER FOOD
LESS EXTREME CONSEQUENCES

CHAPTER 3

"Well, at My High School . . ."

Copaganda and Police-Youth Programming in Schools

Our SRO was a very calm, kind man who went to all of our events, football games, basketball games, baseball games, prom, homecoming, everything. He would take pictures with everyone and made an effort to form relationships with students and would always give a smile . . . and was a very approachable man to go to for whatever. I feel as though students were much more comfortable going to him rather than teachers or administrators, who at my school tended to be more rigid and mean to students.

—Karlie, preservice teacher

Karlie had just started college and was in her first semester learning to be a high school English teacher. The high school that she graduated from the previous semester was close to Oxford High School in Michigan, the site of a 2021 shooting. Karlie said that they experienced many threats to her high school in the weeks after the Oxford shooting; these increased not only the number of police officers who were regularly stationed at her school that fall, but also the frequency with which additional officers were sent there.[1] Indeed, school shootings and threats of violence are often the rationale for which police are placed in schools today. But, as we learned in chapter 1, police were increasingly deployed into schools at various points throughout the twentieth century, often in response to Black student activism, community efforts for civil rights, and families fighting for more just and equitable educational experiences. And police in schools today are sources of violence, punishment, and harm, as we learned in chapter 2. This history and accounting of the contemporary effects of police in schools give us more context about how police do not keep students safe, nor do they make all students feel safer. Yet Karlie, who was learning to be a high school English teacher, recalled the police officer at her high school fondly, describing him as "kind" and "approachable."

Few studies have explored teachers' perceptions about police, broadly speaking. In some school systems, school boards have even prevented teachers from participating in research about school police.[2] Further, research about teachers' perceptions of police often does not take into account theorizing about, for example, racism and the intersection of racism and policing. The research that does exist suggests that even as teachers acknowledge the importance of "race talk" in classrooms, they may minimize or erase the ways that police violence is racialized.[3] Research conducted about teachers' views of police in schools is instead often linked to perceptions about school safety. For example, teachers themselves may sometimes associate police presence with feelings of safety, even while recognizing that some students in buildings with school police may be more fearful.[4]

So how do we make sense of the ways that students like Karlie and other future teachers describe school police: with fondness, admiration, and even as sources of safety, despite what we know about the harm that police cause? One reason could be that many preservice teachers are also white women (like Karlie) and rely on their own positive interpersonal experiences with police (or lack of experiences overall) to inform their perspectives.[5] Broadly speaking, we are more likely to hold positive perceptions of groups when our personal history is marked by positive one-on-one interactions. Perhaps more significantly, though, preservice teachers, as have we all, have been exposed to messages about police that we learn from media—what some cultural studies scholars and abolitionists have called "copaganda," or propaganda that socializes us to see the police as a positive, necessary presence.[6] And preservice teachers who have attended K–12 schools in the last ten to twenty years have likely all experienced some version of police-youth programming, including day-to-day efforts to build relationships with the student body. It is therefore difficult to detangle Karlie's memory of positive interactions with police from the copaganda and police-youth programming that she and her peers were immersed in. In fact, many students who have interactions with school police, including preservice teachers, have been the recipients of years of dedicated funding and resources to programming that essentially has one goal: to improve perceptions of police. This type of police-youth programming in schools, as we learned in chapter 1, has its roots in "Officer Friendly" campaigns in the 1960s—a time when Black folks, for example, were working tirelessly for civil rights, and when police were regularly engaged in upholding segregation, strike busting, and other activities to maintain the status quo.

In this chapter, we first learn about the concept of copaganda—what it looks like, how it circulates, and how it socializes us. Then we hear directly from preservice teachers at several large universities in the Northeast, Midwest, and South as they recall their memories of school police. Through their recollections and reflections, we learn about how police-youth programming socializes students and teachers into believing that police presence in schools is necessary and desirable. The chapter ends with Abolitionist Activities that support preservice teachers in auditing their memories of and thinking more critically about school policing and copaganda, a step toward interrogating copaganda and imagining police-free schools.

COPAGANDA IN MEDIA AND CULTURE

Mainstream media, popular culture, and even police departments present numerous images, narrative and rhetorical choices, and television shows, for example, that introduce and reinforce ideas about criminals, good cops, bad cops, and the necessity of policing. These narratives of police are so pervasive in our lives that they make it seem impossible for us to exist without police. In the news, for example, we often read or hear about "officer-involved shootings," rather than a more accurate description about police perpetrating violence.[7] Or we might read about "police brutality," which implies that there is a type or version of policing that exists without violence.[8] On television, in movies, and on streaming services, we repeatedly see plots about victims in need of police protection or cops arresting and locking up criminals. *CSI*, *Law and Order: SVU*, and countless shows and movies across the decades (even *Paw Patrol*) perpetuate narratives about policing as an integral part of our lives. And we see social media and public relation campaigns by police departments and city offices across the country extolling the virtues of individual officers who have "solved crimes" and "gotten" the bad guys. This latter kind of copaganda, unlike cultural products like television and movies, is "direct and unmediated," where "money and efforts of police departments, police unions, and local government . . . lobby for additional funding, disseminate misinformation and manage public perception."[9] This might look like, for example, the Community Policing in Action Photo Contest, sponsored by the Office of Community Oriented Policing Services (the COPS Office, under the US Department of Justice).[10] Or it might look like sophisticated police social media campaigns, like those in my community in Alabama, that document all the police-youth programming in schools.[11]

As sociologist Derek Denman has written, this type of copaganda—police direction of and influence on media—has a long history.[12] For example, in the mid-twentieth century, former Los Angeles police chief William Parker and the Public Information Division (PID) of the Los Angeles Police Department (LAPD) had close relationships with the press, controlling narratives about police in Los Angeles and beyond.[13] Parker and the PID even vetted the script for the television show *Dragnet* in the 1950s.[14] According to historian Joe Domanick, "The advisors closely examined the script to guarantee that the LAPD officers on Dragnet were ethical, efficient, terse and white."[15] And *Dragnet* was only the beginning: today, police departments and unions around the country are regularly consulted by showrunners, media strategists, and politicians to direct pro-police messaging. Even HBO's recent show *Watchmen*, which critiques some aspects of policing, was developed in collaboration with law enforcement.[16] Regarding print media, as Alec Karakatsanis reported in 2023, the *New York Times* published what were characterized as "independent reports" about police responses to the 2020 racial justice movement, but they were actually authored by LAPD officials.[17]

Whether via news media, television, or movies, copaganda affects all people, across all demographic groups. For example, Mark Anthony Neal, professor of Black popular culture, has written about what he calls "the myth of the good cop."[18] He argues that much of how policing is presented on television socializes us into believing that individual officers are doing good work to solve crimes and protect folks, even if we might acknowledge that there are some systemic issues with policing. Neal writes that narratives and images about cops as hardworking do-gooders work to legitimate the police violence that Black folks regularly experience. He takes particular issue with the ways that even Black folks are socialized by copaganda, especially when the police on screen are Black. These onscreen efforts to "diversify" police mirror reforms in police departments across the country, of course. But we need only remember how Black police officers murdered Tyre Nichols, a Black man in Memphis, for example, to understand how Black officers enact harm just as white officers do.[19] Abolitionists agree that reform efforts like diversification do nothing to transform policing as an inherently violent institution. As Mariame Kaba and Andrea Ritchie remind us, "The notion of 'reform' implies that an institution has strayed from its core responsibilities, that the reins just need to be tightened on individual cops or departments. But there is no 'fixing' something that works as intended."[20]

And it's not just shows and movies that are specifically about policing that socialize us into believing that police are necessary. Abolitionists have argued, for example, that the series *Yellowjackets* perpetuates the idea that, left to our own devices without police and laws, we as human beings are destined to turn on one another.[21] Other types of media, including the classic novel *Lord of the Flies*, emphasize beliefs about innate human cruelty and the necessity of laws, and the enforcers of those laws, as integral to our collective survival. Similarly, sociologist and scholar of policing Tyler Wall has written about what he calls the "patronizing shit" that is the "Thin Blue Line" mythology—the idea that, without law enforcement, societies would descend into chaos and ruin.[22] We also see this type of copaganda commodified on merchandise: shirts, flags, and bumper stickers depicting the "Thin Blue Line" became especially popular amid the racial justice movement of 2020, and that popularity continues. It's a regular occurrence, for example, for me to see college students wearing T-shirts depicting a grayed-out American flag with a blue line running through it as I walk to my office on campus. "Blue Lives Matter" merchandise is just as popular, as is the image of the Punisher skull, overlaid with a blue line.[23]

As abolitionists Mariame Kaba and Andrea Ritchie point out, "There are racial, gendered, and ableist subtexts to this threatened chaotic violence without police—a reflection of the social and economic order that policing upholds." They add, "As currently defined, 'public safety' produces separate camps—people who need to be kept safe and the people from whom they must be kept safe," ideas that we see mirrored in messaging about "good guys," "bad guys," "good cops," "bad cops," and what "safety" means.[24] Consider, however, that the world is already an unsafe place for many marginalized folks. And no amount of policing has prevented crime. Further, these ideas make it seem like some people—those deemed "criminals"—deserve the violence that they experience at the hands of police.

Police-youth programming, from the Officer Friendly program in the 1950s to mentorship programs in today's schools, socializes teachers, administrators, students, and students' families just as copaganda in media and culture does. These programs reinforce messages about criminality and innocence while teaching us that police are here for us, to keep us safe and to act as resources. These messages and assumptions about police are problematic given the violence that comes with policing and the ways that police-youth programming actually diverts resources from things that we know are important for high-quality schooling: well-paid teachers and school staff, relevant curricula, and support services for students and families, to name just a few.[25] Yet police placement in schools continues to be ubiquitous, and police-youth programming is even expanding in some schools across the country as lawmakers call for more and more police after each school shooting.[26] Many school systems are even developing their own police forces.[27] In the next sections, we learn more about preservice teachers' recollections of police in their schools to understand what police-youth programming looked like for them, alongside information about these different types of programming.

POLICE-YOUTH PROGRAMMING IN SCHOOLS

Mentors and teddy bears

Jordan, like Karlie featured at the beginning of this chapter, had just begun college and was learning to be an elementary school teacher. She, like her classmates in their teacher preparation program, had participated in an audit (called "Unlocking Core Memories") of their experiences with school police during a series of lessons that I cotaught at her university. Jordan had attended a large high school near the university and recalled fist bumps with police and School Resource Officers (SROs) who "gave off the vibe of a big teddy bear." Mya, another student in Jordan's university class, also learning to be an elementary school teacher, explained that "in junior and senior year of high school, we had one main cop who would walk around and had his own office. He would always tell students his office is 'right down the hall' if they wanna stop by and say 'hi'. He would walk the halls, but was very interactive with all the students. He was extremely friendly and knew a bunch of the students' names on a personal level."

Likewise, Georgianna, who was learning to be a high school science teacher, remembered, "Our officer would always walk around and stand in the hall in between classes and talk to everyone. He also showed a lot of support at sporting events. He would even sometimes come into the class and talk . . . he let people know that if there was ever an issue we could go and talk to him. His interactions with students were always great and everyone really liked him." And Kathleen, who was learning to be an elementary school teacher, remembered that one of the officers at her school "would do this 'song of the day' thing during lunch where he would sit outside the lunchroom and people could stop and talk to him about it. . . . He always made his presence positive."

These memories from preservice teachers align with dominant narratives that equate school safety with police presence and position police as friendly, benevolent do-gooders. These experiences are also orchestrated by huge investments and efforts on the part of both public schools and organizations like the National Association of School Resource Officers (NASRO), the premier school police training organization, headquartered in my home state of Alabama. Partnering with NASRO, and aided by grants from the COPS program, public schools around the United States invest millions of dollars in training initiatives for school police; some school systems now even boast that their SROs are "NASRO trained."[28] Most notably, NASRO developed the "triad" model of policing that shows up in many public schools today, promising trained officers who are not only responsible for law enforcement on school grounds, but who are also "mentors" and "educators."[29] At its core, this triad model is designed to push officers to interact with students in "friendly" ways, gaining their trust and even encouraging them to share their adolescent problems with them, while also projecting a public image of school police as necessary. Police as mentors and educators, roles better handled by other adults in public education systems, make policing in schools seem necessary and grant them the authority and legitimacy of adults who are responsible for shaping students' lives, just as teachers are. Police are positioned as yet another trusted adult in the building, much as preservice teachers like Jordan, Karlie, and Mya remember them.

This NASRO triad model of school policing is part of a larger, nationwide network of police-youth programming happening in schools across the country that promotes positive views of policing—programming that leaves little room for folks to critique police presence. This pervasive presence of positive policing means that when students do report problems with the police, it makes it easier to chalk up harmful policing to a few "bad apples." After all, how could the sort of "teddy bear" officers that Jordan recalled so fondly also be responsible for harming students? In the next section, we learn more about various police programs in schools, including how preservice teachers remember their experiences with them.

Officer friendly

Police-youth programming in US public schools has its roots in the Officer Friendly efforts that began in the Chicago area in 1966, a joint venture between the Sears-Roebuck Foundation and the Chicago Public School System.[30] Police officers began entering classrooms to "educate" students about how they kept communities safe, and teachers were supplied with related workbooks and activities. Some teacher materials included a "show-and-tell" book with illustrations of a white police officer holding the hand of a small Black boy, captioned with "The policeman is my friend. He helps me cross the street. He holds up his hand and stops the cars. Then it is safe for me to cross. And the policeman smiles at me . . . because he is my friend."[31] Workbooks encouraged students to engage in "crime resistance activities" in lieu of instruction about, for example, math, reading, or other content areas.[32] The context for the program's origin is important: Officer Friendly began in response to antipolice sentiment proliferating around the country as police violence against not just everyday citizens, but also civil rights activists and anti-war activists, became more visible. A spokesperson from the Sears-Roebuck Foundation made the purpose clear: "In the 1960s, it was a very turbulent time. Police were called names and we felt there was a need for the children to see police officers as human beings."[33] By the 1970s, similar programs had spread across the country, with police making routine visits to classrooms to "teach" students about their roles and responsibilities. Indeed, Officer Friendly programs really introduced school police not just as those responsible for law enforcement, but also as educators.

This type of "friendly" education continues today. Meg, a preservice teacher from New York, remembered a school police officer who "would come into different classes and would give advice and talk about his job and crazy stories he had. He . . . gave a great presentation/talk to all of us about law enforcement and his job." Similarly, Ryley, who was learning to be an elementary school teacher, recalled that "we would have our local police come into our classes when we were doing community service projects in our leadership classes." One need only look at the social media accounts of local school systems to see images of police in front of classrooms, giving handcuff demonstrations, presenting slide decks about policing, and even bringing K-9s to classrooms as part of lessons about police.[34] The model of cops-as-teachers started with Officer Friendly programs in the 1960s and expanded in the 1970s. By the time I was in elementary school in the 1980s, it was much more robust.

D.A.R.E.

In the 1980s, police-youth programming started to morph from Officer Friendly programs to take new forms, one of which was the Drug Abuse Resistance Education (D.A.R.E.) program. D.A.R.E. came about at the height of the War on Drugs, when government and media fearmongering instilled anxieties about crime waves and gang violence related to the sale of drugs. In Los Angeles, the site of the first D.A.R.E. program, the LAPD at the time was led by police chief Daryl Gates.[35] Chief Gates and his police department had tried for years to disrupt drug sales in Los Angeles, with little success. While there had been prior iterations of drug prevention programming aimed at youth, including some in public schools, Gates began to zoom in on public schools in a new way. Partnering with the Los Angeles School District, which already had its own school police force (the Los Angeles School Police Department), he deployed uniformed police officers in schools to begin concentrated education programs with K–12 students.[36] To bolster support for the program, the LAPD engaged in a fearmongering campaign of its own. It related drug sales to racialized narratives about gangs, broken homes, and drug use, and went so far as to claim that even very young students were using drugs like marijuana and phencyclidine (PCP; also known as "angel dust"), without any evidence to support that claim.[37] The LAPD asserted, "We are now seeing chronic marijuana use by 12-year-olds and even younger" and claimed that "PCP is frequently used by juveniles in the Los Angeles area and its epidemic proportions give serious cause for alarm."[38] And, according to historian Max Felker-Kantor, "police officers and educators believed that elementary school students in the 1980s were so aware of drugs that teachers were out of their depth in teaching drug prevention. Instead, police officers were the only option for changing student attitudes toward drug use."[39] Notably, as Felker-Kantor details, the early iterations of D.A.R.E. were implemented in a school district that was composed mostly of Black and Brown students, leading to increased contact between police and youth of Color.

The fearmongering campaign worked: parents, teachers, and educational policymakers, not just in Los Angeles but around the country, became convinced that drugs, and the gangs of Color supposedly associated with them, were the biggest new threat to school and student safety, and that police were best equipped to identify its incidence and prevent its further spread.[40] Police were soon routinely delivering instruction in schools across the country in the 1980s and 1990s, including in my elementary and middle school classrooms in North and South Carolina. D.A.R.E. meant cop-teachers were now lecturing about the harms of drug use and encouraging us to "Just Say No!" to drugs and alcohol. Police were now not just regular figures in school contexts; they were also teachers and public health educators, "transform[ing] the image of the police officer from a threatening enemy to a friend and mentor."[41]

Drug prevention instruction was also part of the schooling experiences for the preservice teachers I worked with, who attended K–12 schools in the 2000s and 2010s. However, they also recalled an expanded version of D.A.R.E.-like approaches, indicating both the role creep and topic creep of contemporary police-youth programming. Mackenzie, who was learning to be an elementary school teacher, remembered a police officer who would "give us informative talks during our gym periods about the law and the effects of drugs." And some of this police instruction about drugs and alcohol now expanded to include instruction about social media. Eva, who was studying to be a high school English teacher, recalled an officer at her school who came into her classes to "lecture us on parking violations, to not drink and drive, and to not send naked pictures of ourselves to people." Officers now focused on, for example, education about vaping and even conducted "vape searches" of students, according to Eva and another student, Kennedy, who was studying to be a math teacher. Searches, in tandem with instruction, were quite common. Mikayla, for example, remembered how, along with lectures about drug and alcohol awareness, police would "monitor lockers and bring in dogs to search the school to try and find students with drugs." Nicole, studying to be an elementary school teacher, also remembered drug dogs regularly during high school: "There would be a lot of jokes made from people, wondering if the dogs would find drugs in people's lockers, but from what I know, I don't believe this ever actually occurred."

D.A.R.E. programming, and programs like it, not only successfully position police as essential teachers and health educators, but also reiterate ideas about people who use drugs and even alcohol as "criminals," which has consequences for K–12 students. Imagine, for example, an elementary school student who has a parent at home struggling with drugs, who then must participate in mandatory drug education programming at school that situates their parent as a "bad guy" and criminal who deserves punishment and even incarceration. Or worse, a child reports their parent and is subsequently removed from the home. The oversimplification of drug and alcohol use, in addition to positioning parents as criminals, at once obscure the reasons why people seek out and use substances and also potentially contribute to the disruption of family structures. While reporting positions the student as a hero, they may also be catapulted, often permanently, into what we often call the "child welfare system"—better framed as a "family policing system"—including foster homes or group homes away from parents, guardians, and siblings.[42] These processes overburden youth and also potentially serve as a gateway to institutionalization for both youth and families. Yet police in schools encourage students to report their family members, neighbors, and peers for drinking and perceived illegal drug activity, assuming roles as confidantes and mentors for students.[43] Some children who have reported their parents and/or guardians as part of these drug prevention campaigns to "snitch" on adult family members have even been questioned repeatedly by officers for reports as minor as occasional marijuana use, use that is legal in many states in the United States.[44]

Likewise, students who report peers also may not recognize the consequences of those reports.[45] Rylie, for example, recalled a memorable instance from middle school:

> We were told to shelter in place. We could stay in the classroom and talk but no kids were allowed in the hallways. The situation that occurred was that someone apparently shared that a student brought lots of drugs, and it was in their locker. When it [the shelter in place order] ended, no drugs were found, but *everybody's* lockers were rummaged through and somewhat destroyed. This was middle school, so some girls had wallpaper and mirrors and hanging pencil holders. Other students had snacks or bathroom products in the top of their locker, but everything was messed up.

Police programs that encourage kids to snitch on their families, and each other, are nothing new. They are deep-rooted, stemming all the way back to the early twentieth century, when police recruited children to identify "delinquents" in their communities.[46] Scholars have argued that D.A.R.E. is just another form of police propaganda in schools, with its focus on criminalizing drug users and encouraging ideas about punishment and incarceration.[47] More specifically, these programs socialize us into believing there are "good people" (those who don't use drugs) and "bad people" (those who do), with the police as important and necessary to catch the bad people. While it is difficult to critique programs that purportedly aim to prevent drug use among students, it's worth noting that research has demonstrated just how ineffective D.A.R.E. and other drug abstinence programs have been throughout the decades. In some cases, youth have even reported using drugs at *higher* rates after having completed D.A.R.E. at school.[48] Still, programs like D.A.R.E. continue in public schools and are now sometimes positioned under the umbrella of mentoring programs, which we learn about next.

Mentorship programs

Police mentoring takes several forms for youth. In the community where I live in Alabama, there are programs similar to D.A.R.E. (one called "Too Good for Drugs," for example) that have more explicit focuses on mentoring, as well as programs for students who have been labeled "at risk" by school personnel and/or community members.[49] These programs exist all over the country. For example, education scholar Bettina Love has described mentoring programs called Teen and Police Service (TAPS), where "officers are assigned to youth and paid to mentor them."[50] These programs are problematic because they direct resources away from support systems and toward the institution of policing, part of broader social trends that invest in policing instead of welfare programs, even though we know that the institution of policing itself places students at risk of harm.[51] In other words, instead of providing wraparound services that support students' and families' needs, such as stable housing, food security, health care, mental health resources, and access to high-quality teaching and curricula, to name but a few, these programs locate problems to individual students and position relationships with police as the "solution." Notably, none of the preservice teachers I worked with during this project had participated in a formal police mentorship project. This is likely because few students who enroll in four-year undergraduate degree programs in universities and colleges have been labeled as "at risk" of failure, labels that are bound up with stereotypes about race, gender, ability, socioeconomic status, and sexuality, among other characteristics. But some preservice teachers recalled friends and classmates in high school who had been tapped to work with police after school. Many of those students were labeled "troublemakers." Kristin, learning to be an elementary school teacher, recalled that the common wisdom was that, by working with police directly, these "troublemaker" students would "straighten up."

Finally, for other preservice teachers, school police were not just operating as "role models" and "mentors" in their schools, but were actually members of students' families. For example, Margaret described school police who were the parents of some of her classmates. As she explained, "When someone in a uniform walked down the halls, my first thought wasn't that something was wrong or someone was in trouble, it was, 'Oh, so and so is here to see their son or daughter.'" Likewise, Becca remembered that the police at her school were "super friendly and I would often see them chatting to students in the hallways. One of them was my friend's dad, so a lot of us knew him very well." And, as Alex recalled, "Some [officers] were parents of students, and they didn't want to get their kids' friends in trouble." These preservice teachers highlighted the sometimes-overlapping nature of police and parental authority, which was common in their schooling experience.

Deterrents and crime prevention

Probably the most common placement of police in schools is under the guise of "safety" and "crime prevention." We might also think of this approach as a form of police-youth programming, since police are often interacting with students at school entrances, hallways, cafeterias, and extracurricular events; this presence as a law enforcement officer is one part of NASRO's triad model.[52] Policymakers and community members sometimes argue that this type of police placement acts as a deterrent. The thinking goes that if police are stationed and visible to folks, it will deter criminal acts, potentially preventing them from happening in the first place. Police presence—being "on the beat" on the sidewalk, in patrol cars, or in public spaces—is part of crime-deterrent efforts everywhere. And these assumptions extend to schools: if officers are in schools, they will deter potential threats, and students (and school personnel) will be more likely to abide by rules (and laws) that are in place. Ashley, who was learning to be a secondary math teacher, remembered police who "would just walk around eyeing students, bring dogs to sniff lockers out, and would pose as a threat to students if we broke any rules."

But some preservice teachers noted that police in schools did not actually act as deterrents, counter to what many policymakers and even NASRO officials posit as a primary justification for police presence.[53] Cameron, who was studying to be a high school English teacher, recalled police in her schools who "just walked around. . . . This doesn't mean the school resource officer didn't do anything, but it always seemed he wasn't doing anything. One time we had a person that was breaking into cars, and the school resource officer was getting updates. It seemed like people didn't take the school resource officer seriously because they would still break the rules."

Here, according to Cameron, police presence did nothing to deter crime. And some preservice teachers even remembered how police at their schools were not taken seriously by many students. Tyler, who was learning to be an elementary school teacher, recalled, "At the high school I graduated from, the SROs were a joke. The biggest problem facing them was sophomores vaping." Implicit here is that police at Tyler's school should have been concerned with more pressing issues; since there were none, students did not see the officers as necessary.[54] Similarly, Kelly, learning to be a special education teacher, pointed out that "they [police] were also kind of a joke because as long as you were friends with them, you got away with everything."

Research supports these preservice teachers' skepticism in that, in many places, schools with police may report more crimes, but researchers are doubtful that criminal behavior is more likely in schools with police.[55] For example, students across two public high schools in the mid-Atlantic region generally viewed surveillance and "safety strategies," including school police, as unnecessary, for a number of reasons: "Because their schools are safe; they feel that the SRO is only one person and, therefore, can't prevent all crimes; or they think that students who are intent on committing a crime at school will do so regardless of the presence of the police officer."[56] Similarly, across four schools in Missouri, students did not view police presence as deterrents for potential misbehavior.[57] And more broadly, police presence does not prevent crime from happening, despite much political rhetoric that would have us believe in the crime-deterring and crime-solving power of police.[58] Instead, more police potentially means more documentation of "crimes" since police make decisions about what and who to focus on as criminal. Police therefore have the potential to transform things that folks do every day into criminal acts, and everyday people into criminals. Put another way, police produce crime in decisions about on what and whom they choose to focus. In schools, this might look like police officers interacting with students about things like wearing hats, using phones, or being outside of class without a hall pass, escalating issues such that students ultimately receive both school-based punishment and maybe also a criminal charge. This move toward the criminalization of young people (discussed in chapter 1) undermines our commitments to teaching and supporting youth. Moreover, however, a focus on crime at schools among students obscures the ways that police themselves have been the cause of particular types of crime and violence in schools, like physical altercations with and even sexual violence against students.[59] The result is that students of Color, female students, and queer and trans students often report that the presence of police makes them feel *less* safe.[60]

Bullying

Police are also sometimes placed in schools as an effort to deter bullying among students.[61] However, research continuously shows that school police do not keep students from bullying or from being bullied.[62] Even when they intervene in an ongoing bullying situation, this intervention may not benefit students, since in some schools, "intervention" might look like arresting students who were accused of bullying.[63] This carceral approach again reinforces ideas about students as criminals and relies on punishment instead of investing in adults who are trained to support students' relationship-building. This approach also fails to implement principles of transformative justice that emphasize accountability without relying on punishment, which we will learn more about in chapter 5.[64] And we might also remember that there are countless incidents where school police themselves act as bullies, like the officer in South Carolina who dragged Shakara from her desk when she refused to give up her cell phone. Students at the school later reported that he had the nickname "Officer Slam."[65] Police also routinely harass and demean students in their day-to-day interactions with them.[66]

TEACHER AND STUDENT PERCEPTIONS OF POLICE PRESENCE AND SCHOOL SAFETY

Of course, we also know that the most widely touted justification for police in schools is to prevent school shootings. Unfortunately, research suggests that there are very few instances where school police have stopped active shooters. We need only remember the police who stood by while shooters massacred students at Marjory Stoneman Douglas High School in Florida and Robb Elementary School in Texas to illustrate this point. Researchers actually have found that more people have died when police or armed guards have been on the scene of active school shootings.[67] Referencing the continuation of mass shootings in schools across the country despite so much police presence, preservice teachers like Josh questioned what they were "actually there to do," and, as Hailie asked, if they were capable of "really keeping students safe."

My own experience as a teacher and researcher in public schools, including in predominantly Black and Latinx schools and in alternative schools, suggests that many students generally take police presence (and broader police presence in the community) for granted, even if they are sometimes wary of it. Students may resent surveillance tactics like police in hallways, metal detectors, and random classroom and personal searches by police. But they also may have internalized dominant narratives about policing and safety (such as "it's for our own good") or even that they are "bad kids" who deserve to be surveilled and scrutinized.[68] Indeed, police in many educational communities still enjoy broad support as part of efforts to keep schools "safe," despite counternarratives from students and families about how police enact harm, even in "progressive" communities.[69]

Therefore, teachers' and students' perceptions about police presence are complicated and nuanced, in that school police are sometimes equated with safety even as they inflict harm on students. As previously stated, some teachers may view police as necessary for school safety, but they may also acknowledge students' discomfort with or fear of school police.[70] In some communities, school boards have prevented teachers from participating in research about school police, which limits not only our understanding of teachers' perspectives, but also the possibilities of imagining schools without them.[71] In some communities, K–12 students may view police as just another member of school personnel, may be ambivalent about their presence, or may be skeptical of their efficacy.[72] And in other school communities, students have acknowledged that school police do not make them feel safe at all, and instead make them feel as if school is a prisonlike environment.[73] Some students feel so unsafe with police at school that they have successfully organized around issues of policing, creating and advocating for demands that they say will make their schools and communities safer without police. Some of their demands have come to fruition, like the removal of police from schools. Researchers have also found that students' perceptions of school police are often shaped by racial identity and interactions with police.[74] In one study of almost two thousand middle and high school students, researchers found that white male students were more likely to feel safe with SROs at school, while African American students of all genders were more likely to feel unsafe with police at school.[75] Further, education scholars like Maisha Winn, Monique Couvson, and Subini Annamma have detailed how Black girls and girls of Color with disabilities experience harm and criminalization in schools, including in their interactions with police.[76]

Preservice teachers like Josie were keenly aware of the tension between messaging about how police are in schools to keep students "safe," along with the knowledge that police can be agents of harm. She recalled, "In middle and elementary school, everyone was scared of the [officer] at my school because he had a gun. . . . I felt safe because people told me that he kept us safe, but I was still scared that he had a gun." Danny remembered that "at my first high school, the SRO was feared and respected. He used intimidation tactics to achieve results. I remember whenever I would hear the crackle of a walkie talkie, or the jingle of keys and my stomach would drop to my shoes. I wasn't even doing anything . . . usually. He was terrifying, but he had to be."

And Florence noticed, especially after the Oxford, Michigan, shooting close to her school, "Walking into school every single day, seeing many groups of police officers standing against the wall, observing each and every student in the hallway. They were rarely smiling and had a stern look on their faces and had their hands resting over their firearm on the belt. I could never tell if their presence scared me or made me feel secure and safe. I always wondered if it was a good thing that seeing this was the new normal."

THE (NEW?) NORMAL AND WHAT IT MEANS FOR TEACHER EDUCATION

What Florence describes as a "new normal" reflects both a scaling-up of police in schools and police-youth programming, but also illustrates how she had not learned about just how deeply intertwined schooling and policing are. Police have almost always been in schools in some capacity, which we learned in chapter 1, and there has been a huge increase in the amount of both individual police officers and police-youth programming over the years. And the social media and public relations campaigns that document police programming in schools circulate narratives of positive police presence to the broader community. NASRO even has a public relations campaign of its own, where it disputes claims that police in schools criminalize youth, going so far as to write on their website that "amid the movement for social justice, school resource officers have become a soft target for anti–law enforcement sentiment."[77] Its social media program, titled "Reality over Rhetoric," claims that NASRO-trained officers "do not contribute to the school-to-prison pipeline" and argues that SROs should not be involved in school discipline matters. They write, "A student's behavior should only warrant SRO involvement if it would prompt a 911 call in their absence."[78] Yet research clearly documents that the placement of NASRO-trained SROs leads to increased exclusionary discipline for students, like suspensions and expulsions.[79] A group of researchers in Pennsylvania even found that NASRO-trained officers were more likely to resolve some school-based disciplinary incidents with a more formal response, such as a court referral, referral to the juvenile justice system, or school suspension.[80] Similarly, researchers have found that police who have apparently built "positive relationships" with students also then engage in criminalizing behaviors, such as searches and requests for information about suspected criminal activities in their schools and neighborhoods.[81]

Further, many NASRO-trained officers have only completed an additional forty hours of training beyond basic policing programs.[82] And more training does not equate to more safety. Instead, we continue to invest billions of dollars in school policing and police training, not to mention the police-youth programming happening outside of schools around the country, but we continually see patterns of police sexual assault, physical assault, and criminalization of students in public schools.[83] Consider, too, how many viral videos exist of trained officers who are actively engaging in disciplining students in matters like possession of cell phones and other incidents that we read about in chapter 2, which certainly do not warrant 911 calls. And we need only remember the tragic murders of students like Trayvon Martin to consider how many 911 calls have been made to report "suspicious behavior" of Black students outside of school, in addition to the vast numbers of viral videos where white people have called the police on Black people (and people of Color) walking, driving, swimming, studying, sleeping, or even birding in Central Park. Put another way, NASRO's "Reality over Rhetoric" campaign does not consider the ways that we in the United States are socialized to view Black people and people of Color as "criminal," and white people as "normal" and "innocent," a socialization that plays out in nearly every context across the country, including among police, teachers, and administrators in schools.[84]

Taken together, this means that preservice teachers, just like all of us, have experienced vast amounts of powerful socialization telling us that police keep us safe when, in instance after instance, the opposite is true. Copaganda, whether as police-youth programming or the media that we consume, presents narratives that policing is a necessary and desirable part of life, including schooling. And what exposure to all this copaganda also means is that we might experience a bit of cognitive dissonance: we have to reconcile the narratives that we receive about police as helpful and necessary with the patterns of police violence against both students and everyday people that have been so thoroughly documented. Reconciling this cognitive dissonance often looks like chalking up police violence, or what some folks perceive as ineffective policing in schools, to "bad apples" interacting with "bad kids." This "bad apples" mentality also means that preservice teachers like Karlie and Jordan are able to reconcile their fond memories of school police even as they might be aware of instances of police violence against students. This mentality also means that preservice teachers might enter schools operating under the assumption that policing is necessary and helpful, prompting them to rely on police as they become teachers.

But just because we have a positive experience with individual officers does not mean that policing as an institution is not harmful—to students, teachers, or communities. Indeed, any positive experiences have actually been engineered and financed by sophisticated mechanisms to counter the police violence that happens all around us, all the time, and sometimes even *to* us, shaping our perceptions of the system of policing. Abolitionists argue that we fail to decrease the violence of policing when we forgo a "systems-based analysis" to instead focus on "individual behaviorist approaches to intervention."[85] As quarterback and activist Colin Kaepernick has written, "It is not a matter of bad apples spoiling the bunch but interlocking systems that are rotten to their core."[86]

BEYOND "BAD APPLES": PRESERVICE TEACHERS' CRITICAL ANALYSIS OF SCHOOL POLICING

There are preservice teachers who take up a more systemic analysis of policing as it intersects with issues of race, gender, class, sexuality, and all the other markers of our identities and the systems that intersect to oppress us and privilege us along those identities. In other words, these future teachers recognized the inherent violence of policing. Here, we focus on their recollections since interrogation of policing as harmful instead of focusing on individual officers is really part of abolitionist thinking. These preservice teachers' memories and perspectives serve as counterstories to the often cheery, positive narratives around policing in schools. They also demonstrate the importance for teacher educators to create space for future teachers to examine policing more critically, including room to voice their critiques, which can often feel risky.

Some preservice teachers with whom I worked attended schools without police-led education programs, about drugs or any other topics. For example, Lucy, a preservice teacher in New York, never experienced D.A.R.E., but she began questioning its effectiveness and utility after talking with a teacher friend and seeing a TikTok video about the "failure" of D.A.R.E. programming. She recalled that the video outlined how instruction by police officers relied on a singular message—"drugs are bad"—in lieu of any information about why people choose to do drugs or connections between drugs, mental health, and trauma. Similarly, Jocelyn, who was studying to be an elementary school teacher, did not see the necessity of having police engage in instruction with students about drugs. She mused, "We have health and safety classes that can teach that . . . we just have other people that can teach that. I don't think police are needed for that." These perspectives are reminiscent of those of early critics of drug education programs in Los Angeles, which historian Max Felker-Kantor has noted. For example, a Board of Education member voiced concerns about using police to teach about drugs, noting that "there are better agencies" to do that work; and even a member of the Police Commission questioned the fundamentals of the D.A.R.E. program, asking, "Do we want our military and paramilitary teaching moral values in our schools in a democracy?"[87] Indeed, there are many adults in school buildings, like teachers themselves, who might better embody the roles that police have increasingly taken on in public schools. Yet D.A.R.E. and programs like it, in addition to mentorship programs, police-youth camps, and even police-led sports leagues, today regularly employ police who have expansive roles and authority and meet little community opposition or critique.

Interestingly, preservice teachers who had not experienced much "Officer Friendly" programming issued some critiques of police in schools, largely related to their perceptions about safety. Some preservice teachers recalled officers in their building who, they said, relied on scare tactics to control students but did not make them feel safe. According to Hillary, who was studying to be an elementary school teacher in New York, police at her school "were there, trying to look intimidating . . . it made me uncomfortable because I felt like the goal was to intimidate students as if we were 'juveniles' [delinquents] rather than students." Mikeila added that "they were there to intimidate students and basically let students know that if they were to do something bad that they could be arrested. They were there to raise the level of discipline to out-of-school consequences." Ava recalled, "I never wanted to interact with them. I was pretty scared that they were there in the first place and tried to avoid them as much as possible." She also noted, "A police officer's job, as it was taught to me, was to protect from danger. So, if a police officer is in the school, it leads me to think that something is there that I need protection from." These perceptions about police as scary are the very perceptions that copaganda in schools and in the media are created to counter. Without mentorship programs, police as educators, or demonstrations where students get to "pet the K-9," for example, the reality of policing as a scary project was made clear to these preservice teachers.

Some preservice teachers even referenced police violence that they had experienced themselves, or witnessed, as they articulated their desire for police-free schools. For example, a police officer in Jocelyn's small community sent her sexually explicit messages online, in addition to previously engaging in sexual harassment and abuse of other women in surrounding communities. Jocelyn knew of patterns of police violence, particularly abuse against women, and explained, "This police officer had a background, and they still hired him here" and, she said, he did "a lot of other nasty stuff to women."[88] She said, "It makes me feel scared and unsafe around police officers . . . like just driving in my car and driving past a police officer, I can feel my heart rate go up." She reasoned that kids also "hear bad things about police," including stories on the news, or maybe they even experience violence, and then they feel "even less safe in schools." These experiences, coupled with her desire to keep kids safe in her future classrooms, informed her commitment to police-free schooling.

Elizabeth, who was learning to be a special education teacher, had actually experienced K–12 police-youth programming at her school aimed at, she said, "promoting trust and positive perceptions." Yet she was also well aware of copaganda in media, having seen shows like *SVU* and *Paw Patrol*. She was steadfast in her belief that police have no place in schools, and she drew on a particular instance that she had witnessed in high school:

> Next door [to the class I was in,] they called a police officer. She was a Latina girl, like me . . . and I'm not sure what happened, but she was kind of resisting, and so they literally put her on a stretcher and took her out. I cried because I went to kindergarten, like all of elementary school with her. I could just see the lack of empathy, or trying to de-escalate a situation and kind of just wanting to take her out . . . like her being the problem and wanting to take her out.

This incident, along with images of police violence toward students that she had seen online, left her "heartbroken," she said. She added:

> I just have so many questions in my head . . . did they really analyze the situation correctly? Was there a legitimate threat? Is this the proper way to go about this? . . . Is this creating more of a hostile environment? And then I think of, afterwards, what that could do to the student, you know? Are they embarrassed to come to school? Could they possibly, at a high school level, drop out? Could they isolate and just not speak? So those are the things that go into my head. You know, it really makes me emotional because that one instance could change the trajectory of their life, and how they view relationships, and school.

Lucy, also learning to be a special education teacher, had also borne witness to police violence online and in the media. She cited the murders of George Floyd and Breonna Taylor as a turning point for her, saying, "It's not like I was like 'Blue Lives Matter' before, but in 2020, with George Floyd and Breonna Taylor . . . [*she paused*]. And even now, I see these TikToks of cops . . . they're so ridiculous for no reason. It's almost like, if you're treating an adult like shit, then how would you treat a child?"

Lucy identified as a queer woman and talked about her identity in relation to a history of police violence. Referencing Pride as an extension of the Stonewall Rebellion in 1969, she argued, "This [police violence] is how you've treated my community in the past. You're still treating communities shitty, so . . ."[89] Again, rather than approaching each of these stories with an individualistic mindset, we should examine them as emblematic of the larger patterns of police violence—patterns that are deep-rooted in the history of policing as an institution, which we learned about in the last two chapters.

Preservice teachers also recognized the costs that came with police placement, in lieu of funding for other types of adults in the buildings. For example, Paulina, who had police officers stationed in her schools, recounted, "I remember the officer walking around the building, trying to look intimidating. . . . Thinking back, I do not believe these officers would have been well equipped to deal with issues related to mental health or other adolescent-related issues." Mara, who had a part-time job while learning to be an elementary school teacher, was also frustrated by the resources devoted to police in schools. She noted, "I don't pay much in taxes from my part time job at an ice cream shop," but questioned, "Are my limited taxpayer dollars paying for cops to relive their high school glory days and hang out with each other in the hallways between classes?" This question about resources is important; when school system budgets devote more funding for police programming in schools, there are fewer financial resources available for many of the things that *are* important for schools, like well-paid and qualified teachers, high-quality curricular resources, and support staff. Indeed, in contexts where public and social services have shrunk—from summer school nutrition programs to afterschool activities for youth—the institution of policing becomes a resource provider.[90] Take, for example, the ways that local police agencies step in to run food distribution services, host summer camps for kids, or even help "Clear the List" for teachers' school supply requests.[91] As abolitionist Mariame Kaba points out, "We're stuck in a position where because everyone's concepts of safety are subjective, they actually have so much power to keep demanding more, and then we end up in a position where education, parks and libraries are always defunded. And it leaves us with no way to be able to say: if all those other things were funded at the levels of this behemoth [policing] and more, what could our society actually be?" She reminds us, though, to "ask what else is possible, and let's make those things possible."[92]

AUDITING MEMORIES AND UNLEARNING COPAGANDA

As evidenced by the reflections in the last section, some preservice teachers come to the profession having already begun to unlearn the ways that copaganda socializes us into believing that police keep us safe. This is a step toward asking what else is possible and moving toward police-free schools. However, these perspectives are not the majority; what this means is that many preservice teachers, if unchallenged during teacher preparation, enter public schools as teachers who believe that police are resources for them and their students, despite so much evidence to the contrary. Herein lies a central tension that we must acknowledge and navigate: preservice teachers like Karlie, who believe that policing keeps us safe, will work in schools where the institution of policing harms students, teachers, and communities, as preservice teachers like Elizabeth, Lucy, and Jocelyn recognize and have experienced. Moreover, when preservice teachers like Karlie and others are not pressed to question police presence and instead take police in schools for granted, they may be more likely to rely on them for lots of different reasons, including, but not limited to, issues relating to student behavior and school discipline. This tension therefore underscores how recollection of personal experiences with police and memory auditing is necessary for preservice teacher unlearning. Even if this memory audit does not prompt an immediate shift in thinking about police in schools, it is important for preservice teachers to hear from one another and learn from those who are more skeptical of police, or have even had negative experiences with police, to recognize that positive experiences with police are not universal. Given that many preservice teachers are young white women and not reflective of the demographics who will be in their future classrooms, critical reflection and unlearning are crucial. Memory audits also model what we ask teachers to do in their classrooms when they introduce new content to students: to access students' prior knowledge and experiences about a topic.

In chapter 4, we will learn how to challenge future educators to confront evidence about policing in schools, opening even more space for unlearning and toward dialogue about and potential critique of policing, especially as it intersects with school discipline. We also will learn about the ways that teachers socialized to surveil and monitor students, engaging in the work of "soft policing."

ABOLITIONIST ACTIVITIES: COPAGANDA AND CRIMINALIZATION

While the following chapters will explore more detailed activities to challenge and extend future educators' thinking about police presence in schools, teacher educators might use these initial prompts to support preservice teachers in auditing their own memories, in tandem with the culture of policing in their local school communities and exposure to broader narratives via copaganda:

- Start by jotting some ideas about your memories with police-youth programming. What interactions do you remember with school police when you were a student? What are the ways that police were positioned as a "resource" when those resources may have been defunded elsewhere? If you didn't experience police in your schools, why might that have been? Where might those resources have been directed instead?
- Next, audit both your past and present consumption of media, including streaming, television, movies, and social media. Which are sources of messages about police? About criminals? About your own potential for "criminality"? How do they shape your understanding of what constitutes a "crime," and what should be punished as such? How do they shape your understanding of who criminals are? How do those messages shape your understanding of the roles and responsibilities of police, both broadly and specifically in schools?
- Teacher educators can scaffold sense-making of preservice teachers' answers to these questions by tracing, for example, the history of fighting or vaping in school systems local to them. Vaping, once punished by teachers and administrators with detention or in school suspension (ISS) at worst, has been increasingly criminalized. In some places, students are poised to face possession charges in juvenile courts and families are asked to pay hefty fines if kids are caught vaping at school. This shift—from in-house discipline by teachers and administrators to more formal charges in the courts—underscores how what constitutes "criminality" and who is "criminal" shifts and changes over time.

STUDENTS ADVOCATING FOR THEMSELVES
OPEN-MINDED TO ALL TYPES OF LEARNING
MORE WINDOWS
MORE COMFORTABLE
OCTAVIA BUTLER

CHAPTER 4

"What Happened to Those Kids?"

School Discipline Data and "Soft Policing"

It was my first day as a guest instructor with a class of preservice teachers at a university in the Northeast. I had collaborated with their lead instructor to design lessons about school discipline and school police.

I ask the class: "Raise your hand if you ever had detention."

A few hands go up.

"Any volunteers who'd like to disclose why you had detention?"

MACKENZIE: "I couldn't get to school on time. . . . I kept sleeping through my alarm and being late."

"Anyone else?"

ZAK: "Same, except it was third block after lunch that I was always late to."

"Other folks?" [*I use my "teacher wait time" to make sure that folks had some space to answer.*] Heads shake no.

"How about suspensions—did any of y'all ever have in school suspension [ISS] specifically?"

A couple of hands go up.

"Anyone want to share what happened?"

MAKAYLA: "I skipped school on Senior Skip Day, and we all had ISS for the next week as punishment."

"What about OSS? Did anyone get out of school suspension?"

No hands go up.

"Anyone ever go to an alternative school?"

KATE: "No, but I know folks who were sent there after the principal said they had weed on them at school."

"What about arrests?"

Heads shaking no; no hands go up.

DJ: "Some kids at my school got arrested because the cops said they had tagged a building next to the football field. They made a big show of coming in and arresting students at lunchtime in front of like half the school."

EMMA: "What happened to those kids?"

DJ (*SHRUGGING*): "I don't know."

Many preservice teachers experience police in schools as a function of the police-youth programming that is so pervasive, as we learned in chapter 3. These programs often start in elementary schools, like Drug Abuse Resistance Education (D.A.R.E.) and Career Day activities, into high school, where students experience what the National Association for School Resource Officers (NASRO) has termed the "triad model" of school policing, including not just law enforcement, but also police attempts to build relationships with and mentor students. Yet few preservice teachers have experienced direct intervention from police in their roles as law enforcement officers at school. While they may have known their School Resource Officer (SRO) or D.A.R.E. officer, none of the preservice teachers I worked with during this project had ever been involved in any incidents that resulted in punishment or discipline from that officer. It is also rare for preservice teachers to have experienced the type of school discipline that results in the removal of students from peers, teachers, and classrooms, as Makayla did: suspensions, expulsions, or referrals to alternative schools—types of discipline that are exacerbated by the presence of school police.[1]

But what we know about school discipline is that it is wrapped up with school police: student contact with police does not always happen in hallways, in cafeterias, or even at football games after school. While there are instances of student arrests for things like graffiti, as DJ recalled, instead, it is often a student's teacher who calls police to their classroom about some perceived misbehavior. Indeed, when police are present, teachers and administrators might be more likely to outsource school discipline, sometimes without thinking about "what happens to those kids" as a result.[2] Part of preparing teachers for police-free schools also means creating opportunities for them to grapple with the reality that teachers, too, police students' behavior. Preservice teachers must come to understand that their school experiences are not universal to all students; in fact, confronting the realities that not everyone learns like they do, had access to the same classes and resources, or has had the same relationships with adults in public schools they did are some of the most powerful "light bulb" moments that preservice teachers can have. Importantly, given that many preservice teachers are young white women, many of them have not been explicitly confronted with or experienced the harmful nature of policing in schools and school discipline more broadly. That's why it is important for teacher educators to extend and challenge preservice teachers' positive personal experiences with police (as explored in chapter 3) with stories of police harm in schools and the numeric data about school discipline that teach us about patterns in punishment and their lasting effects.

In this chapter, we will learn first about school discipline, including how we are socialized to engage in the "soft policing" of student behavior that sometimes escalates to interactions with police officers. We next explore preservice teachers' confrontations with school discipline data as a step toward understanding the nature of school discipline and its systemic effects, teacher and administrator referrals to law enforcement, and school-based arrests by police. The chapter next emphasizes several "traps" and "tropes" that teacher educators and preservice teachers must move beyond as we envision police-free schools. The chapter ends with Abolitionist Activities that support confrontation of data and critical examination of data patterns.

DISCIPLINE DATA FROM THE OFFICE FOR CIVIL RIGHTS

The Office for Civil Rights (OCR) is a federal office of the US Department of Education whose core mission is "preventing, identifying, ending, and remedying discrimination against America's students."[3] OCR administers the Civil Rights Data Collection (CRDC), which aggregates data from public schools across the country, every other year. Those data include, for example, demographic information of students for each school in the country, like students' racial and ethnic identities and disability statuses; information about the curricula offered in schools and school districts, such as Advanced Placement (AP) courses; and disciplinary information, including student suspensions, expulsions, and referrals to law enforcement for things that happen at school.

These data demonstrate how, in some places, schools are more segregated than they have ever been since *Brown v. Board of Education*, how some schools offer more advanced curricula than others, and how some schools have more support staff than others. For many Black students and students of Color, these data might confirm what they already know to be true: that each of them was one of only a few Black kids or students of Color in their graduating class; or if they were a Black student attending a predominantly Black school, they had less access to advanced French or Spanish classes than their white peers at a predominantly white school across town had; or if they were at a Title 1 school, they had few opportunities to engage in advanced curricula like AP courses; or teachers, administrators, and/or police disciplined them or their friends more frequently and more harshly than their white classmates.[4] Most germane to this book, these data make clear that, year after year, educators and administrators suspend, expel, and refer more Black and Brown students and students with disabilities to alternative schools and law enforcement than white students.[5]

In my last book about school discipline in Alabama, my coauthor and I analyzed these OCR data about lots of different school districts.[6] We found that teachers and administrators suspended, expelled, and sent more Black and Brown kids and kids with disabilities to alternative schools and law enforcement than white students in almost every place we looked. Importantly, this is the case not just in Alabama, but across the country.[7] In the next sections, we read about preservice teachers' reactions as they explore these data about schools from their local communities, including myths and misconceptions that are often used to explain patterns in school discipline.[8]

CONFRONTING EVIDENCE WITH PRESERVICE TEACHERS

> *My school suspended so many Black students! And, oh my God, it says there were seven students referred to law enforcement during that school year!*
>
> —Brittany, future elementary school teacher

Brittany, who was learning to be an elementary school teacher, was stunned by what she found in the pie charts about the high school that she'd attended in New York. As she scrolled down her laptop screen, she made notes about what she was finding: how many students had been enrolled at the school in a particular year, how diverse the school was, and the percentages of students of Color that appeared in the graphs in front of her. One set of graphs indicated that Black students comprised only 43 percent of students enrolled at the school, but 72 percent of the students suspended that school year were Black. Another data table on her screen indicated that, as Brittany had pointed out, school personnel had referred seven students to law enforcement during the same school year.[9]

Other students seated around Brittany were looking at similar graphs and percentages. Lala explained, as she looked at the data from her school, that the "school was 17 percent Asian students, but the percentage of students who received in school suspension was 11.4 percent Asian, and for out of school suspension, it is 10.5 percent." She paused and moved her finger up her laptop screen. "Oh, and here it looks like the percentage of Black students who were suspended is much higher than their demographics." Nicole, seated a few rows over from Lala, found that the school that she attended was comprised of only 2.5 percent Black students, but they comprised almost 10 percent of those students who were suspended both via ISS and OSS. She reasoned that "if most of the school is white students, they will have the highest percentages, but these Black students still have a high [suspension] percentage for such a small overall percentage." And Emma, who had remembered the SRO at her high school with admiration, was surprised to learn that school personnel had referred nine students to law enforcement during the 2017–2018 school year, including seven Black students, even though the school that she attended was overwhelmingly white.

These class activities were part of a series of lessons that I designed and co-instructed with teacher educators. In these lessons, preservice teachers confronted data from both their local contexts, including the schools that they had attended and were placed in as part of their observation and future student-teaching assignments, as well as aggregate reports that summarized the data more nationally. Some even explored the data about the schools that they hoped to work in once they had finished their degree. I worked with dozens of preservice teachers in five different classes across multiple states as they explored and learned about these data. And almost to a person, they found the same patterns. Some preservice teachers, like Nicole, were resistant to our subsequent conversations about these patterns in teaching and policing. We will learn more about what this resistance looks like in the "Traps and Tropes" section of this chapter. But others, like Emma, were adamant that they would not become teachers who contributed to "the patterns in those graphs." To support preservice teachers like both Nicole and Emma in fulfilling these commitments, we have to confront how these patterns represent the effects of the soft policing that educators engage in every day in schools and classrooms across the United States. These patterns represent real, actual students' experiences, and without shifting them, we continue to inflict real harm on students via the processes of policing and punishment.

Exploring soft policing in teachers' work

Public schools, health-care systems, and even the child "welfare" system, are all entities in our US society that participate in the regulation and distribution of resources.[10] Guiding that regulation and distribution are policies that dictate to whom and under what circumstances those resources become available. And how do we enact "policy"? By "policing."[11] As abolitionists Mariame Kaba and Andrea Ritchie explain, "When policing is understood as the control and regulation of access to safety, resources, and space to enforce relations of power, we see that police are not the only mechanism of surveillance, control, and punishment, and that force does not require weapons."[12] Further, they point out that "the authority figures who make up the 'soft police'—including medical professionals, social workers, and government bureaucrats—engage in policing in their own right, and are often entangled with traditional law enforcement."[13]

This definition of policing, and the "soft police," can also be extended to encapsulate teachers' work. Consider, for example, how we think about students' very presence in school: we have policies that guide what students wear (dress codes), how they behave (codes of conduct), and even attendance (truancy policies). To ensure compliance with these policies, school practitioners surveil—or "police"—students day in and day out. This does not mean that we always call actual police officers to interact with students, although teachers are responsible for many police interventions with students. Instead, with regard to student behavior, this means that we are often primed to look for specific violations of policies. Those policies may be explicitly written in a code of conduct or policy document—like dress codes, for example—or they may be implicit expectations about behavior that we've been socialized to think are "normal," like expecting quiet, obedient students. And we might label students who do not comply with these expectations as "troublemakers," as education scholar Carla Shalaby has described—labels that we apply more often to Black and Brown students.[14] In other words, we all have a "cop in our heads" . . . even as teachers.[15] Put simply: as educators, we police students and punish them when we think that they are misbehaving.

To punish students, we restrict students' access to safety, resources, and space, relying on disciplinary incident codes like "defiance," "disorderly conduct," "disobedience," and even "Other," which often includes dress code violations.[16] These incidents and infractions may then result in removal procedures like detention, ISS, OSS, and transfers to alternative schools.[17] Again, "policing" students in schools happens regardless of actual police officer presence, although the consequences for students who are perceived to violate policy or to misbehave are often worse when police officers are in school buildings. And when teachers feel like students can't be controlled, or when they become frustrated that students are not complying, they might call the police to intervene; this happens via "red buttons" on the walls of classrooms, walkie-talkies carried by teachers or school administrators in hallways, or even simply by a teacher looking into the hallway to see if a police officer is nearby.

The subjectivity of soft policing

The soft policing that teachers and administrators engage in regarding student behavior happens in ways that are subjective—that is, teachers interpret behaviors differently from one student to the next, much as police make subjective decisions about, for example, who to pull over for traffic stops. What teachers and administrators might perceive as student misbehavior includes talking out of turn, refusing to comply with a direction that a student might deem unimportant or irrelevant, or being in a space that teachers do not expect them to be—all often labeled as "defiance," "disruptive behavior," or "disorderly conduct." Yet how those labels are applied, and to which students they are applied, shift according to teacher, administrator, student, school, and district—applications that are rooted in how we are socialized to think about schools, students, and behavior.[18] And when some teachers and administrators feel that they cannot control students for these subjectively interpreted behaviors in a particular moment, they escalate issues, perhaps even relying on police intervention. Indeed, as I reported in my last book, in the 2014–2015 school year in Alabama, almost 27 percent of referrals made to police were for subjective incidents like student "defiance," "disobedience," and/or "disorderly conduct."[19] By the 2018–2019 school year, that number had risen to almost 42 percent. These patterns, including referrals to law enforcement for really subjective interpretations of behavior like "defiance," are common throughout schools in the United States—so much so that community organizers in some places have pushed for legislation that prevents schools from suspending and disciplining students for them.[20] These types of referrals occur in conjunction with reports for supposedly "objective" offenses, like weapons and drugs, which often have zero-tolerance consequences attached to them.[21]

How we have interpreted, and punished, student behavior has also shifted over time, lending another dimension to this subjectivity in approach. Education scholar Decoteau Irby, for example, has studied the ways that our interpretations of behavior, the consequences that we issue, and even the personnel responsible for enacting school discipline policies have shifted, constituting a type of subjectivity in approach over the last two decades of school discipline. This has led Irby to conceptualize contemporary discipline policies and practices as "nets of social control" for many students.[22] This subjectivity looks like, for example, the increasing criminalization of student behavior that we learned about in chapter 1, like implementation of zero-tolerance policies around fighting and the resulting mandatory suspensions that occur for students. As of 2015, twenty-two states had revised their approaches to zero-tolerance policies in efforts to limit exclusionary discipline, although some of those policy changes have not resulted in meaningful reduction of student punishment.[23] We can also look to legislation in California that now prohibits suspensions for subjective offenses like "defiance" as a result of community organizing around school discipline, and yet punishment of students continues.[24] And, of course, we can see the ways that school police placement has increased, resulting in police intervention around student behaviors like cell phone use, "defiance," or even dress codes, representing a disciplinary shift away from teachers and administrators and toward police.[25]

Despite all this subjectivity—from disciplinary shifts over time to the inherent subjectivity in interpretation of student behavior—both "soft policing" by educators and police officer intervention are still playing out with real consequences, as numeric data from the OCR, school-level data at districts around the country, and countless stories of students and families make clear. Teachers and administrators suspend, expel, and send Black and Brown students, queer and trans students, and students with disabilities to alternative schools at rates higher than their white, straight, cis, and able-bodied peers for alleged "misbehavior." Teachers and administrators refer these students to police more frequently, and police arrest these students at school more frequently.[26] In the next section, we examine our socialization about student behavior, including how those tendencies to police students mobilize stereotypes and tropes about racial identity, in addition to other identities.

Socialization about student behavior

Starting from the time that we are children, we are socialized to think about student behavior in school in particular ways. We are taught that "good" students sit in rows, are quiet and compliant, and follow all their teachers' directions. We might remember teachers who expect students to listen attentively, taking notes and filling in worksheets while they engage in direct instruction in the front of the room. This type of instruction, and the behavioral expectations associated with it, have been written about (and critiqued) for many years. Education scholar and theorist Paulo Freire, for example, called this the "banking model" of education.[27] In this approach, teachers are thought of as experts who "deposit" knowledge into students; students, by extension, are positioned as "deficient" until these "deposits" have been made by the teacher. Yet we know that students bring a wealth of their own knowledge from families, culture, and their lives outside of school.[28] In other words, students are not "empty vessels" just waiting for teachers to "deposit" information. We also know that learning is often chaotic and messy. Deeper learning can happen when students are engaged in dialogue and activities not just with their teacher, but with one another. Sometimes learning even comes in places we least expect it, in some of the most unregulated environments. I regularly hear from teachers that students just "don't want to learn" and clearly prefer spending time on their phones or social media. But think about, for example, how quickly students are able to learn a new dance from TikTok or the lyrics to their favorite new song—a testament to how kids are often willing to learn and share knowledge freely and creatively on their own terms.

In school, being attentive and quiet, raising a hand to talk in class, and following directions are all still often thought of as "desirable" classroom behaviors of "good" students. When students do not enact these behaviors, some teachers punish them, labeling them as "disruptive," "defiant," or "disorderly." Because we are so used to thinking about "controlling" or "managing" students, or making them compliant and obedient so teachers can engage in direct instruction, we often end up focusing on those behaviors that we've also been told are "undesirable": students who "talk out of turn," aren't sitting still, are "off task," or refuse to follow our directions. And, importantly, these behavioral expectations, as well as our surveillance of them, are bound up with stereotypes about race, just as we are socialized to think about behavior and gender in particular ways (like girls as "quiet" and boys as "rowdy"). While teachers may think that they are supporting a learning environment by removing students who they deem to be disruptive, they are really privileging compliant classroom engagement, while also potentially affixing lifelong labels to "disruptive" students. Those labels are consistently applied at higher rates to Black students and students of Color (in addition to students with disabilities and queer and trans students).[29] To support teacher decision-making for supportive learning environments, therefore, we must also grapple with socialization about race and student behavior.

Racial socialization

Racial socialization happens in a number of ways, throughout our lives. For example, in the United States, we have long been socialized to believe in whiteness and white people as "natural," "normal," "desirable," "smart," and even "beautiful"; when invoking descriptions of "race," white people usually do so about folks of Color.[30] Put another way, white people often consider themselves "raceless." This "racelessness" is also linked to an emphasis on socialization about "colorblindness" or color-evasiveness as an ideal state in our US society.[31] In this framing, the misguided assumption is that focusing on race is divisive and even racist. To this end, white folks, including teachers, often say things like "I don't see color." Yet if we claim not to "see color," how do we then see racism and work against it? We know that white supremacy and racism exist; they permeate all aspects of our lives, from interpersonal interactions to our systems of schooling, lending/banking, housing, health care, and, of course, policing and prisons.[32] Part of the ideologies that keep these systems going are the socializing messages that we receive about whiteness as normal and desirable and Blackness and Black people as "unnatural," "undesirable," "ugly," "dumb," "loud," and even "criminal." These constructions can be traced, of course, to the period of enslavement in the United States, when white people in power perpetuated dehumanizing tropes about and relied on the criminalization of Black people to maintain an economic system built on enslaved labor—tropes that continued after the abolition of slavery into the period of Reconstruction, and that continue today in the "afterlife of slavery."[33]

Abolitionists remind us that it is not just ideas about race that are part of carceral ways of thinking about criminality and consequences: ideas about, for example, gender, sexuality, ability, nationality, and socioeconomic status are bound up with who is considered disposable, dangerous, disruptive, and deserving of surveillance and punishment via policing and incarceration. Policing and prison systems are directed at people of Color, women, immigrants, poor people, people with disabilities, and queer and trans people.[34] Conversely, socialization about identities and criminality, in addition to statistics about policing and incarceration, reinforce stereotypes about people with majoritized identities, like white people or cis people or straight people, as more "innocent."[35] We also receive messages that Other and stereotype people along identity domains: people of Color and immigrants face stereotypes about who is considered "white" or "American."[36] Queer and trans people face stereotypes about being "deviant."[37] And people with disabilities face stereotypes that they are burdensome or abnormal—all of which serve to marginalize aspects of identity within our systems and assign degrees of danger. Folks who hold and embody multiple identities may experience oppression and discrimination at the intersection of systems of power; we might think of some folks as "multiply marginalized" and systems of oppression as "intersectional."[38] And when people who hold marginalized identities also hold prominent positions of power, the discourse shifts to portray them as exceptional. We often point to them as examples: "They succeeded, so why can't everyone else who is like them succeed too?" Despite all our efforts toward diversification of all our institutions like schools, corporations and businesses, health care, and the court and prison systems—we continue to see systems of oppression and their effects, like racism, sexism, homophobia, transphobia, and ableism. Stereotypes of different groups of people, including police and criminals, inundate our social media feeds, mainstream news media, television and movies, and even the work that police do in schools, as we learned in chapter 3. Police might be cheery and smiling, as they are presented in the books that they often read to elementary school students in school, or the demeanor with which they interact with small children or their K-9 companions. Meanwhile, police are also interacting with Black students and students of Color, for example, in harmful, dehumanizing ways, treating them as criminals in classrooms and schools.

Much as we learn about race, gender, ability, and "good guys" and "bad guys," we are socialized into thinking in particular ways about "good students" and "bad students." We receive messages about students, behavior, and identity not only from our own experiences, but from the media and popular culture. Take, for example, images of seemingly unruly, uncontrollable students in still-popular teacher movies like *Dangerous Minds* and *Freedom Writers*, or the students of the more recent television show *Abbott Elementary*, who have been criticized as being too well-behaved to seem "real."[39] And, as previously noted, we are socialized into behavioral expectations and what constitutes "good" and "bad" student behavior based on our own experiences as students. Taken together, how we are socialized about what "good" and "bad" students do, which is bound up with racial socialization and socialization about gender norms, sexuality, socioeconomic status, and even linguistics, shapes how we engage in surveillance and soft policing in schools. That is, teachers (and police) might expect students to behave in particular ways based on stereotypes about the identities that students embody, which shape interpretation of behavior. For example, teachers and students alike might misinterpret a Black student's behavior as threatening, which has to do with how we are socialized to think about Blackness as criminal and dangerous, and interpret and even reward a white student's behavior as compliant, which has to do with how we are socialized to think about whiteness as innocent and pure. Teachers (just like police) might be more likely to perceive Black boys as older than they are, Black girls as "combative," or gender nonconforming or trans students as "inappropriately dressed."[40] And again, this socialization about "good students" affects people across all demographics; we see, for example, Black teachers and administrators who discipline Black students based on these stereotypes.[41]

In one telling study conducted at Yale University, researchers showed teachers videos of classrooms, asking them to look for bad behavior. Many of the teachers began to track the Black boys in the videos despite the fact that the researchers had not included any language about race in their prompts.[42] This particular study gives us insight into how socialization works. It also helps us to make sense of the patterns that exist in school discipline data collected every other year by the OCR—patterns that show up along domains of students' race, gender, and ability. Data from schools across the country, including stories and testimonies from students, families, and practitioners, tell us that teachers and administrators are disciplining Black students (in addition to Latinx students, Indigenous students, students with disabilities, queer and trans students, and students at the intersection of these identities) more frequently, and with harsher punishments. For example, in my last book, my coauthor and I detailed a story from a Black high school assistant principal who described how school administration decided that a white student who had a large amount of marijuana and knives in her possession was able to be "picked up from school by a parent," while a Black student who had marijuana "small enough to fit in a gum wrapper" was arrested at school.[43]

BEYOND TRAPS AND TROPES

If not examined critically, numeric data like those from the OCR, in addition to stories about school discipline, have the potential to reinforce stereotypes about Black students, students of Color, students with disabilities, and even teachers and school police officers. Some people who explore these data will assume that Black students or students with disabilities, for example, are more likely to engage in behaviors that deserve punishment via suspension, expulsion, and even arrest. Instead, it is necessary to engage in a more critical analysis of schools as carceral spaces where adults are constantly policing students. While some school-based practitioners might argue that removing supposedly "disruptive" students is necessary for an ideal teaching and learning environment, we might instead engage with the idea that school discipline policies and practices actually create "spaces of trouble" for many students, as Decoteau Irby argues. To approach school discipline more critically, preservice teachers must move beyond the following "traps and tropes" as they examine school discipline data, recognize patterns, and look forward to their own teaching experiences.[44]

Trap 1: Deficit thinking

Many preservice (and practicing) teachers might explore numeric data local to them and think that, since these demographic groups of students are so overrepresented in the data, they must misbehave more. This might look like Kelly, a preservice teacher learning to be an elementary school teacher, labeling students as "behavioral issues," or Ryley talking about students as being "out of control" after looking at the OCR/CRDC data from the schools that they attended.[45] They might invoke one of the oldest myths in education—"Their parents don't care about education"—something that I've heard since I started teaching in the 2000s and something that I continue to hear from public school teachers and administrators in lots of different places. The "their" in this attribution usually refers to Black and Brown students. These interpretations of school discipline data—whether from the OCR or a particular school or classroom—are fundamentally flawed. These common tropes are types of what scholars have called "deficit thinking" about students and families.[46] That is, instead of locating problems within the systems that we have in place in public education, we focus on students and families as problems in need of correction.[47] Deficit thinking about students and families is rampant in education; yet in my twenty-plus years working in public schools and universities, I have never once met a parent or family member who "doesn't care" about a child's education. Instead, I have seen teachers and parents/guardians who care deeply about children, yet might have differing expectations of school, curricula, and even instructional approaches. And I have seen students enact resistance in classrooms and schools, which might look like putting their heads down on desks; drawing, writing poems, or engaging in other creative expressions instead of classwork; or even "talking back" to teachers and administrators. This resistance to unjust learning conditions, irrelevant curricula, and even racist and unfair policies and teachers is often characterized as misbehavior rather than student agency, empowerment, and bravery.[48] Importantly, framing students and families as "deficient" and as problems in need of correction is a poor explanation for patterns in numeric discipline data that show up in almost all school communities across the country.

Teacher educators should acknowledge deficit thinking when it arises in the classroom, pushing preservice teachers to examine where ideas about behavior and students originate. Teacher educators can redirect preservice teachers' attributions about behavior—away from ideas about students, families, and care—and toward understandings about the sociocultural and historical contexts of public education. Specifically, teacher educators can teach preservice teachers about public education in the United States as situated in a legacy of both disenfranchisement and opportunity, as well as how these legacies are bound up with race, gender, ability, sexuality, class, and even language, emphasizing how notions of behavior have been used to justify increasingly punitive practices in school discipline. And preservice teachers should understand how work in their future classrooms will contribute to this legacy of exclusion and removal of students unless they participate in the hard work of unlearning status quo perspectives about behavior, discipline, and punishment.

Trap 2: "Bad apples"

Sometimes examining data, whether they are numeric data from the OCR or stories from those affected by school discipline and school policing, reinforces beliefs about particular police as "bad apples" instead of recognizing patterns in school policing that go beyond individual officers. For example, Katie, after hearing her classmates describe the data indicating just how many students had been arrested at their schools, offered that she "never heard anything negative about my school police." She continued that she now recognized that "this type of personality in a school police is not seen at every school, and when I was in high school, this is something I did not realize and I took for granted." In other words, instead of recognizing a pattern of policing across the schools that she and her classmates attended, Katie attributed those arrests to individual officers who perhaps just needed more training or were simply ill-suited to working in schools. Katie's attributions about individual officers as "good" and "bad" are similar to those made by Abby, featured in the introduction to the book, who argued, "Are there 'bad apple' officers in schools? Of course . . . and they should absolutely be held accountable"; and Karlie, featured in chapter 3, who recalled her school police officer as "kind" and "approachable."

Yet focusing on individual officers as "bad," "mean," or even "racist" toward students is a misunderstanding of policing as an institution of racialized violence, which we learned about in chapter 1. As scholars of policing David Correia and Tyler Wall explain, "As a metaphor, the [bad apples] expression naturalizes the problem of police violence. It establishes that police violence is no more a political problem than a rotten apple. . . . It condemns police for 'unjustified' police violence, but excuses the police as an institution by locating the problem as limited to the individual. After all, an apple tree grows apples, not rotten apples, and thus the bad apple must be understood as an aberration."[49] Just as we must not label individual students as deficient, or as problems to be fixed independent of the systems of schooling that they exist in, we must not decontextualize individual officers from the violence and harm of policing as an institution.

Teacher educators must acknowledge thinking about "bad apples" and individualized notions about officers when they occur in the classroom. Teacher educators must also push preservice teachers to avoid extending this "bad apples" thinking to individual teachers—some might interpret patterns in school discipline to a particular "bad teacher." Indeed, in some places, there may be small groups of teachers who are responsible for large amounts of punishment.[50] But, as we have learned, discipline data are strikingly similar across the country; these patterns teach us that socialization about and expectations of student behavior are in some ways universal, underscoring how preservice teachers must start to unlearn what has been taught about behavior and punishment. This unlearning is especially important for those preservice (and practicing) teachers who might identify with police officers in schools, since both teachers and police are positioned as enforcers of policy and charged with punishing those who are deemed non-compliant. In some schools, teachers may even take their lead from police, especially given the emphasis on police as mentors, creating a tendency to humanize what are actually harmful, carceral practices of discipline and punishment. This might look like teachers observing police interactions with students in hallways, orders to "pull up your pants" or "take off your hat," and the punishments that result if students do not comply; teachers then engage in similar behaviors without considering the consequences for students. Teacher educators must therefore support preservice teachers' interrogation of policing behaviors with an eye toward building relationships with students and abolitionist accountability, which we learn more about in chapter 5.

Trap 3: Parity in punishment

As previously stated, numeric discipline data from schools across the United States indicate racialized patterns. These patterns have been characterized in various ways: as "racial disparities"; or that Black students, students of Color, and students with disabilities, as well as students at the intersections of these identities, are "overrepresented" in disciplinary processes and consequences; or that there is "disproportionality" in school discipline outcomes. And, as in the general research literature and mass media reporting about school discipline, preservice teachers take up this language. Examples of this include Matthew, who explained to his classmate that "African American students are overrepresented here" as he pointed to a pie chart visualizing OCR data about OSS on his computer screen; and Alexandria, who commented about how the "proportion of white students was lower than Black students" as she explored the discipline data from the OCR about the high school that she attended. While engaging in "disparity" inquiries and adopting this discourse might be an initial step toward understanding patterns, this language is misleading.[51] It implies that there is some desirable "parity," or equality of representation, in the ways that we punish students. This language also obscures how school systems are carceral contexts, where educators, administrators, and police rely on systems of surveillance and punishment. As abolitionist and education scholar Erica Meiners reminds us, "'Disproportionality' does not capture the reality of who is actively targeted for state and interpersonal violence: women, queers and those gender non-conforming, poor people, brown–red–black people, people with disabilities and/or others on the margins."[52] Put another way, the solution here is not that we should mete out punishment more "equally" across student groups, racial or otherwise. When we punish students by removing them, whether it be via suspension, expulsion, alternative school placement, or police arrest, we do not engage in accountability that works. Punishment by removal or arrest does not center relationships with students or their safety. And we can't "reform" our way out of these types of punishments. As Meiners explains, we must avoid the trap of aiming for "'better' school suspension and expulsion policies that just remove the 'right' bad kids from schools."[53]

Teacher educators can point out language about "disparity," "over/under-representation," and "disproportionality" when it arises both in classroom spaces and in research literature that they might assign to preservice teachers. Again, although this language might be well-intended, it implies that we can "adjust" our system of punishment to affect students more equally. Yet punishment by removal and police arrest is harmful and undermines our stated professional goals for teaching all children. Teacher educators can instead show preservice teachers how language shapes our understanding of phenomena in schools, emphasizing that we cannot reform our way out of the practices that lead to those disparities. Instead, we must bring an abolitionist analysis to practices like suspension, alternative schools, and school arrests by recognizing the harmful effects of these punishments and imagining how to do things differently.

Trap 4: "I'm going to be an elementary school teacher"

Preservice teachers studying to be elementary school teachers often assume that issues of police and policing are not relevant to their work. Because there are fewer police officers stationed in elementary schools, they may believe that they do not need to grapple with school discipline issues in the same way. But while there may in fact be fewer of them in elementary schools, their numbers are growing. According to the National Center for Education Statistics, in the 2017–2018 school year, over 50 percent of all elementary schools had one or more "security staff" and 36 percent of elementary schools had one or more armed SRO.[54] And, according to data from the 2020–2021 school year, law enforcement arrested over one hundred elementary school students in that year alone.[55] Consider, too, the egregious accounts of police who have arrested students as young as five and six years old, or even accounts of police being called in preschool contexts.[56] Importantly, these numbers do not account for all the police-child contact that occurred that did not result in arrests but still had potentially harmful effects on kids.[57] Nor do they account for the police-youth programming that takes place in elementary schools, like D.A.R.E. instruction or cops reading books to kids in classrooms, which we learned about in chapter 3.

Moreover, elementary school teachers may be charged with the work of soft policing, even if they do not name it as such. For example, Amor, a preservice teacher in New York who had just started her student-teaching practicum, was asked by the special education coordinator at her school to track particular students in her kindergarten class for two weeks to inform their behavior intervention plans. Amor described "literally making tally marks at the end of the day" to note instances of behaviors like "elopement, meaning running out of class," and "aggression"; as she put it, "What does that even mean for a kindergartner?!" The special education coordinator asked her to "scale them," noting different degrees of each behavior. And, Amor noted, all the students about who she was charged with generating "data" were "Black boys." As a Black woman, Amor felt unsettled by these procedures, and that the data she was collecting was "decontextualized." She felt that she was "tallying instances of particular behaviors with no opportunity to describe what had happened before or after." Further, these processes were tied to resources—Amor had been asked to track student behavior so they would receive supports as part of special education services. These processes are similar to what Isla Tauheed, an elementary educator from the Bronx, has described when she points out that "policing happens in the classroom, too, when educators enforce codes, rules, and regulations that students have never agreed upon." She argues further that "classroom policing is often cleverly masked behind color-coded charts, apps with cute avatars, point systems, and weekly trips to the prize box. Teachers dangle carrots as a means to patrol students' language and behaviors, or to regulate their bodies."[58]

Even though scholars have critiqued these systems of rewards and punishments for decades, they exist in classrooms across the country.[59] Systems of rewards and punishments also show up in teacher preparation courses focused on "classroom management," as Ashley and Bella, preservice teachers from New York, described having learned about. They recalled even learning about technologies like "Class Dojo" as a way to "track students" and "reward them for good behavior" in their future elementary school classrooms.[60] Tracking students in this way, while common, is a form of soft policing with historical and contemporary ties to formal carceral practices. It encourages student compliance via reward-seeking behavior in a powered teacher-student hierarchy instead of nurturing authentic classroom relationships.[61] Newer technologies like these are also tied to profit-making enterprises that arguably do not have children's best interests at heart.

Teacher educators can disrupt preservice elementary teachers' misconceptions about police in elementary schools, pointing out the increasing rates of placement there, especially following mass shootings like those at Sandy Hook in Connecticut and Robb Elementary in Texas. They can emphasize that it is highly likely for preservice teachers to work in a school with at least a part-time school police officer or SRO, drawing on both research and news media to demonstrate the harm that comes with police intervention into elementary student behavior. Teacher educators can also underscore the likelihood of police-youth programming in elementary schools that we learned about in chapter 3: programs that encourage positive perceptions of police in communities around the country and shift focus away from the harms that come with policing. And importantly, teacher educators should engage preservice teachers in learning and reflection about the systems of soft policing and punishment that educators engage in every day, like points systems or data collection procedures about student behavior.

Trap 5: It's not just about facts

A final trap has to do with the coming-to-consciousness that many preservice teachers (and others) experience in response to data. When preservice teachers begin to learn about patterns in school discipline, including exposure to the research that details discriminatory discipline patterns and how we engage in the soft policing of students, they often develop some critical analysis. This analysis is vitally important. Yet confronting data about racialized phenomena in particular, especially among white folks, often results in what education scholar and theorist Cheryl Matias has described as a "white racial epiphany."[62] For example, as white preservice teachers explored the demographic data about their schools, some of them were surprised, noting that it was hard to reconcile the data that they were seeing with their memories of school. Ian remarked, "I knew my high school was pretty white, but I didn't know it was *that* white! It's like more than 93 percent white students." Felicia also was taken aback when she learned how many "Hispanic" students were at her school: "I never saw anyone but white kids in any of my classes." Lucy, who attended a "really diverse school" and who said that she had lots of "different classmates," explored some of the other schools in her home district. She was "shocked" by what she found when she saw the overwhelming whiteness of some of the other schools: "I can't believe all these students grew up going to schools with kids who only look like them . . . it's just a *lot*. I'm shocked." Emma, who had recalled her SRO so fondly, wrote, "My eyes have been opened" after exploring the data from her former high school.[63] And Cassidy recalled, "Personally, I feel as though the security guards paid no attention to me because I am a white girl. A security guard stopped me once for running down the hall fast and asked what I was doing. When I told him I was quickly hanging up posters around the school for student council, he let me off the hook and never bothered me again. I now wonder if my race was different if he would've punished me."

As Matias explains, these types of racial epiphanies center the emotions of those who are coming to consciousness (in this case white preservice teachers), rather than the experiences of marginalized folks that teach us about how oppression operates. Further, abolitionist and education scholar Erica Meiners again reminds us that oppression and privilege are intersectional, but often recognition of oppression happens along only one axis, like race.[64] Epiphanies only about race, therefore, fail to account for how racism can also be bound up with heteronormativity, ableism, classism, and misogyny, as well as other forms of oppression. Data collection procedures, in addition to data visualization systems, also make it difficult to see patterns in multiple identity categories, obscuring the ways that systems of oppression interlock to affect students. For example, while there are mechanisms in OCR data websites to explore school discipline and policing patterns by race, gender, and disability status, it is cumbersome to manipulate data so two or more identity axes are overlain. To understand how oppression is intersectional, it is important for testimonials and stories of student experiences to be presented alongside numeric data. Organizations and movements like the In Our Names Network and #policefreeschools present students' stories and experiences with criminalization and policing at school, in addition to the robust research scholarship about students' experiences, much of which is cited throughout this book.[65] As preservice teachers explore both types of data—numbers and stories—teacher educators should be careful to frame and scaffold these activities with an eye toward dismantling oppressive systems and practices rather than a tendency toward saviorism.

Moreover, awareness about oppression and injustices is not enough. As abolitionists Kelly Hayes and Mariame Kaba remind us about mobilizing around particular issues, "It's not just about facts."[66] They underscore how, when moving people toward action, we must remember that "no fact is so shocking or profound that its utterance will spontaneously spark a movement." What this means in moving toward police-free schools is that teacher educators must push preservice teachers to recognize when they might be engaging in "epiphanies," pushing them beyond realization and awareness. After all, it's one thing to learn to critique educational practices; it's another thing altogether to mobilize to change them so that teachers do not, in Emma's words, become part of "the patterns in those graphs." In the next section, as well as in chapter 5, we learn about moving toward abolitionist accountability as a way to disrupt both police intervention with students and the soft policing of student behavior.

MOVING TOWARD ABOLITIONIST ACCOUNTABILITY

In the opening vignette of this chapter, DJ mentioned that he "didn't know" what happened to the kids in his school who had been arrested. But we *do* know. We know that they experienced, firsthand, what happens when punishment is used as accountability. We know that they, like so many students, were caught in a carceral system that centers soft policing rather than relationships. And critical and abolitionist perspectives remind us that "policing cannot produce safety and instead produces harm."[67] This includes the ways that educators engage in soft policing.

The only way out of this system—both for those students at DJ's school and students in schools around the country—is through imagining a different type of accountability structure. And, importantly, we know that this imagination must come from teachers. In chapter 5, we begin to take up and apply imagination, a core principle of abolition, to common scenarios that often end up escalating to school disciplinary proceedings. Specifically, we consider four case studies of student-teacher interactions that start with soft policing and are sometimes even escalated to formal police intervention. We do this so future teachers and their students do not become part of the data patterns documented in this chapter and in decades of other research about school discipline and school policing. In other words, we learn how to move away from soft policing and toward abolitionist accountability.

ABOLITIONIST ACTIVITIES: DATA CONFRONTATION

The following activity is for preservice teachers to begin to confront evidence about schools in their local communities:

- **Navigate to the website for the CRDC.** This collection details data reported to the OCR every other year. (Some of these data were recently removed by the Trump administration and later were reinstated; please note that these data may continue to be affected by shifts in policy and political dynamics. This broader context is something that you might also discuss as a group.)
- **Search for districts or schools in your community.** Depending on the guidance of your instructor, these could be schools that you attended as a student, schools that you anticipate working in as a future teacher, or school communities that you currently work in as a practicing or preservice teacher. First, just examine the demographic data for your school. What do you notice?

- **Navigate to the school discipline reports for the school.** Explore categories of student removal, such as ISS, OSS, and/or school-based referrals to law enforcement. For example, what is the proportion of Black students at the school? Of white students? What is the proportion of Black students receiving ISS? Of white students? Put another way, which demographic groups of students appear to be most affected by suspensions, expulsions, and referrals to law enforcement? As you look at the charts provided by the OCR, remember that these numbers represent actual students; sometimes looking at statistics and pie charts can "erase" the human beings that those numbers represent.
- **Reflect and discuss.** As you review these data, you will likely notice the same patterns described in this chapter. What attributions can you make for why these patterns exist, without falling into deficit explanations about students or the other traps and tropes outlined earlier in the chapter? What commitments can you make to avoid becoming teachers who contribute to these patterns? Specifically, what might it look like to adopt a philosophy of discipline that does not rely on writing referrals for student behavior that result in ISS, OSS, or expulsion? What other resources are available in schools to support you so you do not resort to calling the police on your students?
- **Continuous reflection.** As we have read, unlearning how we are socialized into carceral systems predicated on policing and punishment does not happen all at once, nor does it ever stop; it is a lifelong journey. Moving forward, how might you continue to interrogate your new commitments toward abolitionist thinking and action so you are not relying on deficit or "bad apples" thinking about students, epiphanies/the tendency to embrace savior stances, or a desire to punish more equally?

MORE CONFIDENT STUDENTS
MORE TRUST
BUILDING RELATIONSHIPS AND EMPATHY
KIDS WANT TO BE THERE

CHAPTER 5

What Would Mrs. Sue Do?

From Policing and Punishment to Abolitionist Accountability

WITH LAKENDRICK RICHARDSON

The Big Boy in the Hoodie: A Memory

Mrs. Sue was in the middle of a lesson on linear motion when a rattling knock startled us. We all loved Mrs. Sue. She had taught us, and many of our parents. Mrs. Sue always kept her classroom door locked, mainly because she hated being interrupted, so this intrusion was not welcomed. With a balled fist full of chalk, she marched to the door and swung it open to find a cop standing at the door. We did not have a School Resource Officer (SRO), but occasionally a sheriff's deputy would stop by.

"Good morning Mrs. Sue, sorry to bother you, I just had to speak to one of your students," said the officer.

"Why?" she responded, clearly irritated at the interruption.

"Oh, nothing too serious," he responded. "It's the big boy over there. The one with the gold hoodie."

I was the only one in the classroom with a gold hoodie, so I instantly felt a chill run down my spine, followed by anger. At that age, I did not have the words, but I did not enjoy being reduced to "the big boy in the hoodie." Like any teenager, I was deeply insecure about my weight, and his comment felt like a fat joke. With fire running through my fingers, I got up and followed this cop outside the classroom. A part of me wanted to know what this was about, another part of me wanted to check him for his comment, but nonetheless I remained quiet as I stood outside the door, waiting on him to come outside and address me.

"So, you know why you are out here, right?" he responded.

"No, but the big boy in the hoodie is eager to know what I did," I spit back.

If I were a rattlesnake, I was poised to strike. Was it teenage angst? A feeling of disrespect? Or my father's attitude? I'm not sure what came over me, but I was on the defensive and did not trust this man or his intentions.

He looked at me and laughed before responding, "Watch it, kid. I just want to know why you got that hoodie on when it's against the rules."

I looked at the officer, a bit shocked. Was he serious? A hoodie?!

"So, you pulled me from class because of a hoodie?" I asked rhetorically. "Because it's cold in this building, ain't nobody heater working, but my hoodie is the issue?" I continued on.

"Hey kid, watch it," he said, moving closer, intending to intimidate me.

"Watch what? What did I do?" I responded while taking a step back. "I'm serious, it's cold in here and nobody seems concerned about the raggedy building, but hoodies get y'all attention." At this point I was seeing red and felt the need to challenge, but Mrs. Sue must have heard my raised voice, because the door swung open. She stepped out of the classroom, closed the door, and approached the cop.

"Now look here Lester, I ain't said nothing about his hoodie, so why you bothering him? As I recall, you used to wear earrings when it was against the rules, and I let you get away with it. So stop bothering this kid, before I call the sheriff," she said.

"But Mrs. Sue, rules are there for a reason and he needs to learn them now," he said before Mrs. Sue threw up her hand to silence him.

"The world will teach him enough lessons, but right now it's colder in this hall than in this classroom," she replied. "Let's just continue this discussion on any other day than the coldest one this year. OK?"

Mrs. Sue did not wait for a response. She ushered me into the room, following behind me, and motioned for me to take my seat.

And just like that, Mrs. Sue continued her lesson on linear motion. I was never particularly a teacher's pet, but she took me out of a situation that could have ended badly. I remember thinking that if I ever became a teacher, that's the kind I wanted to be: one that stood up for kids, especially when they were being persecuted over trivial things that were wrapped up in carceral logics.

—LaKendrick Richardson, high school teacher in Alabama

LaKendrick, a practicing high school teacher, wrote this story as part of his reflection about how he came to abolitionist perspectives about school police. In his story, he details how a school police officer was poised to punish him for a supposed dress code violation. But LaKendrick's teacher intervened, choosing to calmly de-escalate the situation rather than focusing on compliance with a policy. She prioritized LaKendrick as part of a learning community instead of allowing the officer to punish him, ensuring that he would not be removed from any more learning time with her and his peers. And because she had a relationship with this particular officer, Mrs. Sue called out the hypocrisy in his focus on LaKendrick's hoodie, reminding the officer that he, too, was not always in compliance with policy when he had been a student. More important, she remained accountable to her values as an educator, prioritizing LaKendrick's place in the learning community over compliance with policy. Taking accountability for ourselves as educators and recognizing students as part of a broader learning community are vital for working toward abolition. They are on the path toward how we might start to think differently about students, behavior, and accountability—what we might call *abolitionist accountability.*

It is rare to see this type of explicit teacher intervention into police-youth contact. Instead, teachers often escalate interactions with students around issues like dress codes, phones, and other school policies—issues of compliance that, as LaKendrick indicates, are "wrapped up in carceral logics." This escalation sometimes even results in police coming to classrooms; indeed, teachers are often the source of many referrals to law enforcement, calling the cops on kids that they deem non-compliant.[1] In earlier chapters, we learned how teachers (and students) have been socialized into believing that police keep us safe and are a resource. And, in chapter 4, we learned about how educators engage in "soft policing" of student behavior even without the presence of police officers.

In this chapter, we learn about carceral logics and how they shape how we think about accountability and safety. We examine how a carceral version of accountability—the structural tendency toward blame and punishment—plays out at a micro level in classrooms and student-teacher interactions. Specifically, we present vignettes that describe common interactions between and among students and teachers that often escalate to police contact with youth. Then we examine how preservice teachers in teacher preparation classes at several large universities across the country responded to these vignettes.[2] The chapter ends with Abolitionist Activities focused on values mapping and analysis of codes of conduct to support preservice teachers' identification and disruption of carceral logics in classrooms and schools.

SCHOOL DISCIPLINE AND CARCERAL LOGICS

As we learned in the last chapter, numeric data collected by the Office for Civil Rights (OCR) from schools across the country indicate that school-based practitioners (teachers and administrators) suspend, expel, and refer students to police many, many times every school year. This results in the removal and exclusion of students from their classrooms, peers, and teachers. And it can lead to police-youth contact. Examination of these data, however, does not tell us the specific infractions that students are punished for—the issues or incidents that lay behind these numbers. But if we triangulate or corroborate these data with other numeric data sources from local and state agencies, in addition to stories about things that have happened in schools around the country, we can piece together a fuller picture of what these incidents are. For example, we know that many educators and administrators deem students to be non-compliant by labeling them "defiant," "disobedient," or "disorderly"—all labels that are rooted in subjective interpretation of student behavior. In chapter 4, I characterized this as "soft policing" in schools—the ways that we surveil and control students for compliance with policies, norms, and rules that we take for granted, and then punish them via removal and exclusion. Soft policing is rooted in carceral logics: the ideas and processes by which punishment and removal become seemingly normal and natural and beneficial to the whole.

Educators communicate carceral ideas to students all the time, especially in our school discipline and classroom management beliefs and practices. For example, as education scholar Carla Shalaby describes, educators determine and post rules in norms in classrooms, reinforcing ideas that rules (like laws) keep people safe. Teachers then develop systems of rewards and punishments to motivate students to abide by those rules. When students do not comply, educators "flag" them and intervene, relying on "punishing, pathologizing, or diagnosing" them, and finally "excluding them."[3] Shalaby explains that these logics communicate to students that "to preserve the classroom community and other kids' rights to learn, the threat to that community must be removed," reinforcing the notion that "community only includes people who are good and follow the rules." In other words, as she writes, "One's place in the community is conditional and contingent." By acknowledging how these carceral logics underpin the seemingly "normal" routines of classrooms, we come to understand that classrooms are not safe for all students; instead, students run the risk of punishment and ultimately removal from their learning environments if we determine them to be unable or unwilling to comply with policies and rules, and harm is done even to those who remain.

Mobilization of carceral ideas about compliance means that we deem some students "bad," and others "good," while we deem certain student behaviors to be "problematic." And, as we learned in earlier chapters, interpretations of student behavior are deeply racialized, classed, and gendered, and they are bound up with perceptions about (dis)ability, sexuality, nationality, and other demographic and identity markers. The behavior that we determine to be problematic tends to threaten the stability of perceptions about order—and, to Shalaby's point, not the actual safety of students. We then trap ourselves as educators into policing for "bad" behaviors, labeling students as "defiant" or "disorderly," often becoming overly focused on dress codes, phones, talking out of turn, or calling out—and maybe even ultimately calling police to classrooms to discipline those "bad" students and behaviors. We do all this in a misguided attempt to "hold students accountable" to the often unjust systems and structures that govern schools and classrooms. Writing about community accountability, organizer and abolitionist Amanda Aguilar Shank points out that abolition is not just about ending our reliance on policing and prisons; it's also about "knowing that the current systems we have put in place to address harm are actually causing additional harm."[4] In schools, that means recognizing that our systems of soft policing and punishment introduce harm to spaces that are supposed to be positive and supportive for youth.

So how do we encourage preservice teachers to resist the carceral logics that lead to punishment and even police-youth contact and move toward abolitionist accountability? One way is to examine micro-interactions in classrooms. In the next sections are four classroom vignettes, each of which was presented to and analyzed by preservice teachers.[5] These vignettes are both hypothetical and familiar: I have observed some version of them in just about every school I've been in, whether as teacher, researcher, or observer. And, importantly, some version of them has also been reported to me from the preservice teachers I worked with during this project, in addition to those practicing teachers I've worked with over the years. The scenarios they detail are everyday occurrences, and yet they are also those that teachers and administrators sometimes escalate to actual police contact with youth. I present these vignettes along with preservice teachers' discourse about them as they work to make sense of how they might respond, integrating abolitionist perspectives to both critique and affirm their perspectives.

Vignette A: Dress Code Surveillance by Mr. Pauly in the Hallway

Mr. Pauly is on hall duty before school one day. He is standing outside his math classroom and notices that two of his students, Jamal and Ryan, are walking through the hall with their hoodies on. He also notices that they are sagging their pants. Both things are against the dress code. Mr. Pauly calls out to them. "Boys, pull up those pants and take off your hoodies, please!" Jamal and Ryan do as they are told and give Mr. Pauly a slight nod as the bell rings.

Mr. Pauly is about to go back into his classroom to start the day, but when he turns around, he notices that they have pulled up their hoods again as soon as he turned away.

"Jamal! Ryan!" he shouts, louder this time over the noise of the crowd in the hallway hurrying to their first class, "What did I just tell you?"

"Yeah, OK, we heard you," Ryan says.

"Then do as you're told," Mr. Pauly yells back. His voice is getting louder and he is getting frustrated.

"We're going to Mrs. Lauden's class," Jamal says as he walks down the hall and passes Mr. Pauly, adding, "She doesn't care."

Ryan walks past Mr. Pauly too, and they begin to head down the stairs.

"Don't walk away from me when I'm talking to you," Mr. Pauly calls after them, "Jamal! Ryan! I need you to take those hoodies down and pull those pants up or I'm going to have to write you up."

Jamal and Ryan keep walking. Mr. Pauly has to decide what to do.

Preservice teachers Emma, Holly, and Lauren read and discussed this vignette in their small group. They suggested that it might be appropriate for the teacher to "explain to the students why it was important for them to follow the dress code." Also, they took issue with the ways that policy was being enforced in different ways by different teachers: "If it's policy, why doesn't the other teacher care?" In another small group, Laura and Christa vocalized some of the tensions that other preservice teachers in their class were wrestling with. They first noticed that Mr. Pauly was yelling at the students. Laura argued, "the teacher was being mean." Christa agreed, pointing out that Mr. Pauly should "ask nicely and not yell when giving directions." They rationalized Mr. Pauly's frustration, however, noting that "the boys weren't listening." Importantly, after their analysis of the vignette, Brianna and Gretchen decided to ask the class, "Why can't they wear hoods or pants that sag?" Emma, Holly, and Lauren argued that dress codes were important because "showing butts is a no-go" and "hoodies and hats are safety issues." When pressed to articulate what they meant, they argued that it was important for adults to be able to see kids' faces in the hallway and on surveillance cameras. Notably, many of the preservice teachers in this class had been in local high schools when the mass shooting at Oxford High School in Michigan had happened. They had endured multiple threats and lockdowns in the days and weeks following the shooting—so much so that, as Emma said, "police were at the school all day, all the time." This presence, coupled with the messages around safety and policing that they received, meant that some preservice teachers were hyperfocused on issues of policy and compliance. While Emma, Lauren, and Holly staunchly defended the need for dress code policies throughout the discussion, they agreed that police were not the answer in this scenario. Preservice teachers in other groups, like Cesar and

Joe, argued that schools should have "open dress codes," emphasizing that "less extreme consequences" and "keeping kids in school" were most important.

Abolitionist perspectives push us to ask questions about policies, including who they punish and who they keep safe. In schools, enforcing rules and policies often does not demonstrate care for students. Specifically, dress codes, and the ways that educators and administrators try to force compliance with them, *police* how youth express themselves via their clothing choices, in addition to Blackness and expectations for what constitutes "masculine" and "feminine" student expression. And dress codes often provide a mechanism by which schools exclude students. For example, as I wrote about in my last book about school discipline, one school system in Alabama suspended so many students for dress code violations that legal advocacy groups, parents, and community members organized to change the policies that led to these suspensions.[6]

Yet these policies that so deeply affect students are often those that practicing and preservice teachers take for granted, like Emma, Holly, and Lauren. Indeed, Brianna and Gretchen's question about why students "can't wear hoods or pants that sag" is important. Dress codes are not only deeply entrenched in racial, gender, sexual, and class politics, but also prisons and policing. Since at least the 1980s, when sagging pants became a pop culture trend, police officers have been stopping Black and Latinx youth on the streets for markers of what they deemed "gang affiliation," like sagging pants, hoodies, braids, and certain colors.[7] From the mid-2000s to now, lawmakers and political officials in states and municipalities across the country have introduced legislative proposals to ban sagging pants and hoodies with varying success, citing that sagging pants were a marker of criminality and hoodies were a "safety issue" both outside of and in school.[8] We need only remember the murder of Trayvon Martin as an indicator of what hoodies represent to many people in the United States. In Florida and Georgia, city officials have even bragged about their "fashion policing" approaches and how much revenue these fines generate for their municipalities.[9] Some of these same legislators and policymakers have also attempted to ban "short shorts" and skirts in public.[10]

Bans centering street fashion outside of schools have mirrored what has happened in school dress codes, which often contain language about tank tops, shorts, sagging pants, belts, hats, and hoodies; some of these are also prohibited in prisons. Although students have organized over the years to assert their right to free expression, many educators and administrators still often interpret students' dress according to these policies.[11] Adherence to these policies indicates that educators have internalized socialization about sagging pants being associated with criminality, or that young women should "dress appropriately," meaning that they should have covered shoulders, midriffs, and legs.

In cases of dress code violations, punishment might look like removing students from class to call a parent/guardian for a change of clothes, a write-up that sends them home with a suspension for a number of days, or even introducing school police to the situation if students do not comply. These punishments do not keep students safe. Instead, punishments for dress code violations communicate to students that not only will they be stereotyped for their clothing, but that they are part of a school community only insofar as they are willing to comply with the rules and norms of schools. Many practitioners continue to argue that these policies are in place for "safety" reasons, as Emma, Holly, and Lauren referenced and what they continued to argue to the other groups who analyzed this vignette. But it is important to ask: How might educators damage relationships if they surveil students in attempts to enforce policy? As Laura and Christa pointed out, the teacher in the last vignette was yelling at students. The shape and tenor of adult talk in schools land on students in particular ways—whether it be yelling or a calm voice. The next vignette illustrates issues of surveillance and treatment of students as well.

Vignette B: Tech Surveillance in Ms. Olsen's Middle School English Classroom

Ms. Olsen, a middle school English teacher, has been working with her students on intertextual connections to a book they've read in class. Her students are working in pairs to ask one another about the connections they're making. One group, Melanie and Onike, are talking about a movie that is an adaptation of a part of the book. Ms. Olsen overhears Melanie say that she doesn't know the movie her partner, Onike, is talking about. Onike gets out her phone to show her partner Melanie the movie on the IMDB app. They are both looking at Onike's phone when Ms. Olsen walks over. Ms. Olsen says, "Onike, put your phone away. You know you're not allowed to have devices in class." Onike replies, "But Ms. Olsen, we're talking about the book!" Ms. Olsen, getting frustrated, tells Onike again to put her phone away. Onike becomes frustrated now too. "Ms. Olsen, we're literally talking about the book. I'm showing Melanie that movie that came out last year." Ms. Olsen responds, loud enough for the whole classroom to hear her now, "Onike, I'm not even sure how you have your phone on you right now. You know you're supposed to put it in your locker before school." Onike is really frustrated now, and she's embarrassed that Ms. Olsen has called her out in front of the class. She slams her phone down on her desk and mumbles under her breath something that Ms. Olsen can't quite make out. Ms. Olsen has to decide what to do now.

Kaitlyn and Monica sat at a table next to each other as they read this vignette. They talked first about tech policies in schools, noting that, when they were in high school, everyone had their phones on them "all the time." They first decided to ask about the vignette: "Was this a classroom policy or a school policy? Is it consistently being enforced?" Kevin and Laura, at another table, briefly discussed tech policies, but they noticed and pointed out to the class that "Onike was actually on task." At their table, Bella, Patsy, and Evie talked about what tech policies had been like at their schools, where they too said "everyone had phones." Yet their group did not emphasize policy but rather the teacher's response: "Ms. Olsen called out Onike in front of the whole class. She didn't have to do that. She could have given her an alternative." Riley and Christina also agreed, arguing, "Ms. Olsen was quick to blame Onike. She created a scene in front of the whole class." And, as Kevin and Laura mused, "if Ms. Olsen were to further escalate, she might write Onike a referral, resulting in her suspension or worse." The class agreed that this type of punishment was not appropriate, especially for a student who was actually engaged in the lesson. Kaitlyn and Monica offered that these kinds of "power struggles" were common in classrooms, but they didn't have to be. The class agreed that emphasizing "empathy," "relationships," and "an open mind to all types of learning" were what teachers should be thinking about. Yet many were unsure of what might happen if there were schoolwide policies that they, as new teachers, didn't follow "to a T," as Evie put it.

Phone and device policies are in some ways more entrenched than dress code policies in schools today. In the mid-2000s, when I began teaching high school, the iPhone and Androids that we are so used to today were not yet on the market. But students were already arriving at school with iPods that they could use to connect to the internet and message one another. In the late 2000s and early 2010s, students as young as elementary schoolers began arriving at school with iPhones, Androids, and all other types of devices. And, of course, phones, iPads, and other devices now are seemingly indispensable parts of childhood, adolescence, and adulthood. In some schools, educators have embraced this technology, integrating student devices for warm-up activities at the beginning of class, as sources of information about the content for the day, and as creative outlets for them to demonstrate their learning. But, in many schools, phones are still strictly prohibited, although enforcement of those policies is not always consistent.

Kaitlyn and Monica's questions about policy enforcement reflect the reality that educators give students mixed signals about technology all the time. For example, we might ask students to rely on Chromebooks or other internet-connected devices while simultaneously prohibiting phone usage, without clear explanations for these distinctions. Or educators might tell students that phones are off-limits while using their own during class, either as part of a lesson or in other contexts.[12] Although we often defend school rules about student phone use in the context of supporting learning, it's worth pointing out that policies prohibiting devices are rooted in carcerality: people in jails and prisons are not permitted to have personal devices, and they are even considered contraband. They must instead work to "earn" communication privileges with friends and families on the outside.[13]

The broader issue in this vignette, though, is how Ms. Olsen is attempting to force compliance with this policy—at the expense of both Onike's dignity and support for Onike to meet the learning objectives for the lesson, as Kevin, Laura, Bella, Patsy, and Evie pointed out. Blaming students for non-compliance, instead of examining our interpretations of behavior and the structures in place that shape those interpretations, is also rooted in carcerality. And, as we have seen in viral videos of incidents in schools across the country, Ms. Olsen could have called a school police officer to intervene, introducing even more punishment and harm.

As Evie points out, though, many teachers, and perhaps especially new teachers, might fear punishment for non-compliance with school policies; this example shows the many nuances of school contexts that teachers are required to negotiate. This fear is also a by-product of how carcerality structures our education system, even for teachers. Teachers at all career stages must be prepared to interrogate policies that may not always be in the best interest of kids and to negotiate the risks that come with advocating for students in the face of those potentially harmful policies. This risk negotiation is part of resisting carcerality and moving toward police-free schools. In the next vignette, we again focus on carceral logics, this time related to surveillance and restricted movement in a middle school science classroom.

Vignette C: Restricted Movement in Mx. Kai's Middle School Science Classroom

Mx. Kai's class is working on a photosynthesis lesson in small groups at stations around the room.[14] *Students are planting a variety of seeds in cups, and each group has been tasked with researching on their Chromebooks how much light each of their seeds needs to grow. One group, Mx. Kai notices, is finished a bit early. One of the students in the group, Leticia, tells Mx. Kai that she needs to go to the bathroom. Mx. Kai says, "Not right now . . . we're getting ready to move stations so that you can explore seeds different from the ones you just planted." Leticia protests, "But Mx. Kai, I really need to go." Mx. Kai is concerned because they know that lots of fights have been happening in the bathrooms during classes, and the principal has asked teachers not to let students leave their rooms except during class change. Mx. Kai again tells Leticia that she can't go to the bathroom, that she'll have to wait until class is over. Leticia looks up at the clock and realizes there are still forty-five minutes to go in the block. She knows Mx. Kai is not going to give her permission, so she quietly gets up during the station transition and leaves for the bathroom. Mx. Kai realizes that Leticia has left. They now must decide what to do when Leticia returns.*

Gracey, Isabella, and Mackenzie talked softly at their table as they discussed this vignette. They were perplexed that there was no bathroom procedure in place for students in this particular class. They emphasized that, to them, it was "clear that the teacher doesn't trust the students, or maybe just this particular student." Courtney and Andrea agreed and pointed out to the class that "Leticia is not typically a white name—we wonder if that [racism] plays a role in the teacher's decision."[15] Several of their classmates nodded, while others were visibly uncomfortable that the "r" word ("racism") had been invoked to contextualize a teacher's decision-making. Preservice teachers Cesar and Luke were quick to emphasize to the class that the "teacher is in the wrong . . . students can't control when they have to use the bathroom." And Katherine, after much discussion with her group, argued to the class that "sometimes kids know what's best for themselves in these situations . . . and aren't afraid to act." While many preservice teachers agreed that the student in this vignette should have been allowed to leave the classroom for the bathroom, they were also not quite able to think through their future classroom procedures for bathroom use without relying on carceral ideas like incentive systems or a "limited number of passes," as suggested by Gracey and her group. The class did agree, however, that students should be trusted more, and even suggested "teacher training for conflict management and de-escalation."

Like policies about dress codes and technology use, policies that restrict student movement in schools are also well entrenched; these policies are also idiosyncratic within and across schools and classrooms. For example, some schools may permit students to be in hallways and classrooms during class or even adopt "open campus" policies, while others have strict rules about who can be where and when. Some teachers may even invent elaborate schemes to deter students from leaving class to go to the bathroom. For example, an art teacher of mine when I was a high school student had a toilet seat as his "bathroom pass." If we wanted to leave class to go to the bathroom, we had to literally carry a toilet seat down the hall![16] These movement policies, often invoked to protect student safety, are predicated on the notion that students cannot be trusted to manage themselves in hallways and bathrooms.

Bathrooms are particularly contested spaces in public education, from fears about fighting and vaping, to anti-queer and anti-trans bills in state legislatures, to "bathroom policies" presented at local school board meetings.[17] Abolitionist perspectives push us to consider how policies that restrict movement for students and students' control over bodily autonomy are contrary to notions of safety. As abolitionist and teacher educator Farima Pour-Khorshid remembers, her elementary school experience was marked by teachers who doled out one bathroom pass per month, "policing our bowel movements to maximize instructional time."[18] A lack of trust again stems from carceral logics: we assume that student movement needs to be controlled, lest things devolve into chaos. While physical fights between and among students are an issue in some schools, as this vignette alludes to, we also know that hypersurveillance, including restrictive movement policies and cameras in hallways to capture movement (while administrators or school police monitor the footage), is often implemented in schools composed of students of Color.[19] And we know that educators stereotype Black students and students of Color, making assumptions about students as "troublemakers" or even "criminals." Indeed, carceral notions over who gets access to which spaces and when have existed since the inception of public education.

Of course, the denial of educational services to Black, Brown, and Indigenous people and, later, attendance at segregated and boarding schools have defined much of the history of public education. For example, prohibiting Black students from particular spaces in schools still happens all the time. In my last book about school discipline in Alabama, my coauthor and I amplified the voice of a Black assistant principal who said that he was asked by white teachers to remove Black students from the wing of the school where most of the Advanced Placement and "higher-level" courses were taught; the teachers argued that the students had "no reason to be in this building."[20] And educators and administrators sanction students for being out of class all the time, even going so far as issuing suspensions or relying on a school police officer or SRO to intervene. Yet policies restricting student movement, especially bathroom policies, are often unrealistic—children are, for example, supposed to suffer or soil themselves in the classroom, creating untold harm, rather than risk a potentially violent encounter (i.e., a fight) in the bathroom. Preservice teachers should therefore recognize that allowing students to have some bodily autonomy is not just integral to development, it's also integral to feeling "safe" in a given context. Allowing students, and even advocating for students to move freely in and out of learning spaces and other spaces, demonstrate that educators trust students, which Gracey, Isabella, and Mackenzie emphasized. Unrestricted movement also means that educators create opportunities for students to break trust, which are also important opportunities for learning and accountability.

In the next vignette, we see how the carceral logics that govern rewards and punishments creep in during whole-class instruction with elementary school students.

Vignette D: Rewards and Punishments in Miss Thomas's first-grade class[21]

Recently, Miss Thomas has become frustrated because a few of her students consistently interject comments loud enough for the whole class to hear while she is giving directions or explaining new information to the class. The student comments are not offensive—she just finds them unnecessary and mildly disruptive because she is talking. As Miss Thomas was reviewing the day's activities with her class, Jamilah called out, "Yes, Miss Thomas! We will be doing great things today!" Miss Thomas responded to Jamilah, "Yes, Jamilah, we will. But please don't interrupt me while I'm talking." A bit later in the class, while she was introducing a new read-aloud book, Isaiah interjected, "I don't really like this book, I like the book about foxes that we read yesterday. Can't we read that one again instead?" Miss Thomas felt her frustration level increase as she responded to Isaiah, "No, Isaiah, we are starting a new book today. And it is disrespectful to interrupt me while I am speaking! We have only been in school for two weeks, and you have interrupted me every day. You just lost five participant points for today." Isaiah seemed bewildered by her sharp response. Miss Thomas has to decide what to do next.

Jocelyn, Gabby, and Sarah Beth, as they talked through this vignette, were frustrated that Miss Thomas was frustrated. They emphasized that Jamilah's interjection was actually expressing "enthusiasm" about their day together in the classroom and what they would be learning. "Miss Thomas might be squashing Jamilah's desire to learn by responding in that way!" they argued. Likewise, Amor and Jesse pointed out that even though Isaiah had interrupted Miss Thomas, "he was clearly excited about reading." Katie agreed, underscoring how "teachers should never associate grades with student behavior, though they do it all the time." Many of her classmates nodded and murmured about how they "hated participation points, even in college." Similarly, Elizabeth argued for her group, "Deducting points from a student's grade because of behavior stuff is basically the same as removing them from the lesson . . . like, if they're not there, they can't earn points anyway, but if they're there and the teacher says they're misbehaving, they also lost points. Seems like a lose-lose."

Preservice teachers presented various options for how Miss Thomas could "do better" in this instance. For example, Gianna and Frankey noted that to de-escalate and avoid imposing any more punishment on students, Miss Thomas could do a number of things: "Listen to the students. Remain calm. Be polite. Keep an open mind. Start a conversation. Be flexible." And Gracie and Olivia agreed, asserting that Miss Thomas, above all, should "not make it a power struggle" because, they said, "the teacher never wins." Amor and Jesse also agreed that Miss Thomas "could have responded more kindly, or even given him the option to work with the fox book later in the lesson." Finally, Julie, Nick, and Robyn reflected that Miss Thomas could invite even more feedback from students: "If she were to ask them, what would students say they expect from her?" They wondered what opportunities for student choice and voice the lesson offered.

Student interruptions in class can indeed be frustrating for many teachers. And when frustration levels rise, some teachers resort to punishment: via grades, as Miss Thomas does here, assigning students to detention or "time out," or even writing referrals that result in suspension, even in elementary school. For example, when we examine incident data from referrals that result in in-school suspension (ISS) or out-of-school suspension (OSS), these are many of the behaviors that are labeled "defiance," "disruption," or "disobedience."[22] And although this vignette takes place in an elementary school classroom, it may surprise some readers to learn that administrators and teachers routinely call police to classrooms for K–5 student behavior, as we learned in earlier chapters.[23] Yet sometimes student interruptions can be displays of engagement, although we are socialized to think that "good" students are those who are quiet, still, attentive, and compliant. It's clear in this vignette that Jamilah and Isaiah are paying close attention to what's happening in their classroom. In some ways, they are giving Miss Thomas real-time feedback about the lesson, which we could argue is a marker of student learning.

Miss Thomas also relied on "participation points" to motivate students to comply with her in-class rules, as Katie and her classmates pointed out, and as many teachers do.[24] Educators everywhere use points systems tied to grades, in addition to rewards like stickers and tokens; but, as educator Kelly Lagerwerff explains, these systems are detrimental to classrooms and relationships since "in order to make the tokens mean something, they cannot be given equally to every student. Inherent in the system is that certain students do not receive tokens. So, inherent also is individualism and competition; children are divided and pitted against each other just like they would be in any exploitative situation."[25] Notably, points systems are also common strategies in alternative schools, prisons, and jails.[26]

Taken together, the vignettes in this chapter push educators to acknowledge how carceral logics underpin the seemingly "normal" rules of classrooms so we come to understand that classrooms—and by extension, schools—are not safe for *all* students. Instead, students run the risk of punishment, lowered grades, and even removal from their learning environments if we deem them unable or unwilling to comply with rules and policies.[27] Importantly, some preservice teachers who analyzed these vignettes were unable to concretely answer what they would do instead without reverting to asking questions like "What does policy say to do in the situation?" This failure of abolitionist imagination is one of the essential reasons why teacher educators must continuously push preservice teachers to engage in discussions about micro-interactions in future classrooms, while also teaching about how carceral logics shape policies and aspects of our relationships. Teacher educators should not expect that preservice teachers' unlearning will happen all at once, or even across entire semesters of coursework; carceral logics are at the root of so much of what happens in schools, classrooms, and the world around us that it is indeed difficult to imagine how we might do things differently without continued analysis and support for that analysis. And, as educators, we will all continue to make mistakes, as will students. It's what we do after those mistakes—the types of accountability that we should engage in—that we turn to now.

ACCOUNTABILITY IN PUBLIC EDUCATION

The previous vignettes represent teachers and students who are under incredible stress in classrooms around the country. Teachers are pressured to cover content and meet pacing guides; to address standards and learning outcomes; to prepare students for standardized tests with scripted curricula and lessons; and even to meet performance metrics, many of which are imposed by those who critique public education from outside the system. Much of the stress that teachers and students face, in addition to low pay and long workdays, can be traced to how we think about accountability in a carceral society, including the "accountability movement" in education. Socialization in a carceral system means that the way we think about accountability is to locate blame to individual people, schools, and communities and punish them, often by deprivation of resources or even removal. In this section, we examine the accountability movement in education as it relates to high-stakes testing and how it is rooted in the same carceral logics as our policies that guide discipline, all as a misguided way to hold students accountable for both learning and behavior and to hold teachers accountable for their practices.

The "accountability movement"

The term "accountability" in public education in the United States is usually associated with a movement that codified the equation of school quality with standardized test scores and graduation rates, as well as other so-called measures of student learning. This movement gained steam in the early 2000s with the implementation of No Child Left Behind (NCLB), an initiative ostensibly intended to bolster student learning, but which had disastrous consequences for many school communities. For example, it accelerated high-stakes, standardized testing in public schools and made these tests the primary measure of student learning. When schools did not meet certain "growth" benchmarks each year, the accountability structures in place meant that those schools lost resources. In other words, schools (and the teachers and students in them) were blamed for their own failure and punished by reductions in funding; in some cases, schools were even closed or threatened with closure, like the high school in North Carolina where I taught.[28] And these accountability measures often affected schools composed of Black and Brown students more than they did predominately white schools, stripping them of resources like funding for high-quality teachers and leaders, curricula, and support staff.[29] By contrast, in schools where students scored well on standardized tests, teachers were rewarded with merit pay. This resulted in a nationwide system of rewards and punishments that supposedly incentivized school communities to facilitate learning. What happened in many places instead was a narrowed curriculum where teachers "taught to the test" and employed "skill-and-drill" lessons, at the expense of relationship-building, culturally responsive curricula, and student-centered instruction.[30] And there are ties between the accountability movement and systems of policing and surveillance.

I first started teaching high school in the mid-2000s, at the height of NCLB implementation and the accountability movement. The school where I taught—predominantly Black and Latinx and high poverty—was ranked among the lowest in the state according to standardized test scores.[31] In response, the North Carolina Department of Public Instruction (NCDPI) regularly sent what we used to call the "SWAT team" to our school. These NCDPI representatives came and did walk-throughs in all classrooms, observed in hallways, reviewed lesson plans, and surveilled us during standardized testing windows, of which there were many. We had not only end-of-course (EOC) tests in many content areas, but also frequent "benchmark testing" to ostensibly gauge how students were progressing during the semester. This surveillance was unnerving for both students and teachers.

One day toward the end of the school year, I was proctoring an EOC Social Studies test in a classroom where Algebra was usually taught. Most of the students had finished their tests and were staring off into space. They weren't allowed to use devices, to read, or to even put their heads down, or else they risked jeopardizing the test session. As the proctor, I was not allowed to use devices, read, or to sit down; I had to be constantly moving throughout the classroom. We had been in the classroom for just over three hours when I stopped at a large table on the side of the room and absent-mindedly flipped through a math textbook on the table. Just then, a member of the "SWAT team" walked by the classroom. She spotted me through the window, motioned for me to close the book, and kept walking. The following week, an administrator at the school called me to the front office, where I was told I would have a "letter in my file." The NCDPI representative had reported me for non-compliance.

This type of surveillance was deployed in schools across the country that had been labeled "failing" in the 2000s. It was also happening at the same time as the numbers of student suspensions and expulsions, and the numbers of school police were beginning to rise as well. Education scholars like Linda Darling-Hammond, for example, documented connections between and among high-stakes testing, student suspensions, and student dropouts, arguing that in some places, accountability measures incentivized suspensions of low-performing students to boost test scores.[32] In this climate, teachers were engaging in soft policing of students, officials were surveilling teachers and administrators, and police were increasingly introduced to schools.

Although some conditions have changed, schools today are constantly functioning (or dysfunctioning) under these accountability regimes, which put all the responsibility onto schools and teachers to increase graduation rates and test scores, in addition to attempts to hold students accountable for learning and behavior. When schools do not meet the standards set by accountability regimes, largely due to conditions outside school, schools—and the people in them—become targets for blame and anger. For example, when students do not pass standardized tests, educators often blame that failure on students or families, expressing ideas about how "their parents don't care about education" or "that student doesn't want to learn."[33] Or administrators blame individual teachers for not raising students' test scores or the pass/failure rates in their classrooms. The punishments for failure to meet measures of accountability often come in the form of cuts: cuts in resources for teacher pay, cuts in resources for meaningful teacher professional development that is centered on high-quality teacher practices and curricula, and even cuts to support staff like counselors.[34] Importantly, though, we rarely ever see cuts to policing and security budgets.

This type of accountability operates to such a degree that we often fail to see the structural forces at play, reducing social problems to the work of "bad" individuals and entities (parents, students, and schools, among others). We blame and punish "bad" teachers for low test scores instead of critiquing—or even eliminating—the standardized testing industry. We blame and punish "bad" students for their behavior instead of asking critical questions about our classrooms, rules, and norms.[35] We blame "bad" police officers for police violence instead of examining policing as an inherently violent institution and trying to imagine life without it. Escaping this cycle requires that we free our understanding of accountability from the trappings of blame and punishment. We look to abolitionist perspectives of accountability to do so.

ABOLITIONIST ACCOUNTABILITY

Much of what abolitionist perspectives teach us about accountability, broadly, is rooted in the experiences of survivors—of interpersonal violence, sexual and gender-based violence, and police violence.[36] Survivors of violence often want resources to keep themselves and their loved ones safe that do not involve the police.[37] Working toward abolitionist accountability, therefore, means making a commitment, first and foremost, to work toward safety without calling police because police do not make us safe. Instead, abolitionist accountability acknowledges that police are part of systems of punishment and control and introduce more harm than support.

As abolitionist Mariame Kaba points out, "Some people may ask, 'Does this mean that I can never call the cops if my life is in serious danger?' Abolition does not center that question. Instead, abolition challenges us to ask, 'Why do we have no other well-resourced options?' and pushes us to creatively consider how we can grow, build, and try other avenues to reduce harm."[38] So how do we support teachers who are committed to keeping children in their classrooms, refraining from involving police in students' lives, and imagining what accountability might look like without punishment? How might teachers structure classrooms differently, guided by the notion that accountability can exist without punishment? What does a "managed" classroom, and school, look like when teachers are accountable to students, as Mrs. Sue was for LaKendrick at the beginning of the chapter? What would it look like for the teachers in the previous vignettes to be accountable to students rather than to top-down policies that are rooted in carceral logics?

First, *abolitionist* accountability means considering individuals, schools, and communities as parts of broader ecosystems that are governed by structures and systems. This type of accountability does not rely on blame and punishment; instead, it is rooted in collectivism, community, and resources to transform.[39] According to activist and abolitionist Amanda Aguilar Shank, "Interpersonal harm is a basic fact of human reality. We can't avoid being harmed and harming others. . . . Abolition is a hopeful vision that means each movement where harm happens is an opportunity to transform relationships and communities, build trust and safety, and grow slowly towards the beautiful people we are meant to be, in the world that we deserve."[40]

Abolitionist accountability means engaging in a critical analysis of how harm comes to be, rather than relying on blaming, shaming, and punishing individuals. It looks like members of a community coming together to seek safety, to develop creative solutions, and to repair damage to relationships in lieu of relying on institutional punishment. That doesn't mean that those responsible for harm do not experience consequences; yet consequences are still humanizing and determined by a collective rather than punishments imposed by institutional and police power. Antiviolence advocate and activist Shannon Perez-Darby emphasizes the importance of seeing accountability as "a process we do *with* ourselves and *for* ourselves."[41] As educators, we must think about acknowledging our own harmful actions and encouraging students to acknowledge their harmful actions as we make efforts toward repair and transformation. But we also have to get clear about what harm is and looks like in schools.

Distinguishing between harm and non-compliance

What's tricky about relationships in schools is that we often collapse and conflate instances of harm with non-compliance. Police and prison abolitionists often encourage a distinction between "harm" and "crime," emphasizing that everything that is criminalized "isn't harmful, and all harm isn't necessarily criminalized."[42] Abolitionists cite, for example, corporations that pay workers low wages to redirect wealth to elite executives and shareholders, or that introduce environmental pollutants to the air and water, all with no criminal liability or consequences. Yet individual citizens may be fined or even jailed for things like littering, loitering, or sleeping in public.

In school, we must similarly evaluate when harm has occurred in our classrooms and school communities and distinguish that harm from what we might deem as rule-breaking or our desires for students to comply with policies—policies that sometimes have nothing to do with safety. In other words, we must not conflate harm with an instance of a student not following policies and rules. When students do not comply with policies, as in the vignettes featured here pertaining to dress codes, tech usage policies, bathroom policies, and even classroom rules about who gets to speak and when, we must first reflect on our school and classroom policies, norms, and expectations. We must ask tough questions of ourselves: Are these policies, norms, and expectations rooted in carceral ways of thinking?[43] Who do these policies *police* in our schools and classrooms? What must we, as educators and school communities, change to support students rather than blaming and punishing them with labels like "defiant," "disorderly," or "disobedient"? We must shift our thinking from policing students for compliance to asking what students' behaviors might be trying to communicate to us about school, including what's happening in classrooms with teachers, peers, and even curricula. Education scholar Carla Shalaby encourages us to develop our skills as teachers here—to be self-aware, reflective in the moment, and to draw on that reflection to "inform love-filled action."[44] That action must also be developed locally within classrooms and schools because context and community matter when unlearning carceral logics. This kind of self-determination is an important aspect of abolitionist work.[45]

When students do not comply with policies but no harm has occurred, this might actually mean taking no action at all.[46] Jamal and Ryan, for example, did not cause harm by wearing sagging pants and hoodies. Onike did not cause harm when using her phone during her class lesson. Leticia did not cause harm when leaving her classroom to use the restroom. And Jamilah and Isaiah did not cause harm by calling out during their teachers' instructions. By contrast, examples of harm between and among students and teachers might include name calling, bullying, physical harm, or even sexual violence. If and when teachers and students do make mistakes and engage in harmful behaviors toward other educators or peers—as we all do—we must rely on abolitionist accountability rather than punishment.

Distinguishing between punishment and accountability

> A world without harm isn't possible and isn't what an abolitionist vision purports to achieve. Rather, abolitionist politics and practice contend that disposing of people, by locking them away in jails and prisons, does nothing significant to prevent, reduce, or transform harm in the aggregate. It rarely, if ever, encourages people to take accountability for their actions. Instead, our adversarial court system discourages people from ever acknowledging, let alone taking responsibility, for the harm they have caused. At the same time, it allows us to avoid our own responsibilities to hold each other accountable, instead delegating it to a third party—one that has been built to hide away social and political failures.[47]

Although abolitionist Mariame Kaba is writing here about courts and prisons, there are parallels with how we treat students (and teachers) in school. For example, in school, we dispose of students by removing them from classrooms, peers, and learning opportunities when they enact harm. This is problematic because "when someone is 'outside'—unaccountable, invisible, not a part of—there is very little possibility of reconciliation, transformation, or healing."[48] We also sometimes delegate punishments to third parties, driven by bureaucratic processes like state-level legislation, school district policies, juvenile justice courts, school board proceedings, or youth tribunals. We must therefore examine the differences between punishment—as it is wielded and dictated by bureaucracy, institutions, and policies—and abolitionist accountability.

Punishment is rooted in a desire to control; it is a tool of power that someone holds over someone else and has the potential to damage relationships. Punishments like student removal and exclusion—from learning contexts, classrooms, and peers—deprive students of supportive resources and opportunities to take accountability for wrongs that they have committed. Smaller punishments also introduce harm. For example, how might Miss Thomas have harmed her relationship with Isaiah and her classroom community by lowering Isaiah's grade? How might Ms. Olsen have harmed her relationship with Onike and her classroom community by calling her out in front of the class? Abolitionist accountability, by contrast, is something that someone has the power to take or enact, and is rooted in transformation. Disability justice activist Mia Mingus reminds us that we "need to move away from 'holding people accountable' and instead work to *support people to proactively take accountability for themselves.*"[49] It gives us the opportunity to examine how harm comes to be, as well as how we are responsible for it. And it is our responsibility to take accountability when we have enacted harm and to encourage others to do so instead of delegating these processes to third parties. We must consider doing this work in-house, although we must carefully engage in skill building to do so.

Mingus argues that accountability requires four things: self-reflection, apology, repair, and changed behavior. She emphasizes apologies in "conflict, hurt, misunderstandings, small breaks in trust, and low-level harm. We begin with these because most of us do not know how to navigate these smaller experiences, and our relationships suffer or even end because of it." And, she argues, when we learn how to navigate small conflicts and breaches of trust, we prepare ourselves to better address violence. Through this process of abolitionist accountability, we do not just simply apologize; we reflect on what we do and why we do it. As we question the conditions, forces, and ideologies that drive our behaviors and confront the impact that we can have on the world around us, we are also doing the work necessary to change our behavior (for the better) in the future. When we take accountability for our actions that cause others harm, we transform ourselves as we work to heal and enact repair.

In the case of Ms. Olsen, she could first self-reflect, asking questions like "What happened?" "What was the impact?" and "What could be done to make it right?" Specifically, she could reflect on why she prioritized phone policy over the learning community in her classroom, acknowledging that she was wrong to assume that Onike was not participating in the lesson just because she was using her phone. She could also reflect on how her response—calling out a student in front of the rest of the class—likely caused harm not only to the individual student but to the broader classroom climate. Her apology to Onike could include acknowledging and apologizing for calling Onike out and admonishing her in front of the class, emphasizing that Onike was actively participating in the lesson with her classmate. Ms. Olsen could work to repair her relationship with both Onike and the classroom community by demonstrating that she will change her behavior. She could commit to refraining from calling out students in front of one another as punishment, emphasizing instead that she will hold herself accountable for creating a safe, trusting classroom climate. Ms. Olsen could go further to interrogate the policies around phone use at the school by asking questions about who these policies benefit, who they punish, and how they might be changed to better serve students. She could also encourage student participation by creating opportunities for students to voice their concerns with school policies. And Ms. Olsen must acknowledge that all of us, including teachers, students, and community members, have made and will continue to make mistakes—it's how we treat each other when we make mistakes that is at the center of abolitionist accountability. As organizer and poet Terisa Siagatonu writes in her poem "Abolitionist Teaching": "Because what's a prison guard but a teacher in wolf's clothing, unless the teacher breaks the rules and humanizes first? Apologizes first. Remembers that my humanity is tied to y'all's forever."[50]

When students engage in harmful behavior, as they inevitably will, we must rely on abolitionist accountability to address that harm rather than relying on police and institutional punishment. The effect is more than improving the learning environment for children—it also means humanizing our interactions with students and approaching the work of teaching from this humanizing stance. Yet refusing to call police on students, or advocating for students in the face of institutional punishments such as removal and exclusion, might mean taking risks.

Taking accountability might mean taking risks

Being accountable to ourselves, the students in our care, and the learning communities we build means risk-taking, especially in the face of policies that—even if well-intended—are potentially detrimental to learning environments. How do we assess the risks for educators involved in intervening in police-youth contact? For example, when thinking about her future teaching practices, Lucy, a preservice teacher from New York, was worried that she would "probably have to call the police on a student at some point." There were some non-negotiables for her, such as a fight in her classroom. She explained that she was fearful that she could lose her job if she did not comply with school policy about when to involve police, including for some of the "zero-tolerance" things that she knew were in place in some schools, like fighting.

Other preservice teachers like Lucy, well-versed in the research around school discipline and racism and committed to doing things differently so their *students* would not become those statistics we looked at in class, also risk becoming statistics of those *teachers* who lose their jobs while advocating for students. And those fears are genuine. Yet we must ask educators to also examine the risks for students when they come in contact with police. We have to hold ourselves accountable for the reality that police aren't protecting us in schools—from mass shootings or otherwise. We have to acknowledge the empirical research that details just how harmful the police are, including research that honors the voices and stories of students and teachers who have shared their experiences of harm via policing. We know, for example, that police presence in schools makes some students fearful; that presence is also interpreted by some students as a symbol of exclusion.[51] We also know that police-youth contact in schools has the potential to thrust students into the juvenile and even adult justice systems; once our systems of punishment enclose students and families, it's very difficult for them to navigate and get out of those systems. And, importantly, we know that contact with the police can even end in police violence against students, as the #AssaultAt map from the Advancement Project documents.[52]

In education contexts, we, as teachers, school administrators, counselors, staff, teacher educators, and other education professionals, say that we value students, families, and learning. So how do we move in ways that demonstrate those values rather than subjecting students to punishment via policing or disciplinary punishment like suspensions and removal from classrooms? In other words, how do we reject blame and punishment, whether they be directed at individual student behaviors or at whole schools full of students and teachers, in favor of supporting students and schools so our actions are more aligned with our values? As activist and abolitionist Mariame Kaba puts it, "When we're being accountable to ourselves, we're acting in a way that honors our values. We're acting with integrity by taking responsibility for who we are in the world and for living in alignment with our values." Here, we might ask ourselves, "What would Mrs. Sue do?" as we gauge our capacities for risk-taking, drawing on our values and a sense of abolitionist accountability to those values, to students, and to learning communities.[53]

In relying on accountability models and structures rooted in blame and deprivation/removal of resources and students, schools operate as part of the carceral state. To get beyond these carceral ways of being, doing, and knowing, we have to shift toward abolitionist accountability—accountability to one another. This means not only unlearning what we've been taught about people as good/bad, carceral ideas, and soft policing as we've started to do in the last few chapters. It also means acknowledging when we ourselves have caused harm. In the next chapter, my coauthors and I trace our journeys to abolition, outlining how we too operated under carceral logics as teachers, and how we are always learning to do better.

ABOLITIONIST ACTIVITIES: ACCOUNTABILITY

Abolitionist accountability includes committing to new ways of interpreting student behavior, including an analysis of how school policies attempt to police and control behavior.

Comparing Values

- On a piece of paper or in a document on your device, list the values that you think should drive responses to harm (such as "affirming students' humanity" or "healing") on the left side of the page. On the right side, brainstorm the main values that underpin how schools—the ones that you have attended or are preparing to teach in—deal with non-compliance with policy (such as the isolation that comes with detention and ISS). Compare and contrast and examine how the two sides differ.[54]

Critically Examining Codes of Conduct

- Examine the codes of conduct and the student handbook of an individual school or school district. This could be a school that you attended, a school where you hope to teach one day, or a school in your local area.
- As you read, reflect on policies about student dress, phone use, bathroom use, and other behaviors like fighting, bullying, and interpersonal harm. Consider and discuss the following questions as a group:
  - What behaviors outlined in these documents have the potential to cause harm?

- When students enact harm, are the consequences outlined in these documents, such as suspension, expulsion, alternative school referral, or police referral, rooted in carceral logics and punishment? Or are there opportunities for school community members to self-reflect, apologize, and enact repair without resorting to institutional punishment like removal and police contact?
- What would those opportunities look like, and how do the opportunities for transformation (or lack thereof) shape your view of this school and its climate?

Revisiting the Vignettes

- Read each of the vignettes presented in this chapter again. What creative practices can you imagine engaging in based on what's happening in these classrooms? How might you engage in behavior toward students that does not result in the data patterns that we learned about in chapter 4 and instead is rooted in principles of abolitionist accountability? What risks might you have to take to interrupt and resist harmful punishments that might be dictated by policy?

MUTUAL RESPECT
AUGUST
MORE SUPPORT SPACES
EMPATHY
SELF-REGULATION WITH STUDENTS

CHAPTER 6

"Red Button" Moments

Teacher Educators' Critical Incidents and Abolitionist Imaginings

WITH ALYSSA HADLEY DUNN AND CRYSTAL SIMMONS

Many people, including educators, move through their personal and professional lives believing that police are resources and support that we can call on in moments of need. As we learned in earlier chapters, we are socialized to believe in policing as a useful, helpful institution from very young ages, both via messages that we receive from media and in school. As former middle school teacher and legal activist Derecka Purnell details, we are all socialized to "call 911" for just about every problem that arises in our communities, knowing that police will arrive on the scene.[1] But as we have also learned in previous chapters, abolitionist perspectives teach us that police do not keep us safe from harm, and they often introduce more harm when we call them.[2]

But can we thrive in communities without police, and what does that look like? There are long histories of abolitionist activism by folks who have resisted, and continue to resist, the harmful effects of prisons and policing, and they push us to reimagine our world. Some of these folks are teacher educators who consider what they do in the four walls of their classrooms (or Zoom spaces) as activism toward police and prison abolition. For example, teacher educator and abolitionist Harper Keenan designed a course for preservice elementary educators about building classroom communities that is guided by the question, "How might we organize classrooms if we were reaching toward a world where prisons and policing were seen as unnecessary?" integrating readings by Angela Davis, for example, to support preservice teachers' understandings of abolition.[3] Sheeva Sabati, Farima Pour-Khorshid, Erica Meiners, and Chrissy Hernandez outline approaches across teaching contexts, teaching us what has to be dismantled, changed, and built to "grow abolition" in teacher education.[4] And, as we learned in chapter 5, Carla Shalaby reframes classroom management as an abolitionist project, detailing the ways that classroom rules and procedures are often rooted in carceral notions of control and disposability; her work pushes us to reimagine our relationship with policy and students so we might move toward abolitionist accountability.[5]

As education scholar and abolitionist Erica Meiners reminds us, most of us are not "born abolitionists," and this includes teachers and teacher educators.[6] In this chapter, my coauthors and I trace our journeys in coming to abolitionist perspectives about school police. We do so by locating critical teaching incidents from our experiences in public schools with the "red button." The red button is both real and hypothetical, serving as a guiding metaphor. It represents the actual button on the wall of many public school classrooms that we are socialized to push as teachers when we feel in need of assistance. Yet what often arrives is not assistance at all—it is potential punishment for students, whether it comes from an administrator or a police officer. The red button therefore represents an opportunity to identify critical incidents where we have engaged in carceral practices in school buildings, including times when we have encouraged police-youth contact.

As middle and high school teachers, we all had "red button" moments. We first detail these incidents to illustrate that, as actors in carceral systems, we continuously make errors and enact harm; we must "call ourselves to account" for that harm as we unlearn carceral ideologies and practices that rely on police.[7] We also detail these incidents to support and participate in a culture, as abolitionists Leah Lakshmi Piepzna-Samarasinha and Ejeris Dixon explain, "in which people feel comfortable sharing stories about when they called emergency services but didn't want to . . . we actually learn about crucial needs for community safety projects."[8] In other words, these critical incidents teach us about needs for classroom and school safety. Finally, we engage with the red button to imagine a hypothetical and abolitionist otherwise: What other futures can we imagine, instead of punishment, when we "push the button"? The chapter ends with Abolitionist Activities to support this imagining.

THE "RED BUTTON" AS PUNISHMENT

Alyssa

When I got off the T, there was a police officer at the corner. I walked two blocks to the high school. At the bottom of the driveway were multiple police cars. I climbed the hill to the main entrance, where another two police officers were stationed at the metal detectors. Above and beside us were windows covered with bars. Their belts were cluttered with walkie talkies, sticks, and guns. They barely glanced at me and did not open my "teacher bag," while the students in front of and behind me were basically interrogated and their bags heavily searched. All the students were children of Color, and I was white. It was shockingly similar to the previous year, when I had worked in a classroom at an all-boys juvenile detention facility, teaching poetry to incarcerated youth (a placement for a university class that required community service).

This was my introduction to Boston Public Schools, where I had my first in-school placement as a college sophomore. At the time, I remember thinking that the police scared me. Their presence reinforced my belief that the students were to be feared, and it seemed counterintuitive that police presence would worry me rather than reassure me. In hindsight, of course, this is part of the goal of school policing, and it was working exactly as planned. Their presence meant that I focused not on the fears of what was outside the school, but what was inside—my students.

My time in Boston Public Schools meant unlearning everything that I had ever learned—explicitly or implicitly—about students of Color. In the process, that meant that I learned about and adopted critical pedagogical stances, antiracist classroom management, and liberatory lesson planning. What I did not learn about was abolition, so I left my early teaching experiences still believing that the problem with police was the "bad apples," as opposed to the entire institution.

Six years later, I was teaching in Atlanta. I had my own classroom with rotating casts of students in my English classes. On the first teacher workday, when

I was setting up my classroom, a School Resource Officer (SRO) came by to introduce himself. Then, as he did for all new teachers, he explained what to do if there was an emergency in the classroom. He pointed to the red button near the door to the hallway and told me that it was my "direct contact" with him and the front office. He told me that I could push it anytime I wanted. I knew other teachers who pushed it multiple times a day, sometimes multiple times in one class period. I knew that I did not want to be one of those teachers, although I again remember attributing my hesitance not to my beliefs in SROs or school policing but because of what I feared hitting the red button would say about me. Especially as a novice teacher, I did not want the administration to think that I couldn't "handle" my students. I did not want my own students to think that I couldn't handle them either.

There came a time, of course, when I did push the red button. This is a moment that I remember vividly, and one that I tell my preservice teachers about as a cautionary tale during our lessons on criminalization and militarization in urban schools. One of my students had been labeled as having an "emotional behavior disorder." He had a one-to-one special educator who worked with him each day. He was frequently upset and shouted his thoughts or responses aloud during our class activities. My co-teacher and I were the only two white people in the room.

On this particular day, he was very upset at having to do an assignment from the previous day. As part of his individualized education plan (IEP), he was given previous assignments to complete if he hadn't finished them. He didn't want to finish this particular assignment because he said it was boring (it likely was); instead, he wanted to shift to what the other students were doing. He had already taken two short "walking breaks" in the hallway during our ninety-minute class period. When he returned from the second break, the special educator told him that it was time to get back to work, and he stood behind his desk, grabbed his chair, and threw it at the board. I was nowhere near the board at the time. He then proceeded to walk to other desks and areas of the room to grab free chairs and throw those as well. The other students jumped up or screamed. Thankfully there were no phone cameras at the time. I was trying to talk to him, and, in the process I got closer to him, just as he threw another chair. I had to duck out of the way. To be clear, chairs had been thrown in my classroom before. Fights happened in the hallway. It was not so much the physicality of it all that bothered me; it was that I thought he had been throwing the chair *at* me, as opposed to *around* me. The other teacher was yelling, "Push the button! Push the button!" So I pushed the button. As promised (threatened?), the SRO and principal (both Black men) appeared almost immediately. They grabbed the student and used physical force to escort him from the classroom.

Later, my colleague and I both gave statements about what happened. I remember crying in the principal's office and begging them not to press charges or get the student in further trouble. I believed then, as I do now, that he had not meant to throw the chair at *me*. I had wrongfully assumed that his IEP would provide support for instances like this and he would not be criminally punished. Unfortunately, none of that mattered. The student was sentenced to a week in juvenile detention. He returned to the school, but never again to my classroom. I was completely devastated that I had pushed the button and gotten my student involved in the criminal justice system. I vowed never to push the button again.

Crystal

I entered the teaching profession as a lateral entry teacher, with no formal undergraduate training or preparation. I was hired to teach eighth grade social studies in the very middle school that I had attended several years prior. During my tenure at this middle school in my hometown, I had very little interactions with SROs or police. I attribute the lack of their presence to the student population. The school district and school served predominately white students from upper middle- to working-class families. Discipline was never perceived to be an issue or problem of concern for administrators and district officials. The racial and social class implications of these preconceived beliefs was overtly obvious to me as a Black, female teacher and member of the community. It was not until my experiences in a different school system that I observed, engaged with, and unfortunately upheld and supported the services of school police.

In the next school district that I taught in, the demographics were completely different from my previous job and hometown. The student population was majority Black and the social class was that of working-class and lower-income families. Unlike the inherent narrative of "security and compliance" that was associated with having a white student population, the opposite rang true for Black and Brown students; here, their very presence was perceived to be a threat. As part of my new employee orientation and professional development at my school, I attended several training sessions from the city police department and SROs. These sessions ranged from identifying gang activity, signs, and paraphernalia to the tactics of students for concealing weapons. I remember distinctly that as the police officer was talking, he was slowly revealing the many ways that weapons like knives and guns could be hidden in the clothes of students. For example, I was really shocked to learn that the whole time he was talking to us teachers, he had a razor hidden under his tongue. He spoke of how a girl in one of the local high schools was able to slash the face of another girl during a fight because she had hidden the razor in her mouth. This was my introduction to school police officers. As someone who at this point in my career had very little training and preparation in classroom management from an academic standpoint, I was being guided by the police. Their messaging stoked sentiments of fear and hypervigilance among myself and my colleagues, as we were always being asked to assess the interactions of and with our students.

The presence of police in our school was overwhelming. On an average day, we had anywhere between two to three officers in the school daily. They even had an office centrally located in the building. At times, I felt like I was their surrogate, as I wanted to ensure that I was doing my job of creating a "safe" learning environment. One way in which I did this was by writing discipline referrals, or "pink slips," as they were often called by students. The accumulation of these referral slips could lead to out of school suspension (OSS) or expulsion. In my first year in this school, I wrote numerous referrals for minor incidents, as I felt the threat of punishment or writing the pink slips would deter students. We also had frequent sweeps where we were asked to lock our doors and to keep the students inside the classroom so they could bring drug dogs into the building and check for drugs. One day, I found a small bag of marijuana in the back of my classroom. I immediately turned it in to the police. My actions and decisions to turn in the drugs and write "pink slips" reiterated the need for police. I was complicit in maintaining this structure, which was demeaning and damaging to the lives of my students.

After my second year at this school, I enrolled in a graduate program where I was introduced to critical theoretical concepts and frameworks like culturally responsive teaching and critical race theory. It was at this time where my practices and philosophical orientation to school police officers were challenged and critiqued. I no longer viewed their roles in public schools as justifiable for maintaining safety or order. Instead, I saw their roles as disruptive to the very essence of being for students, primarily Black and Brown students. Police were only there to control and exert their power and authority. As a result of this revelation, I reflected upon the ways that I was upholding this structure, and I was dedicated to disrupting these practices and notions. I began building relationships and trust among and between my students and their families. I refrained from interacting with the police and writing referrals.

Hannah

I was Mademoiselle Carson, teaching high school French, and we were on day three or four of a testing window. The students were fed up. This was at the height of No Child Left Behind (NCLB), when we were testing all the time—not just end-of-course tests but multiple "benchmarks" throughout the nine weeks to make sure that students were "on track." I had been at the school for a little over a year, fresh out of a master's program that prepared me for a K–12 French teaching license. My preparation had been grounded in "social justice" scholarship and pedagogy; we had talked about inequality in resource distribution across schools, the US public education system as fundamentally both separate and unequal for many Black children, and even "dropout" rates for Black children in local school systems. But we hadn't really talked about what it would be like to be in schools where students were administered standardized tests, week in and week out. We also had not talked about school police—at all.

Like Alyssa and Crystal, I was teaching at a school composed primarily of Black and Brown students. And like Crystal, I had experienced numerous "training" sessions from SROs about gangs, prompting us to look for specific colors in student clothing, drawings of things like crowns and particular numbers, and which student groups were hanging out together in hallways and cafeterias, all supposedly indicating gang membership. We also had "weapon and drug sweeps," where police and administrators pulled students out of classes, lined them up in hallways, and searched them with wands and K-9s. The surveillance made me deeply uncomfortable, and I was always annoyed that the sweeps interrupted my carefully planned classroom instruction. I had also already begun to recognize the ways that police in the hallways at the school where I taught were antagonizing students, yelling at them: "Pull up your pants!" "Take off your hood/hat!" "Out of the hallway! Into the classroom!" And I had seen the way that they escalated interactions with students and fights among students by pepper-spraying and even body-slamming students who were fighting, threatening to fight one another, or even just standing by. But I still hadn't made connections about policing as part of the Prison Industrial Complex (PIC), nor was I aware of the deep-rooted history of policing, including its role as part of the violent suppression of activism in schools. I just knew that I didn't trust the cops—in schools or out.

The day of the incident, I was proctoring another content-area test in my own classroom, so it wasn't "my class" exactly, but some of the students in the classroom were also in my French classes. We had been in the classroom for almost three hours, and a student who I knew only from being in my homeroom class the year prior started to talk. "Maaaannn, this is bullshit. We've been in here for forever!" A few students glanced at him, some side-eyeing him. They knew that if anything out of the ordinary happened during the test, we could be held in "non-compliance" and students would have to re-test. The student, who I'll call Kamal, kept it up: "I'm so bored. We've been in here so long. They won't let us sleep, talk, read, NOTHIN!" And he was right—students weren't allowed to do anything after they were finished with their test. It was boring AF. I walked over to Kamal's desk and looked at him. He had a big grin on his face, a grin I knew from homeroom. He was extremely smart, but administrators often suspended him for disruptions in other teachers' classrooms. I smiled at him. "I know it's boring. We're almost done." I walked over to the other side of the room by the door and our classroom window, thinking perhaps Kamal would have settled down at this point. But he kept it up, louder this time: "This is such bullshit. They lock us in these classrooms with these bullshit tests all the time, for WHAT?"

Other students started to rustle, telling him to be quiet, pointing out that we might have to re-test if he kept talking and a testing administrator came by and heard him. I was still by the classroom window, and at that moment, another teacher on my hall walked by. I opened the door, stuck my head out quickly, and asked if she knew how much longer our testing block might be. "I'm not sure, sorry." What I did not realize was that the SRO was also positioned right at the end of our hallway. He started to walk over, while the other teacher scurried down the hall to her classroom. "Is there a problem?" he asked. "Nah, we got it, thank you," I said quickly.

Just then, Kamal yelled over my shoulder to the officer, "What's good, Mr. Wilson?!" The officer glared at him. Kamal continued, "You here to get me out of this hellhole?" The officer looked at me. "May I?" I kind of shrugged sheepishly, not really knowing what to do. Mr. Wilson pointed at Kamal. "Come on with me now." Kamal, on his way to the door, knocked a stack of books off my desk onto the floor, a clattering sound that cut through the silence and tension in the classroom. Mr. Wilson continued to glare at Kamal, grabbing him by the arm and hauling him around the corner of the hallway, out of my line of sight. As I walked back into the classroom, another student, Laticia, called me out: "Damn Mademoiselle, you just let Mr. Wilson take him out like that?" She was right. I hadn't called the police on this student, but I hadn't intervened either. I felt horrible.

After that day, I promised myself that I would intervene when police were interacting with students in my classes. And I did, a few times, de-escalating situations in the hallway between an SRO and a student in my class, even once telling an officer that a student was due in my classroom for lunch detention "that very minute" to get her out of a tense conversation with him in the hallway. Years later, while learning more about the PIC and prison and police abolition, I began teaching at an alternative school in Alabama. I made similar promises to myself to advocate on students' behalf in matters that involved police. I wasn't always successful, as in the case of Rachel, who left my classroom to go to the bathroom and ended up in an altercation with an officer in the hallway. When the officers came to retrieve her belongings from the classroom, I was so confused that I did not advocate for her in that moment.[9] Each "red button" teaching moment is a moment where I recommit myself to police-free schools.

THE "RED BUTTON" AS PEDAGOGY

The red button moments that we have presented here changed how we think about teaching, students, and policing. These are certainly not the only incidents in our classrooms and schools that have shaped the teachers we have become today, but they are salient with regard to how we think about police in schools. We draw on these moments as a type of pedagogy to remind ourselves of and also to teach future teachers about the harms of policing. For example, the three of us, when working with preservice and practicing teachers, are often asked: "What's something you wish you'd known as a new teacher?"

Of course, we wish we had learned more about the history and consequences of school policing, which has informed much of what Hannah has decided to include throughout the book. But even if we *had* learned about school police in our teacher preparation programs, that learning may not have been as impactful as what we have witnessed and experienced outside schools. Specifically, in addition to our experiences in schools, there were really salient moments that occurred outside of school regarding policing and prisons that informed our commitment to abolition. These are the times that we felt like alarms started to go off for us—flashing red buttons outside of schools. These red buttons also functioned as a type of pedagogy—life alarms that we learned from and with.

By the time we became teachers, we had all witnessed so much police violence outside of school. We were all alive when police brutally beat Rodney King in the streets of Los Angeles in 1991; we were still very young and did not yet have the political consciousness to recognize this event in the context of policing as a historically violent institution. Later, Trayvon Martin's death catalyzed many of our feelings about the consequences of policing and surveillance. While not murdered by a police officer, Trayvon's death came at the hands of a citizen in his community who felt entitled to undertake the project of policing himself. George Zimmerman surveilled, followed, and ultimately killed Trayvon, a high school student who was walking home from the convenience store.

As we learned in earlier chapters, the project of policing and the "copaganda" associated with it teach us to be suspicious of one another—that there are "bad" people and "good" people. These labels, as we have learned, are bound up with stereotypes about race, class, gender, sexuality, ability, and other identity markers. As we have also learned, we are more likely to regard Black boys and men as "criminal" or "threatening" due to this socialization, just as we are more likely to "adultify" Black girls.[10] But for us at that time, it felt like Trayvon could have been a high school student in one of our own classes. Crystal and Hannah were in graduate school but had only left the public school classroom about eight months prior, and Alyssa was teaching at a high school in Atlanta at the time. We also subsequently witnessed the police first refuse to arrest Zimmerman after the murder; and later we watched, in one of the most high-profile trials of the decade, as Zimmerman was acquitted of the charges against him. We wondered what other modes of accountability for his actions could have been possible, rather than a trial in the criminal justice system that seemingly did not bring Trayvon's family any sense of justice. And we also acknowledged that, even if Zimmerman had been convicted and sentenced to jail, the harm that would come to him from incarceration would be no justice, nor would it be equivalent to Trayvon's lost life.

Next was Rekia Boyd, a twenty-two-year-old Black woman in a park in Chicago, who police shot and killed while attempting to fire on another person who, they said, had a weapon. The following year, the movie *Fruitvale Station* was released, which, while fictional in some ways, chronicled the events on the night that police murdered Oscar Grant in San Francisco in 2009. And then there was Michael Brown, who had just graduated high school in Ferguson, Missouri, in 2014 when an officer shot and killed him while his hands were up. The Ferguson uprising spawned protests and movements that demonstrated just how many Black communities and communities of Color were fed up with being surveilled, targeted, harassed, ticketed, and abused by police departments across the country. Preservice teachers also might have had "red button" moments, as when they witnessed global protests in the summer of 2020 after the police murders of George Floyd, Breonna Taylor, and so many others.

Crystal, as a Black woman, has stories of her own about police harassment. And Alyssa and Hannah, in community with Black folks who are teachers, friends, and students, have heard countless stories of police surveillance, harassment, and violence. Now, as teacher educators, we are intentional in ensuring that our students receive preparation that is grounded in abolitionist imagining about police and prisons. As former classroom teachers, we can speak to our experiences and the damaging and consequential effects that our actions have had on students. As the preservice teachers in Crystal's and Alyssa's classes engage in field placements and practicums, they participate in reflective journaling and explicit discussions that call out the wrongful and harmful use of policing in schools. As the practicing teachers, administrators, and researchers in Hannah's classes engage in school-based research and learning about systems of oppression, they also journal and come to terms with the violence of policing. Sadly, so many Black and Brown students, queer and trans students, and students with disabilities, among others, are subjected to police in their schools that there is always something for preservice and practicing educators and educational leaders to write about. Yet this reflection also sometimes pushes those working in and for public schooling to make commitments to the possibilities of police-free schools.

THE "RED BUTTON" AS POSSIBILITY

While critical incidents with school policing and punishment may not always involve a red button, we find it useful to engage the red button as a metaphor, reframing it to instead create an opportunity to reflect and imagine schools without police. Abolitionist perspectives caution us that, regarding calling police, "factors such as race, gender . . . and class can impact your judgment on whether something is 'suspicious' and can be life threatening for those you accuse."[11] This pertains to our work in schools too. We might stop and ask ourselves, "Do we *actually* need to take any action here?" We also see the button as a possibility for imagining what resources might arrive if we push it. For example, what if students could "push a button" when they begin to feel overwhelmed or anxious in a classroom? What if they could request support for teachers when they have had enough of the "humiliating ironies" that they experience in classrooms that tend to push students out of schools altogether?[12]

One day, Crystal witnessed a fairly typical situation in an elementary school hallway where one of her preservice teachers was doing their placement. A young Black boy left a classroom and was running in the halls. A teacher had used her red button to call the office and ask for a police officer. When the police officer came face to face with the young boy in the hallway, the boy immediately dropped to his knees and raised his hands as if surrendering.

Here, let us adopt the abolitionist practice of "imagining an otherwise"—an abolitionist future. Imagine what the teacher might do *instead* of calling the school police officer. Imagine that, instead of pushing the red button, the teacher had spoken to her multiple co-teachers in the classroom and then entered the hallway to find the student. Imagine that she found him around the corner from their classroom, sat down with him, and asked how he was doing and if he was OK. Imagine that they had a brief conversation and then walked back to the classroom, where he was welcomed back by the co-teachers and his classmates. Imagine that this teacher tapped a sign on the door of her room that said "We Keep Each Other Safe," and the student knew what this meant because it was a guiding principle and mantra of the classroom and school. Or imagine that there was a ready-made area in the school for when students needed space and safety from what was happening in their classrooms. Imagine that the boy knew just where to go and that, when he arrived there, he would find comfortable bean bag chairs, fidget toys, calming music, and laminated cards about different kinds of breathing exercises that he could do to regulate himself. Imagine that there were multiple books on the bookshelf, even plants to be tended to, that the boy could choose to engage with if he felt ready to do so. Imagine that he was not surveilled, not accosted, not terrified enough to raise his hands in surrender. Imagine that, instead, he was given the time and space to feel centered and safe.

The original version of this story—one where police confront a Black elementary school student who drops to his knees—is a shameful and telling reminder of how families teach many children to engage and interact with police at an early age. But it is the responsibility and role of educators to prevent these interactions from ever happening in our schools. Our imagined abolitionist retelling of the story may *seem* like a utopian ideal, but the reality is that this future already exists. In schools and classrooms around the country, there are *already* people doing this work, as there have been for decades. It just *feels* hard to imagine because, as we've read in previous chapters, we have been socialized to believe that policing is necessary: that policing is all there is and all there ever has been. Thus, we must look back to look forward, or rather, look *back* and look *now* to look forward. And reimagining school practices and relationships without relying on carceral solutions like policing and punishment transcends schooling contexts; this work has the potential to extend into all aspects of our lives, transforming how we interact with one another in school communities and beyond.

ABOLITIONIST ACTIVITIES: COMMITMENTS

In this set of Abolitionist Activities, we ask readers first to commit not to call the police to their classrooms and to imagine alternatives:

- First, read and take the Sanctuary Pledge developed by the Black Organizing Project. It calls on teachers to refrain from calling the police, ICE, and other policing agencies on students.[13]
- Next, we acknowledge what abolitionists and disability activists Ejeris Dixon and Leah Lakshmi Piepzna-Samarasinha explain regarding calls to police: "So many people experiencing violence or

other emergencies don't want to call the police—or in some cases understand that they should not—but have no idea of what to do instead."[14] Here, we encourage readers to continue imagining an abolitionist otherwise. For example, what could an "otherwise" look like in the instances that Alyssa, Crystal, and Hannah wrote about? Revisit these "red button" moments and imagine what you might do instead without the presence and intervention of police.

- To support this imagining, explore programs and practices at schools where teachers and administrators engage in police-free de-escalation and conflict resolution strategies.
- Finally, engage in some self-education around de-escalation and transformative justice approaches. Resources like Transformharm.org and *Lessons in Liberation: An Abolitionist Toolkit for Educators* are particularly helpful in scaffolding this learning.

We will learn more about resources and safety in chapter 7, drawing on preservice teachers' imaginations to envision safe schools without police.

TEACHERS OPEN ABOUT THEIR OWN LIVES
LISTENING
OPEN COMMUNICATION
OPEN DISCUSSIONS

CHAPTER 7

So, What Keeps Us Safe?

WITH KAITLYN J. SELMAN

Police are in schools to "protect" us . . . but soooo many mass shootings keep happening.

—Sage, preservice teacher

Many people in the United States, including educators, falsely equate policing with safety. And this equation is often the rationale for placing and keeping police in our public schools. But as we read about in earlier chapters, we know that police do not always keep us safe; in fact, abolitionist perspectives underscore how police are actually quite harmful in our communities, including school communities, and how these patterns go beyond "bad apple" officers.[1] Sage, who was learning to be an elementary school teacher, used air quotes when she talked about the "protection" that police were supposed to provide in schools. So if police don't keep us safe in schools, what and who can? To answer this question, we draw from the imaginations of preservice teachers like Sage, who acknowledge that police do not keep students safe—from shootings or otherwise—and who envision what safe schools might entail without police. In this chapter, we interweave abolitionist perspectives that teach us how to nurture safety both inside and outside of our schools with the voices of preservice teachers who imagine police-free schools. We end with Abolitionist Activities that prompt readers to map their experiences with school safety initiatives like the ones featured in this chapter, in addition to seeking resources and advocacy activities that may already exist in their communities.

"BUT WHAT ABOUT SCHOOL SHOOTINGS?"

Our repeated exposure to "copaganda," from Officer Friendly and Police Athletic Leagues (PALs) to media like *Law and Order* and *Paw Patrol* (which sometimes are even shown in classrooms), attempts to ensure that we will continue to believe that police keep us safe, even if personal experience teaches us otherwise.[2] We might think of this as a narrative of "bad faith," wherein the consumer of a story can turn away from a "displeasing truth for a pleasing falsehood."[3] We might also think of narratives about "bad apple" officers as contributing to this bad faith argument that equates policing and safety, since it's easier to blame individual officers for harm that they do than to recognize that the whole system is violent. In other words, it's often easier to accept policing as part of our lives than to admit that such an entrenched, well-funded institution does not actually keep us safe. The bad faith of policing also works to foreclose our imaginations about how to transform our communities so we can keep each other safe without police and prisons. And, importantly, this socialization shows up in how we think about schools and safety—so much so that even when educators and administrators are ready to consider that policing might do more harm than good, they often get stuck: If we can't call the police when bad things happen, who will we call?

The "bad thing" that comes to most minds in the context of education is the mass school shooting. Despite the pervasive presence of school-based law enforcement, school shootings have become more common in recent years.[4] And indeed, Sarah, who was learning to be a math teacher in Michigan, experienced the nightmare of shootings at both her high school in 2021 and again on her university campus in 2023. She described a day of horror in 2021, "waiting, texting my friends and family, and not really knowing anything except that we were all so scared." She recalled how often police were in her high school in the aftermath of the shooting there, as the investigation dragged on and as the school was the target of subsequent threats in the months afterward.

Imagining and manifesting police-free schools do require that we reckon with the reality of school shootings. To do so, we might start by digging into the assumptions that come with the "But what about school shootings?" question.

First, this question implies that police and other armed guards at schools prevent school shootings. Instead, we know that school shootings have happened and continue to happen, regardless of school police presence, as Sage points out. Take, for instance, the catastrophic shooting at Robb Elementary School in Uvalde, Texas, where school police were everywhere and yet failed to prevent mass death.[5] Another example is the shooting at Marjory Stoneman Douglas High School in Parkland, Florida, where the police officer on site remained outside the school as the shooting went on.[6] In fact, researchers have found that there are only a few cases where an armed guard or officer at school actually stopped a school shooting.[7] Perhaps even worse, research indicates that in school shooting instances where police are present, more students actually die.[8] Instead of police, many school shootings and plans to carry out gun violence in schools are thwarted by bystanders—family members, friends, and even teachers. In other words, the community that the shooter is surrounded by matters and is often the catalyst for the shooter to abandon their plans.[9]

Second, the question of school shootings implies that schools and the people who work and learn within them are responsible for the horrors of violence in general, and mass shootings in particular. While the forces of violence might sometimes come to a head for young people at school, their roots often lie beyond school walls. Importantly, young people outside of school are victims of gun violence in ways that we do not account for when we focus exclusively on school shootings. The gun death rate for youth has increased 87 percent in the last decade; guns remain the leading cause of death for children and teens.[10] The majority of these deaths take place in the home or in public spaces, with less than 1 percent of gun-related deaths occurring in school.[11] Yet we often don't hear conversations about this type of gun violence despite these statistics and the sustained activism by groups like, for example, March for Our Lives and the Dream Defenders.[12] It has indeed been incredibly difficult in the United States to move the needle with policymakers on the issue of gun control. Lawmakers have even increased funding to expand school police programs in tandem with "gun control" legislation instead of making guns more difficult to acquire. For example, the Gun Free Schools Act of 1994 was developed alongside the Violent Crime Control and Law Enforcement Act.[13] This bipartisan effort mandated a one-year expulsion for student possession of a gun at school and, more broadly, it banned assault weapons in the United States. But it also created the Community

Oriented Policing Services (COPS) grants program, which has been used to fund the expansion of school police nationwide.[14] Even President Obama's 2013 gun control proposal incentivized the placement of police in schools.[15] As a letter to lawmakers from the Advancement Project and other civil rights groups explained in 2022:

> We must be sure that any action to protect children from gun violence does not include any expansion of measures that have been especially harmful to Black, Latinx, and other students of color, students with disabilities, and LGBTQ students. In response to prior tragic mass shootings, states and localities have increased police presence and surveillance, and expanded school hardening measures. The result has been criminalization and physical harm to students and deterioration of learning environments—not an end to mass shootings.[16]

In other words, focusing on school shootings as a primary justification for the placement of police in schools also means neglecting to address the violence that youth experience off-campus, sometimes at the hands of police, in addition to overlooking the violence that happens at the hands of police in schools.

Finally, the question of school shootings requires us to reckon with the fact that policies ostensibly designed to protect students from violence also place the burden of protection on students, teachers, and school staff. These policies most often bring police into the equation, in addition to K-9s, metal detectors, surveillance cameras, lockdown drills, Alert, Lockdown, Inform, Counter, and Evacuate (ALICE active shooter) trainings, bulletproof glass windows in classrooms, and even calls to arm teachers.[17] These measures are not only informed by flawed assumptions, they are also flawed in that they fail to protect students and teachers, time and time again. Yet despite knowing that things aren't working (a displeasing truth), we continue to turn to the more pleasing (if false) belief that police keep us safe. In other words, the question of "What about school shootings?" is another kind of trap that continues to justify the practices of policing.

Beyond bad faith

To move beyond the bad faith of policing, we must first become accountable to the reality that police are not protecting us in schools, from mass shootings or otherwise. Here, "accountability" means recognizing how invested we have become, as both individuals and as a collective US society, in carcerality and policing; it also means acknowledging the damage that that investment has caused.[18] It means unlearning some of what we have been taught to think about policing and safety, acknowledging the research that details just how harmful police are in schools, honoring the voices and stories of students and teachers who have shared their experiences of harm from policing, and committing to envisioning schools without police. And, as we detail, it means putting that collective knowledge to work in our practices, policies, and personal interactions with students as we reimagine safety without policing. In the next sections, we share the visions of preservice teachers and situate them within and alongside existing theoretical and practical literature to illustrate abolitionist imagination. It is our hope that by sharing these visions, readers—especially teacher educators and other preservice teachers—will gain an understanding of the multifaceted nature of abolitionist safety and feel inspired to exercise their own imaginations. Both experiences—learning and imagining—contribute to police-free schools.

REIMAGINING SAFETY

Reimagining safety looks like divesting from particular practices and diverting resources, repairing the harm that school policing has caused, committing to new ways of interpreting student behavior, and encouraging school community members to take accountability when harm occurs so that neither students nor teachers feel isolated and disconnected. Whatever form it takes (and there are many possible forms), the work to reject a world made by and for policing in favor of one made by and for "us" is undergirded by the desire for *abolitionist safety.*

This idea of safety is best described as "a set of resources, relationships, skills, and tools that can be developed, disseminated, and deployed to prevent, interrupt, and heal from harm."[19] Abolitionist safety, by definition, cannot come from a space of deficit thinking, isolation, suspicion, or blame, which are all characteristics that are paramount to the project of policing and the carceral state, both in our schools and outside of them. As it stands, school districts devote huge chunks of money, time, and energy to outfitting, training, and defending police in schools—not just the presence of actual police, but also the everyday practices of "soft policing" that we often fall prey to in our own interactions.[20] With so many resources devoted to policing, far fewer are available to fund things that are more in line with abolitionist safety. For example, well-compensated and well-prepared teachers are less likely to leave their jobs and the profession at large, which in turn creates more stable school environments for kids.[21] Curricula and instruction that center relationship-building between and among students and school staff and connection to students' lives mean deeper student learning.[22] And treating students with empathy and respect, rather than positioning them as "behavior issues," makes it easier to integrate transformative models of accountability and repair instead of relying on carceral ideas about punishment and removal of kids from classrooms and schools.[23]

Despite the mainstream narrative that policing is the *only* way to achieve safety, there are countless efforts across US schools that fall more in line with abolitionist safety—like demands made by teachers' unions to fund housing for students, agreements from teachers to not call the police or Immigration and Customs Enforcement (ICE), successful campaigns to get cops out of schools, and training in restorative/transformative justice—largely the results of student and community organizing for better schooling. As demonstrated through the community-based creation of services and resources like neighborhood gardens and mutual aid fridges, car repair clinics, and trained street medics, we already know what works to keep communities safe, and how we might imagine systems of accountability that do not rely on punishment when harm occurs. Next, we explore the importance of resources, relationships, and skill sets to building and supporting safe schools. Our inspiration comes partly from the work taking place in schools across the country, but also from the visions articulated by preservice teachers when asked to describe and/or design the characteristics of a safe school. This emphasizes the acts of "reimagining" and "freedom dreaming" from those with fresh and thoughtful perspectives on schools. These ideas have also been integrated into and honored in artwork found throughout this book, providing us with a visual reminder of the unlimited possibilities that are unleashed when we lean into unlearning and wonderment.

Resources

Abolition emphasizes the importance of life-*affirming* resources—ones that honor our interconnectedness and abundance, so we may turn to them—instead of to life-*extracting* resources like suspensions or school police.[24] As we mentioned previously, though, and as preservice teachers well know, very little of our collective time, energy, and money actually go to those life-affirming resources. For example, teachers, the primary resource in the public school system, are overworked, underpaid, and increasingly assigned very large classes, which makes it far more difficult for them to create and sustain classrooms of deep connection, innovation, and joy without quickly burning out and resigning.[25] In 2017, starting salaries fell below $40,000 in almost 70 percent of states and job satisfaction fell to 12 percent in 2022 (down from 29 percent ten years earlier).[26] We know that teachers are struggling both financially and emotionally, even more so since the return to schooling after COVID-19 prompted an emergency shift to remote learning. Teachers are increasingly asked to do more with less, facing, for example, increased demands to engage students in virtual schooling, increased responsibilities for student attendance (which has dropped dramatically since 2020), and increased constraints on what can be taught in their classrooms.[27] This refusal to invest in teachers has spurred a nationwide teacher shortage, further exacerbating the stress (especially from accountability measures and standardized testing) that schools and teachers face. And teachers, especially over the last six years, have also been expected and encouraged to engage in "self-care"—a form of gaslighting that places "the onus for solving the stress on educators themselves rather than on fixing a system that was increasingly pressuring teachers and expecting too much."[28] As teachers have been saying for decades, increasing pay, stabilizing retirement benefits, and reducing class sizes improve not only teacher job satisfaction, but also all sorts of student (and community) outcomes.[29] Despite these poor working conditions, students across the United States, like the ones featured in this book, are studying to become teachers. We must invest in support and professional development for them, just as they invest in their respective schools and classrooms, especially in light of challenges exacerbated by COVID-19 like student truancy and absenteeism, heightened awareness and discourse about racial, gender, and disability justice, and increasingly restricted and narrowed curricula.

Indeed, the practices that happen within the four walls of teachers' classrooms can and should be life-affirming. Curricula and instruction, for example, serve as opportunities for teachers to affirm students' identities and experiences. As Ava, studying to be an elementary school educator, and her classmates detailed, allowing students "a chance to express their ideas and opinions" is crucial to a safe school. These "chances" show up in classrooms with teachers who root their work in culturally relevant curricula, like cultivating Black joy and teaching Black history.[30] Teachers can and should also center students' multifaceted identities by adopting, for example, culturally relevant and sustaining pedagogies and ethnic studies pedagogies.[31] Other pedagogies honor students' experiences outside of school, like engaging students' political trauma during heightened partisan activity, acknowledging the "days after" emotionally fraught events that prompt students' fears and anxieties, and engaging students in the fight for climate justice.[32] Classrooms also serve as sites for interventions and resistance to copaganda and status quo ideas about safety and policing, like learning the history of police violence in school districts and surrounding communities.[33] Advocating for curricula and instruction, especially in the face of right-wing attacks on textbooks and pedagogies that consider identity, also means advocating for affirming students' lived experiences.

Other resources in and around the school are life-affirming for students, but we often neglect them as well. For example, between 2015 and 2019, the number of full-time school librarians dropped by 20 percent, and for the 2020–2021 school year, at least 10 percent of students attended a school without a librarian.[34] Unsurprisingly, this librarian "slide" is not experienced equally, as, for example, majority "Hispanic" districts and majority nonwhite districts are more likely to go without a librarian than their majority white and non-Hispanic counterparts.[35] Evidence suggests that libraries can function as safe spaces for students to escape bullies, heal trauma, and access resources for well-being—while also boosting typical markers of success like standardized test scores.[36] In addition, forty-five states exceed the recommended ratio of students to school counselors (250 to 1), with the national average sitting at 385 to 1. Researchers have documented the benefits of smaller ratios, including increased attendance and grade performance, decreased disciplinary infractions, and overall improved social and emotional development.[37] Joe, a preservice teacher studying to be a science educator, and his classmates echoed this call—insisting that safe schools should have many counselors available to students to both support them and decrease teachers' sense of "overwhelm." Investing in school librarians, counselors, and teachers, then, is an investment not only in students but in communities overall. Calling for districts to fully fund these resources is one way that we can enact a commitment to abolitionist safety. And while funding concerns are often mentioned as barriers to investing in this sort of work, we must remember that budgets are determined by people—they are not implemented by some "invisible hand." Since 2000, city expenditures have shifted away from social services and toward policing, meaning that as funding to services like housing, employment, and parks and recreation decreases, the budget for policing increases.[38] Such a trend *can* be reversed: just look at districts like those in Chicago and Los Angeles, which not only cut their policing budgets but also reallocated those funds to invest in curriculum design, teacher professional development, and restorative justice.

Another resource crucial to school safety is, in the words of Holly and a group of her classmates learning to be special education teachers, "good food," at school and beyond. Many students in the United States experience food apartheid, or "a system of segregation that divides those with access to an abundance of nutritious food and those who have been denied that access due to systemic injustice."[39] This inequity wages violence on many low-income communities, communities of Color, and rural communities, and those who experience this violence carry its pain with them when they arrive at school. For some students, particularly students of Color, this can translate into behavior that might be misinterpreted by teachers as "disruptive" or "disrespectful"; research tells us that students from food-insecure homes face an increased risk of suspension and expulsion.[40] Nutritious and satiating food is yet another resource that our schools can (and sometimes do) provide, as in the federally funded School Breakfast Program. This program actually finds its roots in the Breakfast for Children program, developed by the Black Panther Party for Self Defense, which fed more than 20,000 schoolchildren across twenty-three cities by the end of 1969.[41] Unfortunately, as of early 2024, fifteen states have decided to end their summer food assistance programming, leaving about 8 million kids without access.[42] In the absence of state support, mutual aid projects become even more important. In this vein, we might learn from the Black Panther Party, as well as from the contemporary work of abolitionist organizations like Youth Undoing Institutional Racism (YUIR) and Assata's Daughters. The St. Louis chapter of YUIR created a community garden to place people in direct connection with the earth and their neighbors and promote health and vitality, all while "countering the global capitalist structure" of isolation and deprivation.[43] At the same time, the environmental justice program of Assata's Daughters trains young Black Chicagoans in food sustainability practices that they then put to work in community gardens.[44] And programs like these exist all over the country, like in Alabama, where Hannah lives and teaches. In rural spaces, for example, educators might draw from generations of Indigenous and Black farmers' wisdom to provide fresh, nutritious food.[45] Organizing for school-based gardens or even community refrigerators could be a worthwhile endeavor to support student access to food and nutrition.[46]

Likewise, we often take for granted the spaces and structures within our school buildings—which sometimes resemble prisons more than spaces of learning. For example, few or no windows, blank walls, and locked doors set up our learning spaces to feel carceral, especially when we consider the idea that these spaces separate students from the outside world and students must receive permission to move in, out, and around them.[47] Campaigns like those by Critical Exposure, for example, feature photography exhibits by K–12 students to demonstrate how school spaces are constraining, violent, and hostile, for Black and Brown youth in particular.[48] Cheyenne and a group of her classmates, all preservice teachers learning to be both elementary and secondary educators, underscored the importance of space in their desire for an "open campus." They envisioned a public high school where students had access to many windows and natural light, could move about their campus without strict rules or hall passes, and had the opportunity for both learning time and time to "chill" with friends in an outdoor courtyard. This attention to the built environment, they argued, would support the development of relationships within the school community. We might also draw from partnerships between and among teachers, students, and community members to point us toward the importance of critical evaluation of our learning spaces, helping us to reimagine the architecture of our physical school buildings to provide students with opportunities to interact with the natural environment, like the movement for green schools.[49] Rethink Outside, for example, is an initiative that encourages educators, students, and community members to share stories of how spending time outside benefits us all.[50]

Relationships

Preservice teachers like Parker and her classmates already knew that relationships are at the heart of our work in schools and classroom communities. They envisioned safe schools as relationship-focused, emphasizing "building trust and empathy" between and among students. They argued that schools should be spaces where students can feel free to express themselves "without judgment or facing consequences." As it stands, there are huge amounts of resources and funding structures devoted to *police* building relationships with youth. Police-youth mentoring programs, school field days with police, Drug Abuse Resistance

Education (D.A.R.E.) programming, and even police taking part in drivers' ed classrooms are all predicated on the idea that it's important for youth to have meaningful relationships with adults. These intergenerational relationships are important, of course. So how might we reenvision adult-youth and community relationship building without relying on police?

We might first draw from the work of teachers who build relationship-centered activities into their everyday classroom structures and lesson plans. Preservice teachers like Lisa, studying to be a high school social studies teacher, envisioned classrooms where teachers hold "morning circles" or "morning meetings" with students. This classroom structure affords opportunities for teachers to check in, learn about students' lives, and draw on that knowledge to nurture relationships.[51] This time encourages connections between teachers and students in addition to among students' peers. Teachers might also engage students in "free writing" or journaling activities, or as Alice, a preservice teacher who was beginning her student-teaching practicum, liked to say, "writing for full presence" in the classroom. These activities can give students time to reflect, emote, or simply vent about the things happening in their lives that they inevitably bring into our classrooms. Teachers who build this time into the classroom and scaffold students' writing practices also demonstrate to students that their lived experiences are important to the work of learning. And teachers in classrooms could complete "pod-mapping" activities, in which they ask students to identify trusted adults.[52] Engaging students in pod mapping within the school community means finding adults who can come together to support students in their time of need. This might look like the following, as Amor, a preservice teacher studying to be an elementary school teacher, details: a student visiting a trusted teacher or staff member in a time of crisis or if they need time to "decompress," "cool off," or simply be "alone, together." These pods of trusted adults can then intervene in or interrupt situations of conflict from a space of support, without relying on police officers. Identifying pods also makes it possible to determine the nature and depth of our relationships. Knowing where we are abundant and where we might be lacking in our relationships is imperative to identifying the skills that we might need to develop, and with who we can develop them, if we wish to redefine safety without policing.

Individual teachers can build trust with students by making commitments to keep their students safe from policing structures. For example, the Black

Organizing Project (BOP) in Oakland, California, developed what they call a "Sanctuary Pledge," which we learned about at the beginning of the book and in chapter 6.[53] With it, BOP members alerted teachers and school staff to the devastating impact of school police in their community, citing statistics about how many Black students the Oakland School Police Department disciplined in a given school year. They then asked that educators "pledge to fight to make sure Oakland Unified School District is a sanctuary for all students" and "pledge not to contribute to the criminalization of Black students." Further, they called on teachers to agree not to call police, ICE, or the US Department of Homeland Security on students. These efforts also align with scholar Bettina Love's ideas about abolitionist teaching, one of which is rejecting the use of zero-tolerance policies that criminalize students.[54] These efforts build trust and show a commitment to relationships with students and families, free from the risks of introducing law enforcement to their lives at school. They also help teachers make the case to administrators that involving the police is not always an approach favored by parents, guardians, or community members.

As educator Harley Litzelman writes, "The harder pill to swallow is our own responsibility as educators. We cannot abolish police in schools if educators do not abolish the police in their minds. We must abolish the impulse to escalate conflicts with students, seeking to assert authoritarian power over our students."[55] This means reframing how we think about student behavior, approaching what we often characterize as misbehavior with accountability that is not rooted in punishment, as we learned in earlier chapters. We might even approach student behavior with a spirit of curiosity, since, as Sage underscored: "It's about relationships. It's about having conversations with kids. It's about, 'What's going on?'" We might ask ourselves what students are trying to communicate to us with their behavior, reframing their behavior as resistance—to unjust learning or living conditions, to irrelevant curricula and instruction, or to the systems of power and oppression that guide schooling.[56] Unlearning the impulse to punish and being willing to reframe, however, mean learning some skills to support us along the way.

Skills

So, what skills and tools must we develop to prevent, interrupt, and heal after harm? For educators, getting "skilled up" can take various forms—from training to advocacy work, teachers can hone their ability to cultivate new forms of safety, and in doing so, they provide students and even people outside of school, like parents and community members, to do so as well.[57] Haley and her classmates learning to be secondary education teachers agreed that teachers and counselors need training to make "each student feel seen and heard." They suggested schools where students could check in with the "same person" each day or week, as well as teachers who could facilitate "open communication" when students were having issues with one another.

Much of what these preservice teachers envision can and does happen in schools and is embedded in a "framework for inquiry" known as Transformative Justice. Transformative Justice, as abolitionists Mariame Kaba and Andrea Ritchie argue, prompts us to ask questions like: "How do we respond to violence and harm in a way that doesn't cause more violence and harm? How do we respond to violence and harm in ways that don't rely on the punishing state? How are we actively cultivating the things that will help prevent future violence, like healing and accountability? How do we meet immediate needs in ways that get us closer to the world we want—one that is liberatory and prioritizes collective freedom?"[58] In considering those questions, it becomes clear that "there is no one way to do [Transformative Justice]. It looks different because communities are different, geography is different, violence is different."[59] Unlike our current (and ineffective) responses to harm and violence, there is no standardized, one-size-fits-all blueprint for this work—and that is, perhaps, the beauty of it. With that said, being trained in Transformative Justice involves, in the most general sense, learning how to recognize practices that reproduce harm and violence, building trusting and accountable relationships, and engaging with "bold, small experiments" to prevent and/or intervene in that harm and violence.[60] In schools, this could involve critical analysis of school policies and informal practices for underlying carceral logics (like the Power U Center for Social Change's report on the Miami–Dade County Public Schools), and experimenting with new ways to build community and keep people safe (like Oakland Unified School District has done with restorative justice).[61] It can also look like teachers being "trained in de-escalation and conflict management," as Emily, studying to be a high school science teacher, envisioned. Various community organizations offer training in Transformative Justice, like SOIL, where groups can learn everything from how to give a genuine apology to coordinating a community accountability process.[62] Programs like these can easily be funded by diverting the financial resources that are currently devoted to police programs in schools.[63]

As we hone our ability to identify harmful processes and policies, we find new ways in which to intervene, both within the school and beyond. Take, for example, the Ypsilanti Mutual Aid's pull-over prevention clinics.[64] Volunteers provide free minor car repairs, share their car repair skills, and connect community members with resources like housing or food. Repair clinics like this one developed out of the recognition that automotive issues are sometimes a catalyst for deadly contact with the police, as in the case of Philando Castile, who police say they pulled over for a broken taillight—an incident that ended up with police fatally shooting Castile.[65] As such, these clinics can actually help prevent, or at least delay, contact with police in the first place. Many schools operate automotive repair programs for students and thus are already primed to run similar clinics. For example, at Cordova High School in Memphis, Tennessee, automotive students worked together to provide car repairs without charging for the cost of labor.[66] Both the wider community and students themselves can benefit from this type of training, not only strengthening relationships but also potentially intervening in harmful police-civilian interactions. Or we might consider advocating for medical training for students and staff, like gunshot wound treatment. Ujimaa Medics (UMedics), a Black health collective, was founded after a young person was shot in the founders' neighborhood and died on the way to the hospital. From this tragedy, they learned that "our people needed immediate skills to help until a higher level of care could arrive."[67] UMedics provides all sorts of medical training for neighborhoods, but it also provides courses in asthma attack and gunshot wound treatment in high schools in and around Chicago. This kind of training can enable a teacher, staff member, or student to dispense immediate care to another, and in the most extreme cases, stabilize the wounded enough to get to the nearest hospital. This increases the likelihood for survival and decreases reliance on 911, when police are usually contacted. Essentially, this is yet another way that *we* can keep us safe.

IMAGINING BEYOND

Visionary fiction writer and activist Walidah Imarisha declares, "Once the imagination is unshackled, liberation is limitless."[68] In this way, the driving force of the work toward police-free schools is imagination: "How might we reimagine what a safe school looks like?" In the simple act of asking this question, we begin to intervene in the taken-for-granted nature of policed schools, resisting the narrative that things must go on as they are. And by asking this question specifically of those included in this book (and now, those of you reading it), we hope to free our collective imaginations from the confines of carceral thinking. Imagining and dreaming in this way allow us to resist mainstream ideologies—such as "Police keep us safe"—and instead cultivate the space needed to bring about different futures, specifically those in which "we keep us safe." It is this imagination, then, that fosters the practices that we need to bring such futures to life; and as such, it is a fundamental tool that abolitionist activists and teachers can hone and deploy to bring about police-free schools.

We therefore call on educators, parents, students, and community members to *wonder*: What might a safe school for *all* students look like?[69] How would students and teachers feel? What would the hallways look like? What would discipline policies and procedures look like? What you might find when wondering about safety is that it is not something that we can possess. It is a social relation—between and among ourselves, each other, and the world around us—that must first be imagined and then created (and fought for).[70] When we see safety as a reflection of our proximity to resources, the strength of our relationships, and the skills that we are dedicated to honing, we quickly realize that safety is not a "thing" that can be given to us, and most assuredly not by/through policing. As we imagine, we begin to develop concrete steps to move in closer alignment with those visions, like many of the things that we have discussed here. For educators specifically, attending community protests, speaking up at school board meetings, and engaging in political education about the harms of policing in spheres of influence like professional learning communities are all powerful ways in which we can fight for these imagined futures.

We recognize, however, that teachers put themselves at risk by advocating for abolitionist safety. We see teachers punished for reading "controversial" books, displaying "Black Lives Matter" signs or Pride flags, and allowing students to write letters to political prisoners.[71] But those risks decrease as we invest more—and as more of us invest—in the resources, relationships, and skills needed to cultivate safety. As science fiction writer Ursula K. Le Guin reminds us, "Any human power can be resisted and changed by human beings."[72] Put another way, while schools and the society within which they operate are largely defined by carcerality, punishment, and removal, they do not have to be. Teachers around the country have already shown us that things can be changed. For example, over the last ten years, the Chicago Teachers Union (CTU) has won significant pay raises, affordable city housing, a nurse and social worker in every school, caps on class size, sanctuary policies for undocumented students and non-English-speaking students, and the district's first elected school board.[73] More recently, the CTU supported the #CopsOutCPS campaign . . . which won. In a unanimous vote in 2024, Chicago Public Schools chose to remove school police officers and direct their $11 million budget elsewhere.[74] In response, the CTU intends to demand, as part of their upcoming contract negotiation, that resources be invested in "additional trauma supports, restorative practice training and methods, appropriate personnel, and holistic safety practices."[75]

The current teacher shortage reveals much about the dysfunctional state of education, but it also underscores that teachers have a fair amount of bargaining power right now. And in "right-to-work" states like Alabama, North Carolina, and other places where preservice and practicing teachers do not have opportunities to participate in unions, we see some of the hardest battles fought and the most successful collective campaigns waged. Take, for instance, the strikes in Durham, North Carolina, where teachers and school staff spent much of 2024 engaging in sick-outs and sit-ins as they demanded better pay.[76] Another example was the Wildcat strikes of 2018 that originated in West Virginia, which spread to Kentucky and North Carolina and added to the growing Red for Ed movement in states like Arizona and Oklahoma.[77] Depending on the state, teachers fought for and won raises of 5 to 20 percent; on a more ideological scale, the demands made by teachers and school staff have the potential to shift the narrative about the realities facing education.

While collective action on this scale has been effective in many ways, it isn't the only way to catalyze change. In fact, strikes and union organizing are typically the final step, not the first. What comes before organizing at this level is the work that we do to engage in the process of unlearning and imagining an "otherwise," in our teaching practices, relationships with students, and our classrooms and school structures. We might simply start with an acknowledgment that begins our disruption of the status quo—like Sage, who acknowledged that police are not protecting us. As activist adrienne maree brown points out, change is "fractal"; "what we practice at a small scale can reverberate to the largest scale."[78] As such, we end with Abolitionist Activities that can inspire us to wonder and bring that wonderment into our classrooms—and ultimately, bring police-free schools into being.

ABOLITIONIST ACTIVITIES: ENVISIONING AND IMAGINING

This last set of activities encourages imagination above all else:

- First, envision what "safety" means to you, the reader, whether you are a practicing teacher, preservice teacher, or teacher educator. What comes to mind when you think about safety? How does being safe make you feel? What do you need to feel safe? What things or people in your life make you feel safe? What do they do that makes you feel safe? What do you do to make those in your life feel safe? Also, consider what students' sense of safety might be. What about their families and communities? How can your ideas combine with theirs to create an approach that takes everyone's views into account and affords everyone feelings of safety?
- As you think through and respond to these questions, you might engage in some reflective writing, drawing, pod mapping, or maybe even some curation of songs and/or images that help describe your ideas.[79]
- Finally, consider which of these things are currently available in schools and classrooms most proximal to you. If they are not present, which ones would you like to see in schools? What steps might you take to work toward that imagined school context?

Notes

Introduction

1. Joseph M. McKenna and Anthony Petrosino, "School Policing Programs: Where We Have Been and Where We Need to Go Next," National Institute of Justice (2022), https://nij.ojp.gov/library/publications/school-policing-programs-where-we-have-been-and-where-we-need-go-next.
2. Ethan M. Higgins et al., "School Safety or School Criminalization? The Typical Day of a School Resource Officer in the United States," *British Journal of Criminology* 62, no. 3 (2022): 568–84.
3. Research documents how police also harass students in this way. For example, a report by the organizations Interrupting Criminalization and the In Our Names Network documents police sexual harassment and assault of Black girls, trans, and gender nonconforming youth. Interrupting Criminalization and In Our Names Network, *Sexualization Not Safety: Black Girls, Trans, and Gender Nonconforming Youth's Experiences of Police Presence in Schools: Report* (2024), https://www.inournamesnetwork.com/psvresearch.
4. Nicole Chavez, "A Movement to Push Police out of Schools Is Growing Nationwide. Here Is Why," CNN, June 28, 2020, https://www.cnn.com/2020/06/28/us/police-out-of-schools-movement/index.html.
5. According to data from the National Center for Education Statistics, over half of schools in the United States have "sworn law enforcement officers routinely carrying a firearm." US Department of Education, National Center for Education Statistics, "Percentage of Public Schools with Security Staff Present at Least Once a Week, and Percentage with Security Staff Routinely Carrying a Firearm, by Selected School Characteristics: 2005–06 Through 2019–20," *Digest of Education Statistics*, table 233.70 (2021), https://nces.ed.gov/programs/digest/d21/tables/dt21_233.70.asp.
6. We will read more about this history in chapter 1. See also "School Policing Timeline," #policefreeschools, https://policefreeschools.org/timeline/.
7. Mariame Kaba and Andrea J. Ritchie, *No More Police: A Case for Abolition* (New York: New Press, 2022).
8. Jenny Jarvie, "Girl Thrown from Desk Didn't Obey Because the Punishment Was Unfair, Attorney Says," *Los Angeles Times*, October 29, 2015, https://www.latimes.com/nation/la-na-girl-thrown-punishment-unfair-20151029-story.html.
9. Associated Press, "Deputy Who Tossed a S.C. High School Student Won't Be Charged," *New York Times*, September 2, 2016, https://www.nytimes.com/2016/09/03/afternoonupdate/deputy-who-tossed-a-sc-high-school-student-wont-be-charged.html.
10. Jenn Abelson, Jessica Contrera, and Nate Jones, "A School Cop Was Accused of Sexual Misconduct with Kids. He Kept His Job for Years," *Washington Post*, September 2, 2024, https://www.washingtonpost.com/investigations/interactive/2024/south-carolina-sro-child-sexual-abuse-jamel-bradley/.

11. "A School Resource Officer Helped Capture the Suspect in Oxford. How Many Local Schools Have Them?," WXYZ Detroit, December 8, 2021, https://www.wxyz.com/news/oxford-school-shooting/a-school-resource-officer-helped-capture-the-suspect-in-oxford-how-many-local-schools-have-them.
12. Tim Stelloh et al., "Former Uvalde School District Police Chief Charged with Child Endangerment After Shooting That Killed 21," NBC News, June 27, 2024, https://www.nbcnews.com/news/us-news/former-uvalde-school-district-police-chief-charged-child-endangerment-rcna134848.
13. Meredith Deliso and Leah Sarnoff, "Former Uvalde School Police Chief Charged with 10 Counts of 'Abandoning and Endangering' Robb Elementary Survivors," ABC News, June 28, 2024, https://abcnews.go.com/US/uvalde-shooting-grand-jury-indictment/story?id=111490997.
14. Mark Keierleber, "Federal Data Shows a Drop in Campus Cops—for Now," *LA School Report*, January 30, 2024, https://www.laschoolreport.com/federal-data-shows-a-drop-in-campus-cops-for-now/.
15. Chase S. Burton, "Schools and Delinquency in the Early 20th Century: Rethinking the Origins of School Policing," *British Journal of Criminology* 57, no. 3 (2017): 532–50; Noah Remnick, " 'The Police State in Franklin K. Lane': Desegregation, Student Resistance, and the Carceral Turn at a New York City High School," *Journal of Urban History* 49, no. 5 (2023): 1071–87.
16. Lynn A. Addington, "Black Girls Doing Time for White Boys' Crime? Considering Columbine's Security Legacy Through an Intersectional Lens," *Journal of Contemporary Criminal Justice* 35, no. 3 (2019): 296–314.
17. Elizabeth Davis, "School Resource Officers, 2019–2020," Bureau of Justice Statistics, November 2023, https://bjs.ojp.gov/library/publications/school-resource-officers-2019-2020.
18. US Department of Education, National Center for Education Statistics, "Percentage of Public Schools with Security Staff Present at Least Once a Week, and Percentage with Security Staff Routinely Carrying a Firearm, by Selected School Characteristics: 2005–06 Through 2015–16," *Digest of Education Statistics*, table 233.70 (2018), https://nces.ed.gov/programs/digest/d18/tables/dt18_233.70.asp.
19. Today, there are over four hundred school district police departments, according to *A Cop Is a Cop: The Rise of School District Police Departments and Why They Must Be Dismantled*, a report by the Advancement Project, https://advancementproject.org/wp-content/uploads/2024/05/AP-SchoolDistrictReport-V4-1.pdf.
20. Anna Bryant, "Cops in Schools: Tracking Nationwide Changes After George Floyd," Chicago Justice Project, March 26, 2024, https://chicagojustice.org/2024/03/26/cops-in-schools-tracking-nationwide-changes-after-george-floyd/.
21. "School Policing Timeline," the Advancement Project, Police Free Schools, https://policefreeschools.org/timeline/.
22. Leslie Dominique, "Viral Video: Affidavit Reveals New Details in East Ridge Student's Arrest by SRO," News Channel 9 ABC, September 27, 2022, https://newschannel9.com/news/local/viral-video-shows-east-ridge-students-forceful-arrest-by-hamilton-county-sro-tuesday.
23. Brittany Edney and FOX 5 Atlanta Digital Team, "Mom of Teen Body Slammed, Arrested by School Police Says Wrong Person Was Punished," Fox 5 Atlanta, September 6, 2023, https://www.fox5atlanta.com/news/dekalb-county-school-district-arrested-suspended-after-body-slamming-incident.

24. Kaba and Ritchie, *No More Police*, 151–52. Criminalization, according to the authors, is a "highly racialized process of determining who is deserving of social programs and investment and who is not" (30). Criminalizing student behavior in schools, and then punishing students by removing them from peers, teachers, and classrooms, communicate that they do not deserve to be in school to receive educational services and resources.
25. Mark Lieberman and Caitlynn Peetz, "After Teachers, America's Schools Spend More on Security Guards Than Any Other Role," *EducationWeek*, September 22, 2023, https://www.edweek.org/leadership/after-teachers-americas-schools-spend-more-on-security-guards-than-any-other-role/2023/09#:~:text=Then%2C%20the%20duo%20used%20the,dollars%2C%20or%20%2446.87%20per%20pupil.
26. Davis, "School Resource Officers, 2019–2020."
27. Advancement Project, *Education on Lockdown: The Schoolhouse to Jailhouse Track* (Washington, DC: US Department of Justice, 2005), 15.
28. "School Suspensions, Discipline Policies Ramp up After COVID-19," National Criminal Justice Association, September 13, 2023, https://www.ncja.org/crimeandjusticenews/school-suspensions-discipline-policies-ramp-up-after-covid-19.
29. Benjamin W. Fisher and Emily A. Hennesy, "School Resource Officers and Exclusionary Discipline in U.S. High Schools: A Systematic Review and Meta-Analysis," *Adolescent Research Review* 1 (2016): 217–33.
30. Education for Liberation Network and Critical Resistance Editorial Collective, "Black Organizing Project Sanctuary Pledge," in *Lessons in Liberation: An Abolitionist Toolkit for Educators* (Chico, CA: AK Press, 2021).
31. *#AssaultAtSpringValley Report*, Advancement Project, https://advancementproject.org/resources/assaultatreport/.
32. Eesha Pendharkar, "Students of Color Disproportionately Suffer from Police Assaults at School, Says Report," *EducationWeek*, January 13, 2023, https://www.edweek.org/leadership/students-of-color-disproportionately-suffer-from-police-assaults-at-school-says-report/2023/01.
33. Peter Wagner and Wanda Bertram, "'What Percent of the U.S. Is Incarcerated?' (And Other Ways to Measure Mass Incarceration)," Prison Policy Initiative, January 16, 2020, https://www.prisonpolicy.org/blog/2020/01/16/percent-incarcerated/#:~:text=Nearly%20one%20out%20of%20every,in%20a%20prison%20or%20jail.&text=We're%20often%20asked%20what,state%20prison%20or%20local%20jail.
34. Kaba and Ritchie, *No More Police*, 23.
35. "The Origins of Monday Day Policing," NAACP, https://naacp.org/find-resources/history-explained/origins-modern-day-policing.
36. Ruth Gilmore Wilson, *Golden Gulag: Prisons, Surplus, Crisis, and Opposition in Globalizing California* (Berkeley: University of California Press, 2007).
37. Mark Neocleous, *A Critical Theory of Police Power: The Fabrication of the Social Order* (New York: Verso, 2021), 10.
38. Risa Goluboff, "The Forgotten Law That Gave Police Nearly Unlimited Power," *TIME*, February 1, 2016, https://time.com/4199924/vagrancy-law-history/; "Contribute to Making Society Safer and Pursue a Justice Studies Career: A Focus on Quality, Individualized Instruction," EKU Online, https://ekuonline.eku.edu/blog/police-studies/the-history-of-policing-in-the-united-states-part-2/.
39. Tyler Wall, "The Police Invention of Humanity: Notes on the 'Thin Blue Line,'" *Crime, Media, Culture* 16, no. 3 (2020): 319–36.

40. *The Prison Industrial Complex*, Critical Resistance, https://criticalresistance.org/mission-vision/not-so-common-language/.
41. Erica R. Meiners, *Right to Be Hostile: Schools, Prisons, and the Making of Public Enemies* (New York: Routledge, 2007), 2.
42. Hannah Carson Baggett and Carey E. Andrzejewski, *School Based Police: Evidence and Alternatives*, APA Division 15 Policy Brief, https://apadiv15.org/school-based-police-evidence-and-alternatives/.
43. Sam Davis et al., *The Consequences of Cops in North Carolina Schools* (ACLU North Carolina, 2023), https://static1.squarespace.com/static/5b7ea2794cde7a79e7c00582/t/6550d1bd1f350e20e3afc531/1699795390002/The+Consequences+of+Cops.pdf.
44. Hannah Carson Baggett and Kaitlyn J. Selman, "School Copaganda in the US South: Tinsel, Twinkle, and Police-Youth Programming," *Crime, Media, Culture* 21, no. 1 (2025): 46–68.
45. "In Ferguson, Court Fines and Fees Fuel Anger," NPR, August 25, 2014, https://www.npr.org/2014/08/25/343143937/in-ferguson-court-fines-and-fees-fuel-anger; "Alabama Town's Traffic Ticketing Scandal Leads to Police Chief's Resignation," NBC News, January 28, 2022, https://www.nbcnews.com/news/us-news/alabama-towns-traffic-ticketing-scandal-leads-police-chiefs-resignatio-rcna13801.
46. Annette Fuentes, "The Truancy Trap," *The Atlantic*, September 5, 2012, https://www.theatlantic.com/national/archive/2012/09/the-truancy-trap/261937.
47. Kipton D. Smilie, "Patrolling and Controlling the Streets: The Origin of School Safety Patrols in New York City," *Journal of Urban History* 50, no. 5 (2022): 1046–62.
48. Jon N. Hale and Candace Livingston, "'If You Want Police, We Will Have Them': Anti-Black Student Discipline in Southern Schools and the Rise of a New Carceral Logic, 1961–1975," *Journal of Urban History* 49, no. 5 (2022): 1035–48.
49. Angela Mann et al., *Cops and No Counselors: How the Lack of School Mental Health Staff Is Harming Students* (ACLU Publications, 2019), https://www.aclu.org/publications/cops-and-no-counselors.
50. Amy Yurkanin, "Alabama Launches Vape Courts for Students Busted at School," AL.com, October 10, 2023, https://www.al.com/news/2023/10/alabama-launches-vape-courts-for-students-busted-at-school.html.
51. *New Report on Per Capita Spending for Libraries, Police, and Education*, Every Library Institute, https://www.everylibraryinstitute.org/new_report_per_capita_spending_2023.
52. Benjamin W. Fisher et al., "School-Based Law Enforcement Strategies to Reduce Crime, Increase Perceptions of Safety, and Improve Learning Outcomes in Primary and Secondary Schools: A Systematic Review," *Campbell Systematic Reviews* 19, no. 4 (2023): e1360.
53. Aaron Kupchik, *Homeroom Security: School Discipline in an Age of Fear, Youth, Crime, and Justice*, vol. 6 (New York: New York University Press, 2010); Hannah Carson Baggett and Carey E. Andrzejewski, *The Grammar of School Discipline: Removal, Resistance, and Reform in Alabama Schools* (Lanham, MD: Rowman & Littlefield, 2021); Paul J. Hirschfield, "Preparing for Prison? The Criminalization of School Discipline in the USA," *Theoretical Criminology* 12, no. 1 (2008): 79–101; Monique Morris, *Pushout: The Criminalization of Black Girls in Schools* (New York: New Press, 2016); Victor M. Rios, "The Hyper-Criminalization of Black and Latino Male Youth in the Era of Mass Incarceration," *Souls* 8, no. 2 (2006): 40–54.
54. West Resendes, *Police in Schools Continue to Target Black, Brown, and Indigenous Students with Disabilities. The Trump Administration Has Data That's Likely to Prove It*, ACLU News & Commentary, July 9, 2020, https://www.aclu.org/news/criminal-law-reform/police-in-

schools-continue-to-target-black-brown-and-indigenous-students-with-disabilities-the-trump-administration-has-data-thats-likely-to-prove-it.

55. Jacqueline M. Nowicki, *K–12 Education: Discipline Disparities for Black Students, Boys, and Students with Disabilities, Report to Congressional Requesters, GAO-18-258* (Washington, DC: US Government Accountability Office, 2018).
56. Morris, *Pushout*; David S. Kirk and Robert J. Sampson, "Juvenile Arrest and Collateral Educational Damage in the Transition to Adulthood," *Sociology of Education* 86, no. 1 (2013): 36–62.
57. Wilson, *Golden Gulag*.
58. Derecka Purnell, *Becoming Abolitionists: Police, Protests, and the Pursuit of Freedom* (New York: Astra, 2022), 6.
59. Mariame Kaba, "Yes, We Mean Literally Abolish the Police," *New York Times*, June 12, 2020, Opinion, https://www.nytimes.com/2020/06/12/opinion/sunday/floyd-abolish-defund-police.html.
60. *School-to-Prison Pipeline*, American Civil Liberties Union (ACLU), Juvenile Justice, https://www.aclu.org/issues/juvenile-justice/juvenile-justice-school-prison-pipeline.
61. See also Damien Sojoyner's work on how schools are predicated on carcerality and work to enclose Black life; Damien M. Sojoyner, "Black Radicals Make for Bad Citizens: Undoing the Myth of the School to Prison Pipeline," *Berkeley Review of Education* 4, no. 2 (2013): 241–63.
62. Meiners, *Right to Be Hostile*.
63. Carla Shalaby, *Troublemakers: Lessons in Freedom from Young Children at School* (New York: New Press, 2017).
64. Yolanda Anyon et al., "An Exploration of the Relationships Between Student Racial Background and the School Sub-Contexts of Office Discipline Referrals: A Critical Race Theory Analysis," *Race Ethnicity and Education* 21, no. 3 (2018): 390–406.
65. Sheeva Sabati et al., "Dismantle, Change, Build: Lessons for Growing Abolition in Teacher Education," *Teachers College Record* 124, no. 3 (2022): 177–206.
66. Dan C. Lortie, *Schoolteacher: A Sociological Study* (Chicago: University of Chicago Press, 1975).
67. Olly Costello, "Unlearn," in *Lessons in Liberation: An Abolitionist Toolkit for Educators* (Chico, CA: AK Press, 2021), 151.
68. Sabati et al., "Dismantle, Change, Build."

Chapter 1

1. Lynn A. Addington, "Black Girls Doing Time for White Boys' Crime? Considering Columbine's Security Legacy Through an Intersectional Lens," *Journal of Contemporary Criminal Justice* 35, no. 3 (2019): 296–314.
2. The shooters at Columbine were initially reported to be part of a group of students known as the "Trench Coat Mafia," who wore long, black trench coats to school.
3. Antonis Katsiyannis et al., "An Examination of US School Mass Shootings, 2017–2022: Findings and Implications," *Advances in Neurodevelopmental Disorders* 7, no. 1 (2023): 66–76; Michael G. Huskey and Nadine M. Connell, "Preparation or Provocation? Student Perceptions of Active Shooter Drills," *Criminal Justice Policy Review* 32, no. 1 (2021): 3–26.
4. Kaitlyn Selman, Hannah Carson Baggett, and LaKendrick Richardson, "Carceral Care in Kentucky: The Case of a School Safety Plan," *Urban Education* 60, no. 6 (2025): 1602–33.

5. Matthew B. Kautz, "From Segregation to Suspension: The Solidification of the Contemporary School-Prison Nexus in Boston, 1963–1985," *Journal of Urban History* 49, no. 5 (2023): 1049–70; Brenda J. Child, *Boarding School Seasons: American Indian Families, 1900–1940* (Lincoln: University of Nebraska Press, 1998); Meredith McCoy, *On Our Own Terms: Indigenous Histories of School Funding and Policy* (Lincoln: University of Nebraska Press, 2024).
6. David Correia and Tyler Wall, *Police: A Field Guide* (New York: Verso, 2018), 8.
7. Larry K. Gaines, Victor E. Kappeler, and Joseph B. Vaughn, *Policing in America*, 4th ed. (Cincinnati: Anderson, 1999), 58.
8. For a brief history of police and its connections to policy in England, see Mariame Kaba and Andrea J. Ritchie, *No More Police: A Case for Abolition* (New York: New Press, 2022).
9. Gaines, Kappeler, and Vaughn, *Policing in America*; Gary Potter, *The History of Policing in the United States* (Richmond: Eastern Kentucky School of Justice Studies, 2013).
10. Potter, *The History of Policing in the United States*.
11. Ben Brucato, "Policing Race and Racing Police: The Origin of US Police in Slave Patrols," *Social Justice* 47, no. 3/4 (161/162) (2020): 115–36; Philip L. Reichel, "The Misplaced Emphasis on Urbanization in Police Development," *Policing and Society: An International Journal* 3, no. 1 (1992): 1–12.
12. For an in-depth history, see Sally E. Hadden, *Slave Patrols: Law and Violence in Virginia and the Carolinas* (Cambridge, MA: Harvard University Press, 2003).
13. Michael A. Robinson, "Black Bodies on the Ground: Policing Disparities in the African American Community—An Analysis of Newsprint from January 1, 2015, Through December 31, 2015," *Journal of Black Studies* 48, no. 6 (2017): 551–71.
14. Gloria J. Browne-Marshall, "Stop and Frisk: From Slave-Catchers to NYPD, a Legal Commentary," *Trotter Review* 21, no. 1 (2013): 9; Marlese Durr, "What Is the Difference Between Slave Patrols and Modern Day Policing? Institutional Violence in a Community of Color," *Critical Sociology* 41, no. 6 (2015): 875.
15. Durr, "What Is the Difference Between Slave Patrols and Modern Day Policing?," 875.
16. National Constables Association, "Constable," in *The Encyclopedia of Police Science*, 2nd ed., ed. W. G. Bailey (New York: Garland, 1995), 114; Patricia D. Quijada Cerecer, "The Policing of Native Bodies and Minds: Perspectives on Schooling from American Indian Youth," *American Journal of Education* 119, no. 4 (2013): 591–616.
17. Kelly L. Hernández, *City of Inmates: Conquest, Rebellion, and the Rise of Human Caging in Los Angeles, 1771–1965* (Chapel Hill: University of North Carolina Press, 2017); Sherene H. Razack, "Settler Colonialism, Policing and Racial Terror: The Police Shooting of Loreal Tsingine," *Feminist Legal Studies* 28, no. 1 (2020): 1–20.
18. Philip V. McHarris, "Disrupting Order: Race, Class, and the Roots of Policing," in *Violent Order: Essays on the Nature of Police*, ed. David Correia and Tyler Wall (Chicago: Haymarket, 2021), 31.
19. Charles Houston Harris and Louis R. Sadler, *The Texas Rangers and the Mexican Revolution: The Bloodiest Decade, 1910–1920* (Albuquerque: University of New Mexico Press, 2007).
20. Potter, *The History of Policing in the United States*; Philip S. Foner, *Organized Labor and the Black Worker, 1619–1981* (Chicago: Haymarket, 1982); Andrew Silver, "The Demand for Order in Civil Society: A Review of Some Important Themes in the History of Urban Crime, Police and Riot," in *Theories and Origins of the Modern Police*, ed. Clive Emsley (London: Routledge, 2011), 23–46.
21. Potter, *The History of Policing in the United States*, para. 1.

22. The Fugitive Slave Law, Hartford, Connecticut (1850), https://www.loc.gov/resource/rbpe.33700200/?st=text.
23. Adam Malka, *The Men of Mobtown: Policing Baltimore in the Age of Slavery and Emancipation* (Chapel Hill: University of North Carolina Press, 2018), 5.
24. Douglas A. Blackmon, *Slavery by Another Name: The Re-Enslavement of Black Americans from the Civil War to World War II* (Palatine, IL: Anchor, 2008).
25. Talitha L. LeFlouria, *Chained in Silence: Black Women and Convict Labor in the New South* (Chapel Hill: University of North Carolina Press, 2015).
26. Lynn Weinstein, "The Convict Leasing System: Slavery in Its Worst Aspects," Library of Congress Blogs, June 17, 2021, https://blogs.loc.gov/inside_adams/2021/06/convict-leasing-system/.
27. *Lynching in America*, Equal Justice Initiative, https://eji.org/reports/lynching-in-america/.
28. Vida B. Johnson, "KKK in the PD: White Supremacist Police and What to Do About It," *Lewis & Clark Law Review* 23, no. 1 (2019), https://law.lclark.edu/live/files/28080-lcb231article2johnsonpdf.
29. Gaines, Kappeler, and Vaughn, *Policing in America*; Risa Goluboff and Adam Sorenson, "United States Vagrancy Laws," in *Oxford Encyclopedia of American Urban History* (Oxford: Oxford University Press, 2019), 1350–65.
30. Potter, *The History of Policing in the United States.*
31. Maggie Westover, "Riot, Revolution, and Remembrance: Modern Memory of the Haymarket Affair" (2023), *Honor Scholar Theses*, 219, Scholarly and Creative Work from DePauw University, https://scholarship.depauw.edu/studentresearch/219.
32. Michael Lerner, "Big Picture Essay: Unintended Consequences of Prohibition," on PBS website, *Prohibition*, a film by Ken Burns and Lynn Novick, PBS, October 2, 2011, https://www.pbs.org/kenburns/prohibition/unintended-consequences.
33. *History and Evolution of Public Education in the US*, Center on Education Policy, Graduate School of Education and Human Development, the George Washington University (2020), https://files.eric.ed.gov/fulltext/ED606970.pdf.
34. *History and Evolution of Public Education in the US.*
35. Judith Kafka, *The History of "Zero Tolerance" in American Public Schooling* (New York: Palgrave Macmillan US, 2011), 1–16.
36. Carliss Maddox, "Literacy by Any Means Necessary: The History of Anti-Literacy Laws in the U.S.," Oakland Literacy Coalition, January 12, 2022, https://oaklandliteracycoalition.org/literacy-by-any-means-necessary-the-history-of-anti-literacy-laws-in-the-u-s/#:~:text=Anti%2Dliteracy%20laws%20made%20it,color%20to%20read%20or%20write.
37. Anthony M. Platt, *The Child Savers: The Invention of Delinquency* (Chicago: University of Chicago Press, 1977).
38. Platt, *The Child Savers.*
39. Bayley J. Marquez, *Plantation Pedagogy: The Violence of Schooling Across Black and Indigenous Space* (Oakland: University of California Press, 2024).
40. Chase S. Burton, "Schools and Delinquency in the Early 20th Century: Rethinking the Origins of School Policing," *British Journal of Criminology* 57, no. 3 (2017): 532–50.
41. Burton, "Schools and Delinquency in the Early 20th Century," 538.
42. Burton, "Schools and Delinquency in the Early 20th Century."
43. Burton, "Schools and Delinquency in the Early 20th Century," 539–40.
44. Kipton D. Smilie, "Patrolling and Controlling the Streets: The Origin of School Safety Patrols in New York City," *Journal of Urban History* 50, no. 5 (2022): 1046–62.

45. Smilie, "Patrolling and Controlling the Streets."
46. Ben Brown, "Understanding and Assessing School Police Officers: A Conceptual and Methodological Comment," *Journal of Criminal Justice* 34, no. 6 (2006): 591–604.
47. *School Policing Timeline*, #policefreeschools, Advancement Project and Alliance for Educational Justice, https://policefreeschools.org/timeline/.
48. Advancement Project and Alliance for Educational Justice, *We Came to Learn: A Call to Action for Police-Free Schools*, June 23, 2023, https://policefreeschools.org/resources/we-came-to-learn-a-call-to-action-for-police-free-schools-2/.
49. Kaba and Ritchie, *No More Police*.
50. Tamara Gene Myers, *Youth Squad: Policing Children in the Twentieth Century* (Montreal: McGill–Queen's University Press, 2019), 169.
51. Myers, *Youth Squad*, 170.
52. Hannah Carson Baggett and Kaitlyn J. Selman, "School Copaganda in the US South: Tinsel, Twinkle, and Police-Youth Programming," *Crime, Media, Culture* 21, no. 1 (2025): 46–68; McHarris, "Disrupting Order," 40.
53. Alex S. Vitale, *The End of Policing* (London: Verso, 2018), 203–5.
54. Matthew D. Lassiter and the Policing and Social Justice HistoryLab, *Detroit Under Fire: Police Violence, Crime Politics, and the Struggle for Racial Justice in the Civil Rights Era* (Ann Arbor: University of Michigan Carceral State Project, 2021), https://policing.umhistorylabs.lsa.umich.edu/s/detroitunderfire/page/1958-63.
55. Jacquelyn Dowd Hall, "The Long Civil Rights Movement and the Political Uses of the Past," *Journal of American History* 91, no. 4 (2005): 1233–63.
56. "SNCC: The Student Nonviolent Coordinating Committee," Smithsonian National Museum of African American History and Culture, Washington, DC, https://nmaahc.si.edu/explore/stories/sncc-student-nonviolent-coordinating-committee.
57. Courtney M. Echols, "Anti-Blackness Is the American Way: Assessing the Relationship Between Chattel Slavery, Lynchings, & Police Violence During the Civil Rights Movement," *Race and Justice* 14, no. 2 (2022): 217–32; Elizabeth Hinton, *America on Fire: The Untold History of Police Violence and Black Rebellion Since the 1960s* (New York: Liveright, 2021).
58. "Arrested Development: How Police Ended up in Schools," Have You Heard podcast #91, https://soundcloud.com/haveyouheardpodcast/cops-in-schools.
59. "The Little Rock Nine," Smithsonian National Museum of African American History and Culture, Washington, DC, https://nmaahc.si.edu/explore/stories/little-rock-nine#.
60. Kautz, "From Segregation to Suspension."
61. Lawrence Fellows, "Jansen Opposes Police in Schools: Calls Proposal 'Unthinkable' – Leibowitz Backs Idea," *New York Times*, November 27, 1957, https://www.nytimes.com/1957/11/27/archives/jansen-opposes-police-in-schools-calls-proposal-unthinkable.html.
62. Brown, "Understanding and Assessing School Police Officers"; Lassiter and the Policing and Social Justice HistoryLab, *Detroit Under Fire*.
63. Hinton, *America on Fire*.
64. Potter, *The History of Policing in the United States*.
65. Otis S. Johnson, "Two Worlds: A Historical Perspective on the Dichotomous Relations Between Police and Black and White Communities," *Human Rights Magazine* 42, no. 1 (n.d.), American Bar Association.
66. Baggett and Selman, "School Copaganda in the US South."
67. For a history, see Hinton, *America on Fire*.

68. Jon N. Hale and Candace Livingston, "'If You Want Police, We Will Have Them': Anti-Black Student Discipline in Southern Schools and the Rise of a New Carceral Logic, 1961–1975," *Journal of Urban History* 49, no. 5 (2022): 1035–48; Kautz, "From Segregation to Suspension."
69. Kafka, *The History of "Zero Tolerance" in American Public Schooling*, 1–16.
70. Hale and Livingston, "'If You Want Police, We Will Have Them'"; Kautz, "From Segregation to Suspension."
71. Hale and Livingston, "'If You Want Police, We Will Have Them.'"
72. Kautz, "From Segregation to Suspension," 1052.
73. Kautz, "From Segregation to Suspension," 1054.
74. Heather A. Thompson, "Criminalizing Kids: The Overlooked Reason for Failing Schools," *Dissent* 58, no. 4 (2011), https://www.dissentmagazine.org/article/criminalizing-kids-the-overlooked-reason-for-failing-schools/.
75. Noah Remnick, "'The Police State in Franklin K. Lane': Desegregation, Student Resistance, and the Carceral Turn at a New York City High School," *Journal of Urban History* 49, no. 5 (2023): 1076.
76. Remnick, "'The Police State in Franklin K. Lane,'" 1078.
77. Judith Kafka, "Bureaucratizing from the Bottom Up: The Centralization of School Discipline Policy in the United States," in *Education and the State: International Perspectives on a Changing Relationship*, ed. Carla Aubry et al. (New York: Routledge, 2014), 1078.
78. As Kaba and Ritchie note, this was the same charge that authorities used against Shakara, the young Black student in South Carolina who was dragged from her desk by a school police officer for using her cell phone in 2015; Kaba and Ritchie, *No More Police*, 151.
79. Thompson, "Criminalizing Kids."
80. "June 28, 1969: Stonewall Riots," Zinn Education Project, https://www.zinnedproject.org/news/tdih/stonewall-riots/; "Before Stonewall: The Homophile Movement," Library of Congress, https://guides.loc.gov/lgbtq-studies/before-stonewall; Brett Beemyn, "The Silence Is Broken: A History of the First Lesbian, Gay, and Bisexual College Student Groups," *Journal of the History of Sexuality* 12, no. 2 (2003): 205–23; Stephan Cohen, "Liberationists, Clients, Activists: Queer Youth Organizing, 1966–2003," *Journal of Gay & Lesbian Issues in Education* 2, no. 3 (2005): 67–86.
81. Thompson, "Criminalizing Kids."
82. For a case study, see Remnick, "'The Police State in Franklin K. Lane.'"
83. For a history of student activism in the South, see Jon N. Hale, *A New Kind of Youth: Historically Black High Schools and Southern Student Activism, 1920–1975* (Chapel Hill: University of North Carolina Press, 2022).
84. Elizabeth Hinton, *From the War on Poverty to the War on Crime: The Making of Mass Incarceration in America* (Cambridge, MA: Harvard University Press, 2016); Julilly Kohler-Hausmann, *Getting Tough: Welfare and Imprisonment in 1970s America* (Princeton, NJ: Princeton University Press, 2017).
85. Daryl Gates was chief of police of the LAPD when officers brutally beat and almost killed Rodney King in 1992. He was well known for his racist views on the "physiological" differences between Black people and white people.
86. Bettina L. Love, *Punished for Dreaming: How School Reform Harms Black Children and How We Heal* (New York: St. Martin's, 2023).
87. Max Felker-Kantor, "The DARE Snitches," *Slate*, September 30, 2023, https://slate.com/human-interest/2023/09/dare-history-police-surveillance-schools.html.

88. Max Felker-Kantor, "DARE to Say No: Police and the Cultural Politics of Prevention in the War on Drugs," *Modern American History* 5, no. 3 (2022): 313.
89. McHarris explains, "Once a community becomes labeled as deviant and criminal, it becomes easier for the state to target them with policing, surveillance, and punishment." Despite many myths to the contrary, drug use is not more prevalent in communities of Color or poor communities. Decades of research indicate that folks buy and use drugs similarly across all identity and demographic groups. McHarris, "Disrupting Order," 33; Kaba and Ritchie, *No More Police.*
90. Erica R. Meiners, *For the Children? Protecting Innocence in a Carceral State* (Minneapolis: University of Minnesota Press, 2016); John Dilulio, "The Coming of the Super-Predators," *Weekly Standard*, November 27, 1995, 23.
91. Vitale, *The End of Policing*, 56–57.
92. Dorothy Hines-Datiri and Dorinda J. Carter Andrews, "The Effects of Zero Tolerance Policies on Black Girls: Using Critical Race Feminism and Figured Worlds to Examine School Discipline," *Urban Education* 55, no. 10 (2020): 1419–40; Jonathan Lightfoot, "Zero Tolerance Policies Are Anti-Black: Protecting Racially Profiled Students from Educational Injustice," *Northwest Journal of Teacher Education* 16, no. 2 (2021): 5.
93. Hannah Carson Baggett and Carey E. Andrzejewski, *The Grammar of School Discipline: Removal, Resistance, and Reform in Alabama Schools* (Lanham, MD: Rowman & Littlefield, 2021).
94. Chongmin Na and Denise C. Gottfredson, "Police Officers in Schools: Effects on School Crime and the Processing of Offending Behaviors," *Justice Quarterly* 30, no. 4 (2013): 619–50.
95. Love, *Punished for Dreaming*, 165.
96. Russ Skiba and Reece Peterson, "The Dark Side of Zero Tolerance: Can Punishment Lead to Safe Schools?," *Phi Delta Kappan* 80, no. 5 (1999): 372–82.
97. Kaba and Ritchie, *No More Police.*
98. Kafka, *The History of "Zero Tolerance" in American Public Schooling.*
99. *Cops in Schools: The COPS Commitment to School Safety*, US Department of Justice, fact sheet, March 2004, https://www.ojp.gov/ncjrs/virtual-library/abstracts/cops-schools-cops-commitment-school-safety.
100. To be clear, the solution to this issue is not to mete out punishment more "equally"—to arrest fewer Black and Brown students and more white students, for example. The solution is to stop arresting students at school altogether. We must begin by examining our own interpretations of what constitutes misbehavior, as well as approaching students with more developmental perspectives, leaning on ideas about abolitionist accountability when we believe that students are "misbehaving." We will learn more about this in chapter 5 of this book.
101. Johanna Lacoe and Matthew P. Steinberg, "Rolling Back Zero Tolerance: The Effect of Discipline Policy Reform on Suspension Usage and Student Outcomes," *Peabody Journal of Education* 93, no. 2 (2018): 207–27.
102. See, for example, the scholarship of Russell Skiba, who has documented what is often called "racial disproportionality" in school discipline patterns. Other scholars like Maisha Winn, Subini Annamma, and Erica Meiners have also written about school discipline in relationship to Black girls, Black girls with disabilities, and queer and trans students, respectively.

103. This report by the National Education Association details these patterns, in addition to featuring the perspectives of a teacher and parent who is concerned about police in her local schools: James Paterson, "Making Schools Safe and Just," *neaToday*, April 28, 2022, https://www.nea.org/nea-today/all-news-articles/making-schools-safe-and-just.
104. My coauthors and I wrote in 2021 in *The Grammar of School Discipline* about how one school system in Alabama accounted for a huge percentage of student referrals to law enforcement for things like "defiance," "disorderly conduct," and "disobedience" all disciplinary infractions that can be handled by teachers and administrators. See chapter 3, "A Portrait of Removal: Cotton County Schools," in Baggett and Andrzejewski, *The Grammar of School Discipline*, 57–68.
105. West Resendes, *Police in Schools Continue to Target Black, Brown, and Indigenous Students with Disabilities*, ACLU News & Commentary, July 9, 2020, https://www.aclu.org/news/criminal-law-reform/police-in-schools-continue-to-target-black-brown-and-indigenous-students-with-disabilities-the-trump-administration-has-data-thats-likely-to-prove-it.
106. Monserrat Avila-Acosta and Lucy C. Sorensen, "Contextualizing the Push for More School Resource Officer Funding," Urban Institute, September 8, 2023, https://www.urban.org/research/publication/contextualizing-push-more-school-resource-officer-funding.
107. Sarah Muller, "The Obama Administration Funds Police Officers in Schools," NBC News, September 27, 2013, https://www.nbcnews.com/id/wbna53128915.
108. Addington, "Black Girls Doing Time for White Boys' Crime?"
109. Keep Students in School (SB 274), ACLU California Action (2023), https://aclucalaction.org/bill/sb-274/.
110. Sabrina Franza and Marissa Perlman, "Chicago Board of Education Votes to Remove Chicago Police Officers from Schools," CBS News Chicago, February 22, 2024, https://www.cbsnews.com/chicago/news/chicago-board-of-education-to-vote-resource-officers/; Mark Keierleber, "Federal Data Shows a Drop in Campus Cops—for Now," *LA School Report*, January 30, 2024, https://www.laschoolreport.com/federal-data-shows-a-drop-in-campus-cops-for-now/.
111. Baggett and Selman, "School Copaganda in the US South"; Baggett and Andrzejewski, *The Grammar of School Discipline.*
112. Kaba and Ritchie, *No More Police*, 183.
113. Shannon M. Gonzalez, "Making It Home: An Intersectional Analysis of the Police Talk," *Gender & Society* 33, no. 3 (2019): 363–86.
114. Baggett and Selman, "School Copaganda in the US South"; Love, *Punished for Dreaming*; Myers, *Youth Squad.*
115. Felker-Kantor, "DARE to Say No," 313.
116. Arriel Vinson, "I Did Shop with a Cop as a Kid. Now I Realize It Was Police Propaganda," *Vox*, September 10, 2020, https://www.vox.com/first-person/2020/9/10/21427923/police-black-lives-matter-shop-with-a-cop.
117. Remnick, " 'The Police State in Franklin K. Lane,' " 1072.
118. Kaba and Ritchie, *No More Police*, 151.

Chapter 2

1. During the 2019–2020 school year, 65 percent of schools had at least one school security officer on site. Many datasets, and even education researchers, distinguish among school security officers, school police officers, and SROs by emphasizing that SROs have undergone training to work in school settings. Yet, regardless of their intended roles, the effects

of officers in schools are the same in that they normalize police presence and contribute to our belief in policing to keep schools safe. US Department of Education, National Center for Education Statistics, "Percentage of Public Schools with Security Staff Present at Least Once a Week, and Percentage with Security Staff Routinely Carrying a Firearm, by Selected School Characteristics: 2005–06 Through 2019–20," *Digest of Education Statistics*, table 233.70 (2021), https://nces.ed.gov/programs/digest/d21/tables/dt21_233.70.asp.

2. Chelsea Connery, *The Prevalence and the Price of Police in Schools*, UConn Center for Education Policy Analysis (CEPA), issue brief, October 27, 2020, https://education.uconn.edu/2020/10/27/the-prevalence-and-the-price-of-police-in-schools/; American Civil Liberties Union (ACLU), "Schools Without Police Are Better Schools," press release, August 24, 2021, https://www.aclu.org/press-releases/aclu-schools-without-police-are-better-schools.
3. "About NASRO," National Association of School Resource Officers (NASRO), https://www.nasro.org/main/about-nasro/.
4. Anna Bryant, "Cops in Schools: Tracking Nationwide Changes After George Floyd," Chicago Justice Project, March 26, 2024, https://chicagojustice.org/2024/03/26/cops-in-schools-tracking-nationwide-changes-after-george-floyd/.
5. Congressional Research Service, Community Oriented Policing Services (COPS) Program, May 9, 2024, https://crsreports.congress.gov/product/pdf/IF/IF10922.
6. Lisa H. Thurau and Lany W. Or, *Two Billion Dollars Later*, Strategies for Youth (2019), https://strategiesforyouth.org/sitefiles/wp-content/uploads/2019/10/SFY-Two-Billion-Dollars-Later-Report-Oct2019.pdf.
7. Montserrat Avila-Acosta and Lucy C. Sorensen, "Contextualizing the Push for More School Resource Officer Funding," Urban Institute, September 8, 2023, https://www.urban.org/research/publication/contextualizing-push-more-school-resource-officer-funding.
8. West Resendes, "Police in Schools Continue to Target Black, Brown, and Indigenous Students with Disabilities. The Trump Administration Has Data That's Likely to Prove It," American Civil Liberties Union (ACLU), July 9, 2020, https://www.aclu.org/news/criminal-law-reform/police-in-schools-continue-to-target-black-brown-and-indigenous-students-with-disabilities-the-trump-administration-has-data-thats-likely-to-prove-it.
9. Liz Schlemmer, "NC Again Ranks Near Bottom for Effort to Fund Public Schools," WUNC, December 13, 2024, https://www.wunc.org/education/2024-12-13/nc-ranks-49-school-funding-effort-education-law-center-making-the-grade; ACLU North Carolina, "The Consequences of Cops in North Carolina Schools," https://www.acluofnorthcarolina-bts.org/cops-in-schools.
10. Jemma Stephenson, "Alabama State Department of Education Requests Large Increase in Security Funding," *Alabama Reflector*, October 21, 2024, https://alabamareflector.com/2024/10/21/alabama-state-department-of-education-requests-large-increase-in-school-security-funding/; Rob Sneed, "State of Alabama Gives More Funding to Help Keep Kids in School," WAAY31 ABC, July 9, 2024, https://www.waaytv.com/news/state-of-alabama-gives-more-funding-to-help-keep-kids-in-school/article_17afd3cc-3e78-11ef-9511-276e61d96bf8.html.
11. Ronnie Casella, *"Being Down": Challenging Violence in Urban Schools* (New York: Teachers College Press, 2001); Aaron Kupchik and Nicole L. Bracy, "To Protect, Serve, and Mentor? Police Officers in Public Schools," in *Schools Under Surveillance: Cultures of Control in Public Education*, ed. Torin Monahan and Rodolfo D. Torres (New Brunswick, NJ: Rutgers University Press, 2010); Kathleen Nolan, *Police in the Hallways: Discipline in an Urban High School* (Minneapolis: University of Minnesota Press, 2011).

12. *Bullies in Blue: The Problem with School Policing [Infographic]*, American Civil Liberties Union (ACLU), https://www.aclu.org/news/juvenile-justice/bullies-in-blue.
13. *Referrals to Law Enforcement and School-Related Arrests in U.S. Public Schools During the 2020-21 School Year* (Washington, DC: Civil Rights Data Collection, US Department of Education Office for Civil Rights, 2023), https://www.ed.gov/media/document/crdc-law-enforcement-school-arrests-snapshotpdf.
14. *Bullies in Blue.*
15. Chongmin Na and Denise C. Gottfredson, "Police Officers in Schools: Effects on School Crime and the Processing of Offending Behaviors," *Justice Quarterly* 30, no. 4 (2013): 619–50; Amir Whitaker et al., *Cops and No Counselors: How the Lack of School Mental Health Staff Is Harming Students*, American Civil Liberties Union (ACLU), March 4, 2019, https://www.aclu.org/publications/cops-and-no-counselors.
16. Paul J. Hirschfield, "Preparing for Prison? The Criminalization of School Discipline in the USA," *Theoretical Criminology* 12, no. 1 (2008): 79–101; Paul J. Hirschfield and Katarzyna Celinska, "Beyond Fear: Sociological Perspectives on the Criminalization of School Discipline," *Sociology Compass* 5, no. 1 (2011): 1–12.
17. *Data on Equal Access to Education, The 2020-21 Data Collection*, US Department of Education, Office for Civil Rights (OCR) Biennial Civil Rights Data Collection Project (2021), https://civilrightsdata.ed.gov/.
18. *School Climate and Safety*, 2015–16 Civil Rights Data Collection, US Department of Education, Office for Civil Rights (2018), https://www2.ed.gov/about/offices/list/ocr/docs/school-climate-and-safety.pdf.
19. Although not all referrals to police result in arrests, they do involve contact between police and youth. *K–12 Education: Differences in Student Arrest Rates Widen When Race, Gender, and Disability Status Overlap*, US Government Accountability Office (GAO), GAO-24-106294, July 8, 2024, https://www.gao.gov/products/gao-24-106294.
20. Resendes, "Police in Schools Continue to Target Black, Brown, and Indigenous Students with Disabilities."
21. *K–12 Education: Differences in Student Arrest Rates.*
22. "Denton ISD Faces Scrutiny After Officer Seen Handcuffing, Pinning Down Autistic Child," CBS News Texas, August 11, 2018, https://www.cbsnews.com/texas/news/denton-isd-officer-seen-handcuffing-pinning-down-autistic-child/.
23. "'Stop, You're Hurting Me': Body Cam Video Shows 11-Year-Old with Autism Handcuffed at School," CBS News Colorado, March 10, 2021, https://www.cbsnews.com/colorado/news/child-autism-handcuffed-lawsuit-douglas-county-aclu/.
24. "Police Who Handcuffed 10-Year-Old Girl at School Not Protected by Qualified Immunity," Equal Justice Initiative, July 16, 2024, https://eji.org/news/police-who-handcuffed-10-year-old-girl-at-school-not-protected-by-qualified-immunity/.
25. Ginger Allen, "Questions Surround the Handcuffing of a 10-Year-Old Texas Girl with Special Needs While at School: 'I Was Scared,'" CBS News Texas, August 21, 2024, https://www.cbsnews.com/texas/news/questions-surround-the-handcuffing-of-a-10-year-old-with-learning-disabilities-i-was-scared/.
26. Chris Hacker, Aparna Zalani, and Stephen Stock, "New Data: Over 100 Elementary-Aged Children Arrested in U.S. Schools," CBS News, November 16, 2023, https://www.cbsnews.com/news/school-arrest-children-new-data/.
27. Mike Hellgren, "Handcuffs in Hallways: Mother of Handcuffed 5-Year-Old Speaks as WJZ Looks at Child Arrests in Maryland Schools," WJZ News, CBS Baltimore, November 16,

2022, https://www.cbsnews.com/baltimore/news/handcuffs-in-hallways-mother-of-handcuffed-5-year-old-speaks-as-wjz-looks-at-child-arrests-in-maryland-schools-elementary-schools/; *Bullies in Blue.*

28. Denise C. Gottfredson et al., "Effects of School Resource Officers on School Crime and Responses to School Crime," *Criminology & Public Policy* 19, no. 3 (2020): 905–40.
29. Decoteau J. Irby, "Net-Deepening of School Discipline," *Urban Review* 45 (2013): 197–219.
30. Elizabeth Davis, *School Resource Officers, 2019–2020*, Bureau of Justice Statistics, US Department of Justice, November 2023, https://bjs.ojp.gov/library/publications/school-resource-officers-2019-2020.
31. *Bullies in Blue.*
32. *#AssaultAtSpringValley: 2023 Analysis of Police Violence*, update, #PoliceFreeSchools, Advancement Project, https://policefreeschools.org/resources/assaultatspringvalley-2023-analysis-of-police-violence/.
33. #AssaultAt map, #PoliceFreeSchools, Advancement Project, https://policefreeschools.org/map/.
34. Interrupting Criminalization and In Our Names Network, *Sexualization Not Safety: Black Girls, Trans, and Gender Nonconforming Youth's Experiences of Police Presence in Schools: Report* (2024), https://www.inournamesnetwork.com/psvresearch.
35. Interrupting Criminalization and In Our Names Network, *Sexualization Not Safety*, 4.
36. Jenn Abelson, Jessica Contrera, and Nate Jones, "A School Cop Was Accused of Sexual Misconduct with Kids. He Kept His Job for Years," *Washington Post*, September 2, 2024, https://www.washingtonpost.com/investigations/interactive/2024/south-carolina-sro-child-sexual-abuse-jamel-bradley/.
37. Matthew T. Theriot and John G. Orme, "School Resource Officers and Students' Feelings of Safety at School," *Youth Violence and Juvenile Justice* 14, no. 2 (2016): 130–46; Interrupting Criminalization and In Our Names Network, *Sexualization Not Safety.*
38. Victor J. St. John, Andrea M. Headley, and Kristen Harper, "Reducing Adverse Police Contact Would Heal Wounds for Children and Their Communities," Trauma & Resilience, *Child Trends*, June 14, 2022, https://www.childtrends.org/publications/reducing-adverse-police-contact-would-heal-wounds-for-children-and-their-communities, 2.
39. Terry Allen and Pedro Noguera, "A Web of Punishment: Examining Black Student Interactions with School Police in Los Angeles," *Educational Researcher* (2023).
40. "Alex S. Vitale on Rethinking Policing in the Wake of Uvalde," interview, *Current Affairs*, July 21, 2022, https://www.currentaffairs.org/news/2022/07/alex-s-vitale-on-rethinking-policing-in-the-wake-of-uvalde.
41. Jay Farlow, "SRO Success Story: Strong Relationships Help School Resource Officer Remove Gun from School," NASRO National Association of School Resource Officers, June 13, 2024, https://www.nasro.org/news/2024/06/13/news-releases/sro-success-story-strong-relationships-help-school-resource-officer-remove-gun-from-school/; Stephanie Saul, Timothy Williams, and Anemona Hartocollis, "School Officer: A Job with Many Roles and One Big Responsibility," *New York Times*, March 4, 2018, https://www.nytimes.com/2018/03/04/us/school-resource-officers-shooting.html.
42. See the stories compiled about youth organizers by the Advancement Project and the Alliance for Educational Justice, such as "Our Stories," #PoliceFreeSchools, Advancement Project, https://policefreeschools.org/stories/.
43. Bryant, "Cops in Schools," para. 19.

44. Ann D. Helms, "CMS Board Evaluates Removing Police from Schools," WFAE 90.7 Charlotte, June 29, 2020, https://www.wfae.org/education/2020-06-29/cms-board-evaluates-removing-police-from-schools, para. 23; Stacia Brown and Frank Stasio, "NC Communities Examine the 'Resource' School Resource Officers Offer," WUNC North Carolina Radio, June 17, 2020, https://www.wunc.org/show/the-state-of-things/2020-06-17/nc-communities-examine-the-resource-school-resource-officers-offer.
45. Aissa W. Neese, "Columbus High Schools Reopen Without Police Officers for First Time in 25 Years," *Columbus Dispatch*, March 30, 2021, https://www.dispatch.com/story/news/education/2021/03/30/columbus-high-schools-reopen-without-police-resource-officers/6957868002/.
46. *School Safety*, Policing Project, https://www.safetyreimagined.org/papers/school-safety.
47. Evan Douglas, "As a Former Cop, I Know We Need Police-Free Schools," *EducationWeek*, opinion, February 11, 2022, https://www.edweek.org/leadership/opinion-as-a-former-cop-i-know-we-need-police-free-schools/2022/02.
48. Maya Rise-Kositsky, Stephen Sawchuk, and Holly Peele, "School Police: Which Districts Cut Them? Which Brought Them Back?," *EducationWeek*, June 29, 2022, https://www.edweek.org/leadership/which-districts-have-cut-school-policing-programs/2021/06; Bryant, "Cops in Schools."
49. "We Demand Police Free Schools NOW: Call to Action from CPS Students," Grassroots Collaborative, https://grassrootscollaborative.salsalabs.org/policefreeschools2020/index.html; Healthy Schools Campaign, "Police Do Not Belong in Our Schools," June 16, 2020, https://healthyschoolscampaign.org/blog/police-do-not-belong-in-our-schools/; Amy Arneson et al., "Removing Police Officers from Chicago Schools: Trends and Outcomes," UChicago Consortium on School Research, brief, June 2024, https://consortium.uchicago.edu/publications/removing-police-officers-from-Chicago-schools.
50. "Education and Resources," Black Organizing Project, https://blackorganizingproject.org/education-and-resources/.
51. Madeline Fox, "Milwaukee Public Schools Terminates Contract with Milwaukee Police Department," Wisconsin Public Radio, June 18, 2024, https://www.wpr.org/education/milwaukee-public-schools-terminates-contract-milwaukee-police-department.
52. "Our Victories," #PoliceFreeSchools, Advancement Project, https://policefreeschools.org/victories/.
53. Theriot and Orme, "School Resource Officers and Students' Feelings of Safety"; Danielle Layton and Paula Gerstenblatt, "'They're Just, Like, There': A Constructivist Grounded Theory Study of Student Experiences with School Resource Officers," *Journal of Community Psychology* 50, no. 8 (2022): 3470–86.
54. #AssaultAt map.
55. Deana Lewis, Andrea J. Ritchie, and Brendane Tynes, *Sexualization Not Safety: Black Girls, Trans, and Gender Nonconforming Youth's Experiences of Police Presence in Schools: Report Synopsis*, https://www.interruptingcriminalization.com/resources-all/sexualization-not-safety-black-girls-trans-and-gender-nonconforming-youths-experience-of-police-presence-in-schools.

Chapter 3

1. This shooting, which occurred in 2021, also stalled conversations and activism by community members in Oxford and adjacent communities in Michigan to remove police from schools, despite continued community discourse about the harm they were causing.

2. Chris Wickert, "Madison School District Administration Blocked Survey of Teachers on School-Based Police," *Wisconsin State Journal*, May 26, 2019, https://madison.com/news/local/education/local_schools/madison-school-district-administration-blocked-survey-of-teachers-on-school-based-police/article_134c0f37-a5bc-532a-947c-a29c921e3bff.html.
3. Adam Alvarez and H. Richard Milner IV, "Exploring Teachers' Beliefs and Feelings About Race and Police Violence," *Teaching Education* 29, no. 4 (2018): 383–94.
4. Brandon J. Wood and Eric Hampton, "The Influence of School Resource Officer Presence on Teacher Perceptions of School Safety and Security," *School Psychology Review* 50, no. 2–3 (2021): 360–70.
5. While the teaching force has diversified somewhat, approximately 80 percent of all teachers are white women, according to the 2020–2021 National Teacher and Principal Survey, Institute of Education Sciences, National Center for Education Statistics, April 30, 2024, https://nces.ed.gov/pubsearch/pubsinfo.asp?pubid=2024032.
6. Mariame Kaba and Andrea J. Ritchie, *No More Police: A Case for Abolition* (New York: New Press, 2022).
7. Kaba and Ritchie, *No More Police*, 183.
8. Kaba and Ritchie, *No More Police*, 186.
9. Derek S. Denman, "The Cinematic Universe of Copaganda: World-Building and the Enchantments of Policing," *Culture, Theory and Critique* 64, no. 1–2 (2023): 3.
10. Amanda M. Petersen, "Community-Oriented Copaganda: Anti-Black Violence in a Visual Archive of Policing," *Crime, Media, Culture* 21, no. 1 (2024): 96–118.
11. Hannah Carson Baggett and Kaitlyn J. Selman, "School Copaganda in the US South: Tinsel, Twinkle, and Police-Youth Programming," *Crime, Media, Culture* 21, no. 1 (2025): 46–68.
12. Denman, "The Cinematic Universe of Copaganda."
13. Parker, who popularized the phrase "the Thin Blue Line," was known for an explosive temper, racist rhetoric, and public intoxication while on the job, and he also was the predecessor and mentor of LAPD Chief Daryl Gates. For further reading, see Mike Davis and Jon Wiener, "How LAPD Chief William H. Parker Influenced the Depiction of Policing on the TV Show Dragnet," *Verso*, June 16, 2020, https://mronline.org/2020/06/18/how-lapd-chief-william-h-parker-influenced-the-depiction-of-policing-on-the-tv-show-dragnet/.
14. Travis Linnemann, *The Horror of Police* (Minneapolis: University of Minnesota Press, 2022).
15. Joe Domanick, *To Protect and Serve: The LAPD's Century of War in the City of Dreams* (New York: Pocket, 1994), 95.
16. Jessica Hatrick and Olivia González, "*Watchmen*, Copaganda, and Abolition Futurities in US Television," *Lateral* 11, no. 2 (2022), https://doi.org/10.25158/L11.2.2.
17. Alec Karakatsanis, "How the Media Enables Violent Bureaucracy: Part 3," *Alec's Copaganda Newsletter*, February 5, 2023, https://equalityalec.substack.com/p/how-the-media-enables-violent-bureaucracy-bc9.
18. Mark Anthony Neal, "The Myth of the 'Good Cop': Pop Culture Helped Turn Police Officers into Rock Stars—and Black Folks into Criminals," in *Abolition for the People*, ed. Colin Kaepernick (New York: Kaepernick, 2021), 39–44.
19. Sean Campbell, "Tyre Nichols Was Brutally Killed by Five Black Police Officers. How Did We Get Here?," *The Guardian*, September 7, 2024, https://www.theguardian.com/us-news/article/2024/sep/07/tyre-nichols-black-police-officers-memphis-history.
20. Kaba and Ritchie, *No More Police*, 117.

21. Molly Lipson, "Yellowjackets Shows a World Without Police as Disorderly. Abolitionists Aren't Buying It," *Scalawag*, September 13, 2022, https://scalawagmagazine.org/2022/09/yellowjackets-apocalypse-tv-critique/.
22. Tyler Wall, "The Police Invention of Humanity: Notes on the 'Thin Blue Line,'" *Crime, Media, Culture* 16, no. 3 (2020): 319–36.
23. Travis Linnemann discusses these ideas regarding police in movies more thoroughly in his book *The Horror of Police*, where he also ties beliefs about police righteousness to Christian doctrine.
24. Kaba and Ritchie, *No More Police*, 181.
25. "Funding Meant for High-Need Student Programs Given to Police in Many Southern CA Districts," ACLU Southern California, March 5, 2020, https://www.aclusocal.org/en/press-releases/report-millions-student-funds-illegally-diverted-school-police; Aaricka Washington, "What Happened After Los Angeles Schools Cut Police Funds and Hired Mental Health Staff for Black Students," *The74*, March 24, 2022, https://www.the74million.org/article/what-happened-after-los-angeles-schools-cut-police-funds-and-hired-mental-health-staff-for-black-students/.
26. "More School Safety Funding to Come, NC Lawmakers Say," WRAL News, February 9, 2023, https://www.wral.com/story/more-school-safety-funding-to-come-nc-lawmakers-say/20712584/; Jeff Amy, "Georgia School Superintendent Seeks More Safety Money After Apalachee High Shooting," Fox5 Atlanta, September 17, 2024, https://www.fox5atlanta.com/news/georgia-school-superintendent-seeks-more-safety-money-after-apalachee-high-shooting.
27. *A Cop Is a Cop: The Rise of School District Police Departments and Why They Must Be Dismantled*, Advancement Project, https://advancementproject.org/wp-content/uploads/2024/05/AP-SchoolDistrictReport-V4-1.pdf.
28. School Violence Prevention Program (SVPP), Community Oriented Policing Services (COPS), US Department of Justice, https://cops.usdoj.gov/svpp; "SRO Corporal Pam Revels a.k.a. Keeping Our Kids Safe," episode 022, https://www.lee.k12.al.us/cms/lib/AL02210054/Centricity/Domain/3014/022%20-%20Corporal%20Revels.pdf, Lee County Schools Edcast; John Sharp, "'We Don't Want to Leave Anything to Chance': After Uvalde, Alabama Schools Weigh Increases in Resource Officers," AL.com, July 31, 2022, https://www.al.com/news/2022/07/we-dont-want-to-leave-anything-to-chance-after-uvalde-alabama-schools-weigh-increases-in-resource-officers.html.
29. "About NASRO," National Association of School Resource Officers (NASRO), https://www.nasro.org/main/about-nasro/.
30. Sears-Roebuck was a company that shaped modern American consumerism. The Sears catalog, arriving in mailboxes across the country, expanded access to consumer goods for women, immigrants, and Black folks who could order products by mail that they otherwise may not have been allowed to buy in stores. The company profited handsomely from this new access, while also actively undermining efforts for racial and social justice. For further reading, see Vicki Howard, "The Rise and Fall of Sears," *Smithsonian Magazine*, July 25, 2017, https://www.smithsonianmag.com/history/rise-and-fall-sears-180964181/.
31. Sylvia Tester, *My Friend, the Policeman* (Elgin, IL: David C. Cook, 1967).
32. Valerian Derlega, James Heinen, and Nancy Eberhardt, "Officer Friendly: Changing Children's Attitudes About the Police," *Journal of Community Psychology* 7, no. 3 (1979): 220–27.
33. Sharon L. Bass, "Police Officers Give Lessons in School," *New York Times*, January 26, 1986.

34. Baggett and Selman, "School Copaganda in the US South."
35. Gates was also the architect of Special Weapons and Tactics (SWAT) teams, units that were deployed after the Watts riots of 1965 and specifically designed to quell urban protest; he was ultimately forced to resign after the Rodney King riots in the 1990s. For further reading, see Elizabeth Hinton, "Los Angeles Had a Chance to Build a Better City After the Rodney King Violence in 1992. Here's Why It Failed," *TIME*, May 18, 2021, https://time.com/6049185/los-angeles-rodney-king-misunderstand-what-happened/.
36. Max Felker-Kantor, "Arresting the Demand for Drugs: DARE and the School–Police Nexus in Los Angeles," *Journal of Urban History* 49, no. 5 (2023): 1108–29.
37. PCP is a drug that gained popularity in the 1980s and 1990s. It can cause hallucinations and make people feel like they have superhuman powers.
38. Felker-Kantor, "Arresting the Demand for Drugs," 1111.
39. Felker-Kantor, "Arresting the Demand for Drugs," 1113.
40. Max Felker-Kantor, *DARE to Say No: Policing and the War on Drugs in Schools* (Chapel Hill: University of North Carolina Press, 2024).
41. Felker-Kantor, "Arresting the Demand for Drugs," 1109.
42. For further reading about the "family policing system," see resources provided by the Movement for Family Power, https://www.movementforfamilypower.org/.
43. Max Felker-Kantor, "The DARE Snitches," *Slate*, September 30, 2023, https://slate.com/human-interest/2023/09/dare-history-police-surveillance-schools.html.
44. Felker-Kantor, "The DARE Snitches."
45. Students who report their peers may also be unaware that their reports may be used as evidence to arrest students at school, often introducing them to juvenile and even adult court proceedings.
46. Joshua Reeves, "Recognize, Resist, Report," Reason, May 2017, https://reason.com/2017/04/16/recognize-resist-report/.
47. Baggett and Selman, "School Copaganda in the US South"; Felker-Kantor, *DARE to Say No*.
48. Lee V. Gaines and Nicole Cohen, "'Just Say No' Didn't Actually Protect Students from Drugs. Here's What Could," *All Things Considered*, NPR WNYC, December 19, 2023, https://www.npr.org/2023/11/09/1211217460/fentanyl-drug-education-dare.
49. Education scholars like Gloria Ladson-Billings have critiqued this language and what it represents, arguing that there is nothing innate about a student that makes them "at risk" of failure, dropping out, or criminal behavior. Instead, these scholars argue, there are inequitable and unjust systems that govern our lives that place students at risk, like segregated neighborhoods, food apartheid, unequal tax funding structures for schools, and culturally irrelevant curricula that both marginalize and privilege students according to race, class, gender, sexuality, and ability. Yet police programs for so-called at-risk youth are well entrenched in educational systems. See, for example, the Strategic Home Intervention and Early Leadership Development (SHIELD) program as described in Phelan A. Wyrick, *Law Enforcement Referral of At-Risk Youth: The SHIELD Program* (US Department of Justice, Office of Justice Programs, Office of Juvenile Justice and Delinquency Prevention, 2000).
50. Bettina Love, *Punished for Dreaming: How School Reform Harms Black Children and How We Heal* (New York: St. Martin's, 2023), 165.
51. Kathleen Nolan, "Neoliberal Common Sense and Race-Neutral Discourses: A Critique of 'Evidence-Based' Policy-Making in School Policing," *Discourse: Studies in the Cultural Politics of Education* 36, no. 6 (2015): 894–907; Interrupting Criminalization and In Our Names Network, *Sexualization Not Safety: Black Girls, Trans, and Gender Nonconforming*

Youth's Experiences of Police Presence in Schools: Report, https://www.inournamesnetwork.com/psvresearch; #AssaultAt Map, #PoliceFreeSchools, Advancement Project, https://policefreeschools.org/map/; Corey Mitchell, Joe Yerardi, and Susan Ferriss, "When Schools Call Police on Kids," Center for Public Integrity, September 8, 2021, https://publicintegrity.org/education/criminalizing-kids/police-in-schools-disparities/.

52. "About NASRO."
53. Rudolph Pratt Jr., "SRO Appreciation Day," National Association of School Resource Officers (NASRO), https://www.nasro.org/main/sro-appreciation-day.
54. Note, however, that in some states, like in Alabama where I live and teach, legislators have sponsored bills that would make vaping at school a crime; while this legislation has not yet passed, there are school districts that liaise with local judges to hold "vape court," where students and families must attend to pay fines and fees for vaping on campus. Other school districts have instituted vape detection technology, leading to disciplinary action for students, such as referrals to alternative schools, and/or tickets issued to students. John Sharp, "How Alabama Schools Continue to Crackdown on Vaping," AL.com, August 23, 2023, https://www.al.com/news/2023/08/how-alabama-schools-continue-to-crackdown-on-vaping.html; Amy Yurkanin and Savannah Tryens-Fernandes, "Alabama Launches Vape Courts for Students Busted at School," AL.com, October 10, 2023, https://www.al.com/news/2023/10/alabama-launches-vape-courts-for-students-busted-at-school.html.
55. Shabnam Javdani, "Policing Education: An Empirical Review of the Challenges and Impact of the Work of School Police Officers," *American Journal of Community Psychology* 63, no. 3–4 (2019): 253–69.
56. Nicole L. Bracy, "Student Perceptions of High-Security School Environments," *Youth & Society* 43, no. 1 (2011): 374.
57. Arrick Jackson, "Police-School Resource Officers' and Students' Perception of the Police and Offending," *Policing: An International Journal of Police Strategies & Management* 25, no. 3 (2002): 631–50.
58. Hassan Kanu, "Police Are Not Primarily Crime Fighters, According to the Data," Reuters, November 2, 2022, https://www.reuters.com/legal/government/police-are-not-primarily-crime-fighters-according-data-2022-11-02/.
59. #AssaultAt map, #PoliceFreeSchools; Interrupting Criminalization and In Our Names Network, *Sexualization Not Safety*.
60. Carly Domicolo, "Reallocating Funds to Education: A Better Chance for Youth," *Chicago Policy Review*, October 26, 2021, https://chicagopolicyreview.org/2021/10/26/reallocating-funds-to-education-a-better-chance-for-youth/; for a review, see *Fulfilling the Promise: A Blueprint to Build Police-Free Schools*, Center on Gender Justice & Opportunity, Georgetown Law, https://genderjusticeandopportunity.georgetown.edu/report/fulfilling-the-promise-a-blueprint-to-build-police-free-schools/.
61. Gabriel R. Paez, "School Safety Agents' Identification of Adolescent Bullying," *Children and Youth Services Review* 113 (2020): 104942.
62. Deanna N. Devlin, Mateus Rennó Santos, and Denise C. Gottfredson, "An Evaluation of Police Officers in Schools as a Bullying Intervention," *Evaluation and Program Planning* 71 (2018): 12–21.
63. Gabriel R. Paez and Roddrick Colvin, "Identifying and Intervening to Stop School Bullying: The Role of School Resource Officers," *Safer Communities* 20, no. 3 (2021): 189–207; Dominique LaVigne, "Two Golden Valley High School Students Arrested in Apparent Bullying Incident," 23ABC turnto23.com, August 27, 2024, https://www.turnto23.com/news/in-your-neighborhood/bakersfield/two-golden-valley-high-school-students-arrested-in-apparent-bullying-incident.

64. We will learn more about "abolitionist accountability," or accountability to students and school communities that does not rely on punishment, in chapter 5.
65. Associated Press, "Deputy Who Tossed a S.C. High School Student Won't Be Charged," *New York Times*, September 2, 2016, https://www.nytimes.com/2016/09/03/afternoonupdate/deputy-who-tossed-a-sc-high-school-student-wont-be-charged.html.
66. "Sexualization Not Safety (IONN)," #PoliceFreeSchools, Advancement Project, May 14, 2024, https://policefreeschools.org/resources/sexualization-not-safety-2024/.
67. Jillian Peterson, James Densley, and Gina Erickson, "Presence of Armed School Officials and Fatal and Nonfatal Gunshot Injuries During Mass School Shootings, United States, 1980–2019," *JAMA Network Open* 4, no. 2 (2021): e2037394.
68. Hannah Carson Baggett and Carey E. Andrzejewski, *The Grammar of School Discipline: Removal, Resistance, and Reform in Alabama Schools* (Lanham, MD: Rowman & Littlefield, 2021).
69. Caroline Crichlow-Ball, Dewey Cornell, and Francis Huang, "Student Perceptions of School Resource Officers and Threat Reporting," *Journal of School Violence* 21, no. 2 (2022): 222–36; Erica O. Turner and Abigail J. Beneke, "'Softening' School Resource Officers: The Extension of Police Presence in Schools in an Era of Black Lives Matter, School Shootings, and Rising Inequality," *Race Ethnicity and Education* 23, no. 2 (2020): 221–40.
70. Wood and Hampton, "The Influence of School Resource Officer Presence on Teacher Perceptions."
71. Chris Rickert, "Madison School District Administration Blocked Survey of Teachers on School-Based Policy," *Wisconsin State Journal*, May 26, 2019, https://madison.com/news/local/education/local_schools/madison-school-district-administration-blocked-survey-of-teachers-on-school-based-police/article_134c0f37-a5bc-532a-947c-a29c921e3bff.html.
72. Danielle Layton and Paula Gerstenblatt, "'They're Just, Like, There': A Constructivist Grounded Theory Study of Student Experiences with School Resource Officers," *Journal of Community Psychology* 50, no. 8 (2022): 3470–86. This article also contains a review of research literature about K–12 students' perceptions of school police.
73. Monique W. Morris, Rebecca Epstein, and Aishatu Yusuf, *Be Her Resource: A Toolkit About School Resource Officers and Girls of Color* (Washington, DC: Center on Poverty and Inequality, Georgetown Law, 2018); Carla Shedd, *Unequal City: Race, Schools, and Perceptions of Injustice* (New York: Russell Sage Foundation, 2015).
74. Johnathan Nakamoto, Rebecca Cerna, and Alexis Stern, *High School Students' Perceptions of Police Vary by Student Race and Ethnicity: Findings from an Analysis of the California Healthy Kids Survey*, 2017/18, research brief, *WestEd* 1, 5 (2019); Uriel Serrano, "Feeling Carcerality: How Carceral Seepage Shapes Racialized Emotions," *Social Problems*, spae059 (2024).
75. Matthew T. Theriot and John G. Orme, "School Resource Officers and Students' Feelings of Safety at School," *Youth Violence and Juvenile Justice* 14, no. 2 (2016): 130–46.
76. Maisha T. Winn, "Paradigm Shifting for Black Girls: Toward a Futures Matter Stance," in *Investing in the Educational Success of Black Women and Girls*, ed. Lori D. Patton, Venus E. Evans-Winter, and Charlotte E. Jacobs (New York: Routledge, 2022), 227–40; Monique Couvson (formerly Morris), *Pushout: The Criminalization of Black Girls in Schools* (New York: New Press, 2016); Subini A. Annamma, *The Pedagogy of Pathologization: Dis/abled Girls of Color in the School-Prison Nexus* (New York: Routledge, 2017).
77. "How to Advocate for Your School Resource Officers," National Association of School Resource Officers (NASRO), https://www.nasro.org/membership/how-to-advocate-for-your-school-resource-officers/.

78. "Reality over Rhetoric When It Comes to School Resource Officers," National Association of School Resource Officers (NASRO), https://www.nasro.org/membership/reality-over-rhetoric-when-it-comes-to-school-resource-officers.
79. For a review of research about SROs and school discipline, see, for example, Denise C. Gottfredson et al., "Effects of School Resource Officers on School Crime and Responses to School Crime," *Criminology & Public Policy* 19, no. 3 (2020): 905–40.
80. Philip C. Bolger, Jonathan Kremser, and Haley Walker, "Detention or Diversion? The Influence of Training and Education on School Police Officer Discretion," *Policing: An International Journal* 42, no. 2 (2019): 255–69.
81. Terry Allen and Pedro Noguera, "A Web of Punishment: Examining Black Student Interactions with School Police in Los Angeles," *Educational Researcher* (2023), https://doi.org/10.3102/0013189X221095547.
82. "Training Courses," National Association of School Resource Officers (NASRO), https://www.nasro.org/training/training-courses/.
83. Kaba and Ritchie, *No More Police.*
84. Baggett and Andrzejewski, *The Grammar of School Discipline.*
85. Colin Kaepernick, Connie Wun, and Christopher Petrella, "A Journey to Safer Futures," in *Abolition for the People*, ed. Colin Kaepernick (New York: Kaepernick, 2021), 15.
86. Colin Kaepernick, "Introduction," in *Abolition for the People*, ed. Colin Kaepernick (New York: Kaepernick, 2021), 26.
87. Felker-Kantor, "Arresting the Demand for Drugs," 1114.
88. For further reading, see chapter 2, "Who Do You Serve, Who Do You Protect?" in Geo Maher, *A World Without Police: How Strong Communities Make Cops Obsolete* (New York: Verso, 2021), 47–69, in addition to firsthand accounts of police violence from women and students in "Community Responds to Domestic Violence," Creative Interventions, Resources for Everyday People to End Violence, https://www.creative-interventions.org/community-responds-to-domestic-violence/; and Interrupting Criminalization and In Our Names Network, *Sexualization Not Safety.*
89. Dean Spade, "Queer and Trans Liberation Requires Abolition," in *Abolition for the People*, ed. Colin Kaepernick (New York: Kaepernick, 2021), 99–104. See Annika Butler-Wall et al., eds., *Rethinking Sexism, Gender, and Sexuality* (Milwaukee: Rethinking Schools Publications, 2016), for resources for teaching and learning about gender and sexuality, https://rethinkingschools.org/books/rethinking-sexism-gender-and-sexuality/.
90. Associated Press, "Why Did Alabama and 13 Other States Turn Down Federal Money to Feed Kids This Summer?," AL.com, February 16, 2024, https://www.al.com/news/2024/02/why-did-alabama-and-13-other-states-turn-down-federal-money-to-feed-kids-this-summer.html.
91. "Tapping the Police to Distribute Food," Food Bank News, March 10, 2020, https://foodbanknews.org/tapping-the-police-to-distribute-food/; "Youth Camp," City of Opelika, https://www.opelika-al.gov/256/Youth-Camp; "Help Us 'Clear The List' for Lee County Teachers!," Lee County Alabama Sheriff's Office, June 5, 2024, https://x.com/LeeCoSheriffAL/status/1798384356932591726.
92. Sam Levin, " 'Police Don't Produce Safety': The Black Feminist Scholars Fighting for Abolition," *The Guardian*, August 29, 2022, https://www.theguardian.com/us-news/2022/aug/29/police-defund-abolition-mariame-kaba-andrea-j-ritchie.

Chapter 4

1. Shabnam Javdani, "Policing Education: An Empirical Review of the Challenges and Impact of the Work of School Police Officers," *American Journal of Community Psychology* 63, no. 3–4 (2019): 253–69.
2. Advancement Project and Alliance for Educational Justice, *We Came to Learn: A Call to Action for Police-Free Schools* (2018), #policefreeschools, June 23, 2023, https://policefree-schools.org/resources/we-came-to-learn-a-call-to-action-for-police-free-schools/; Ar'Reon A. Watson and Margaret C. Stevenson, "Teachers' and Administrators' Perceptions of Police-to-Student Encounters: The Impact of Student Race, Police Legitimacy, and Legal Authoritarianism," *Race and Justice* 12, no. 4 (2022): 736–54; Libby Nelson and Dara Lind, "The School-to-Prison Pipeline, Explained," *Vox*, October 27, 2015, https://www.vox.com/2015/2/24/8101289/school-discipline-race. In California, for example, teachers are required to file a police report if a student "assaults" them and actually may face prosecution if they fail to do so. Some teachers, however, are adamant that police contact with their students is harmful and have resisted this requirement. See Zuleima Baquedano's story about her advocacy for her students in Jenna Peterson, "When Should Teachers Call the Police?," *The74*, September 9, 2024, https://www.yahoo.com/news/teachers-call-police-170100875.html?guccounter=1&guce_referrer=aHR0cHM6Ly93d3cuZ29vZ2xlLmNvbS8&guce_referrer_sig=AQAAABoJpfKnnI8DjeIFkPbTscDuyAF475j1WJW85AcxqG-F47_a_BYANNrbYk3WJoON9_itYKYjj0M7SdRxYbMfyloKH4CuJP1_zuP2DwT-Q_nhi_qMymSAmOPZA09TWcJM2s8PVdHgA9loXmFtc5qwTTMrl77sqJ9kQqC52XL-5SqlG#:~:text=Research%20has%20shown%20that%20when,hallways%20or%20knocking%20on%20doors.
3. "About OCR," para. 6, US Department of Education, https://www2.ed.gov/about/offices/list/ocr/aboutocr.html.
4. As a former high school French teacher, access to language instruction has been an important topic to me. My dissertation study was in part about students of Color and access to world languages.
5. *Data on Equal Access to Education 2020–21*, Civil Rights Data Collection, Office for Civil Rights, US Department of Education, https://civilrightsdata.ed.gov.
6. Hannah Carson Baggett and Carey E. Andrzejewski, *The Grammar of School Discipline: Removal, Resistance, and Reform in Alabama Schools* (Lanham, MD: Rowman & Littlefield, 2021).
7. In my last book, *The Grammar of School Discipline*, my coauthor and I characterized this "exclusionary" school discipline as a type of removal—a removal that has historical roots in the enslavement of Black people, the displacement of Indigenous people, and the protection of spaces, like classrooms, deemed to be "white." In other words, school discipline that results in our removal of students is just a modern iteration of what has always been.
8. Many focused on the 2017–2018 data, as those were the most recent data available at the time of these class activities. Some preservice teachers also compared across survey years, and others explored the preliminary results for the next data collection cycle (2020–2021).
9. A distinction exists between OCR definitions of arrests and referrals: all arrests are recorded as referrals, but not all referrals lead to arrests. Regardless of outcome, each means that youth have been in contact with police.
10. Mariame Kaba and Andrea J. Ritchie, *No More Police: A Case for Abolition* (New York: New Press, 2022).
11. Brendan McQuade and Mark Neocleous, "Beware: Medical Police," *Radical Philosophy* 2, no. 8 (2020): 3–9.

12. Kaba and Ritchie, *No More Police*, 140.
13. Kaba and Ritchie, *No More Police*, 140.
14. Carla Shalaby, *Troublemakers: Lessons in Freedom from Young Children at School* (New York: New Press, 2017).
15. Paula X. Rojas, "Are the Cops in Our Heads and Hearts?," S&F Online, https://sfonline.barnard.edu/paula-rojas-are-the-cops-in-our-heads-and-hearts/. Similarly, Geo Maher writes about how we are all part of the "pig majority" in *A World Without Police: How Strong Communities Make Cops Obsolete* (New York: Verso, 2021).
16. Baggett and Andrzejewski, *The Grammar of School Discipline*.
17. Russell J. Skiba, Mariella I. Arredondo, and Natasha T. Williams, "More Than a Metaphor: The Contribution of Exclusionary Discipline to a School-to-Prison Pipeline," *Equity & Excellence in Education* 47, no. 4 (2014): 546–64.
18. Tasminda K. Dhaliwal, Mark J. Chin, Virginia S. Lovison, and David M. Quinn, "Educator Bias Is Associated with Racial Disparities in Student Achievement and Discipline," *Brookings*, July 20, 2020, https://www.brookings.edu/articles/educator-bias-is-associated-with-racial-disparities-in-student-achievement-and-discipline/.
19. Baggett and Andrzejewski, *The Grammar of School Discipline*.
20. CBS/Bay City News Service, "California Law Will Make Student Suspensions for 'Willful Defiance' Illegal," October 10, 2023, https://www.cbsnews.com/sanfrancisco/news/california-law-will-make-student-suspensions-for-willful-defiance-illegal/.
21. In my last book, *The Grammar of School Discipline*, my coauthor and I wrote about "subjective" offenses like "defiance," as opposed to "objective" offenses like weapons and drugs. We argued that because of stereotypes about race, gender, and other identity domains, school practitioners are more likely to monitor Black and Brown students, queer and trans students, and students with disabilities, which results in punishment for both subjective and objective offenses.
22. Decoteau J. Irby, "Trouble at School: Understanding School Discipline Systems as Nets of Social Control," *Equity & Excellence in Education* 47, no. 4 (2014): 513–30.
23. Johanna Lacoe and Matthew P. Steinberg, "Rolling Back Zero Tolerance: The Effect of Discipline Policy Reform on Suspension Usage and Student Outcomes," *Peabody Journal of Education* 93, no. 2 (2018): 207–27.
24. Rui Wang, "The Impact of Suspension Reforms on Discipline Outcomes: Evidence from California High Schools," *AERA Open* 8 (2022), https://doi.org/10.1177/233285842 11068067.
25. Baggett and Andrzejewski, *The Grammar of School Discipline*.
26. West Resendes, *Police in Schools Continue to Target Black, Brown, and Indigenous Students with Disabilities*, ACLU News & Commentary, July 9, 2020, https://www.aclu.org/news/criminal-law-reform/police-in-schools-continue-to-target-black-brown-and-indigenous-students-with-disabilities-the-trump-administration-has-data-thats-likely-to-prove-it; Jacqueline M. Nowicki, *K–12 Education: Discipline Disparities for Black Students, Boys, and Students with Disabilities, Report to Congressional Requesters, GAO-18-258* (Washington, DC: US Government Accountability Office, 2018); Monique Morris, *Pushout: The Criminalization of Black Girls in Schools* (New York: New Press, 2016); Neal A. Palmer and Emily A. Greytak, "LGBTQ Student Victimization and Its Relationship to School Discipline and Justice System Involvement," *Criminal Justice Review* 42, no. 2 (2017): 163–87; Christopher A. Mallett, "Police in Schools: The Complicated Impact on Students, School Environments, and the Juvenile Courts," *Juvenile and Family Court Journal* 73, no. 2 (2022): 37–49;

"Liberated Education: The Need for Police-Free Schools," webinar, GLSEN, https://www.glsen.org/policefreeschoolswebinar.

27. Paulo Freire first cited and critiqued this "banking" model of education in 1970 when he theorized that learning was deeper, and more liberatory, when instructors and students were in dialogue with one another about the world and our experiences in it. See Paulo Freire, *Pedagogy of the Oppressed: 50th Anniversary Edition* (New York: Bloomsbury, 2020). In addition, we know that students learn via storytelling, observation, experimentation (and failure!), and, broadly, interaction with the world around them, including their teachers and peers.
28. Scholars like Norma González, Luis Moll, and Cathy Amanti have written about students and families who bring communal "funds of knowledge" to learning; Tara Yosso, writing about "community cultural wealth," also pushes back on ideas of students and families as deficient. Norma González, Luis C. Moll, and Cathy Amanti, eds., *Funds of Knowledge: Theorizing Practices in Households, Communities, and Classroom* (Mahwah, NJ: Routledge, 2006); Tara J. Yosso, "Whose Culture Has Capital? A Critical Race Theory Discussion of Community Cultural Wealth," *Race Ethnicity and Education* 8, no. 1 (2005): 69–91.
29. Melanie Leung-Gagné, Jennifer McCombs, Caitlin Scott, and Daniel J. Losen, *Pushed Out: Trends and Disparities in Out-of-School Suspension* (Palo Alto, CA: Learning Policy Institute, 2022).
30. Scholars from across disciplines and time periods, from James Baldwin and Toni Morrison to Derrick Bell and bell hooks, have written about whiteness and its relationship to the US context. In addition to their work, resources including videos and definitions can be found here: "Whiteness," Talking About Race, Smithsonian National Museum of African American History & Culture, https://nmaahc.si.edu/learn/talking-about-race/topics/whiteness. For a discussion of whiteness and teacher education specifically, see Cheryl E. Matias, *Feeling White: Whiteness, Emotionality, and Education* (New York: Springer, 2016).
31. Some education scholars, like Subini Annamma, have advocated for a reframing of this concept such that it does not rely on ableist language about blindness, and better articulates how white folks are actually very aware of race and racism and yet choose to "evade" these topics in strategic ways; see Subini A. Annamma, *The Pedagogy of Pathologization: Dis/abled Girls of Color in the School-Prison Nexus* (New York: Routledge, 2017).
32. Francesca López and Christine E. Sleeter, *Critical Race Theory and Its Critics: Implications for Research and Teaching* (New York: Teachers College Press, 2023).
33. Jim Crow Museum of Racist Imagery, https://jimcrowmuseum.ferris.edu/index.htm; Saidiya Hartman, *Scenes of Subjection: Terror, Slavery, and Self-Making in Nineteenth-Century America* (New York: Norton, 2022).
34. Andrea J. Ritchie, *Invisible No More: Police Violence Against Black Women and Women of Color* (Boston: Beacon, 2017); Kaba and Ritchie, *No More Police.*
35. Again, scholars from James Baldwin to Toni Morrison have written about whiteness and innocence. Contemporary abolitionist and scholar Erica Meiners has argued that the way that we think about innocence with regard to children is limited to views about children as white cis children who adults perceive as embodying "normative" conceptions of childhood; see Erica R. Meiners, *For the Children? Protecting Innocence in a Carceral State* (Minneapolis: University of Minnesota Press, 2016). For a study about racialized and gendered conceptions of Black children as deserving of police violence, see Phillip A. Goff et al., "The Essence of Innocence: Consequences of Dehumanizing Black Children," *Journal of Personality and Social Psychology* 106, no. 4 (2014): 526–45.

36. Ian Haney Lopez, *White by Law 10th Anniversary Edition: The Legal Construction of Race* (New York: New York University Press, 2006); Michael Omi and Howard Winant, *Racial Formation in the United States from the 1960s to the 1990s*, 2nd ed. (New York: Routledge, 1993); Derald Wing Sue et al., "Racial Microaggressions Against Black Americans: Implications for Counseling," *Journal of Counseling & Development* 86, no. 3 (2008): 330–38; Annika Butler-Wall et al., eds., *Rethinking Sexism, Gender, and Sexuality* (Milwaukee: Rethinking Schools Publications, 2016), https://rethinkingschools.org/books/rethinking-sexism-gender-and-sexuality/; Annamma, *The Pedagogy of Pathologization*.
37. See Ren-yo Hwang for a reframing of "deviance": Ren-yo Hwang, "Deviant Care for Deviant Futures: QTBIPoC Radical Relationalism as Mutual Aid Against Carceral Care," *Transgender Studies Quarterly* 6, no. 4 (2019): 559–78.
38. The Combahee River Collective, an organization started by Black queer women, first began conceptualizing these ideas back in the 1970s. Read its statement here: *The Combahee River Collective Statement* (1977), BlackPast, https://www.blackpast.org/african-american-history/combahee-river-collective-statement-1977/.
39. These two movies have been heavily critiqued for how they both stereotype Black and Brown kids and rely on white savior narratives. For an example of that critique, see Brittany A. Aronson, "The White Savior Industrial Complex: A Cultural Studies Analysis of a Teacher Educator, Savior Film, and Future Teachers," *Journal of Critical Thought and Praxis* 6, no. 3 (2017): 36–54; Selome Hailu, "'Abbott Elementary' Star Lisa Ann Walter Makes Meatballs While Discussing the Teacher Shortage," *Variety*, October 12, 2022, https://variety.com/2022/tv/news/lisa-ann-walter-abbott-elementary-teacher-shortage-1235400917/.
40. "Sexualization Not Safety (IONN)," #policefreeschools, Advancement Project, May 14, 2024, https://policefreeschools.org/resources/sexualization-not-safety-2024/.
41. Muhammad Khalifa, "Can Blacks Be Racists? Black-on-Black Principal Abuse in an Urban School Setting," *International Journal of Qualitative Studies in Education* 28, no. 2 (2015): 259–82.
42. Walter S. Gilliam et al., "Do Early Educators' Implicit Biases Regarding Sex and Race Relate to Behavior Expectations and Recommendations of Preschool Expulsions and Suspensions?," *Yale University Child Study Center* 9, no. 28 (2016).
43. Baggett and Andrzejewski, *The Grammar of School Discipline*, 105.
44. Researchers and abolitionists have written about these types of conundrums in equity work and abolitionist visioning. See, for example, Jamila Dugan, "Beware of Equity Traps and Tropes," *Educational Leadership* 78, no. 6 (2021), https://www.ascd.org/el/articles/beware-of-equity-traps-and-tropes; and "Tricks and Tensions," in Mariame Kaba and Andrea J. Ritchie, *No More Police: A Case for Abolition* (New York: New Press, 2022), 202.
45. This is similar to the way we label students as "failing" if they do not pass a standardized test rather than considering what the test itself measures.
46. Richard R. Valencia, *The Evolution of Deficit Thinking: Educational Thought and Practice* (New York: Routledge, 2012).
47. Gloria Ladson-Billings, in her decades of work on culturally relevant pedagogy, pushes us to ask, "What is 'right' with Black students?" See, for example, Gloria Ladson-Billings, *Culturally Relevant Pedagogy: Asking a Different Question* (New York: Teachers College Press, 2021).
48. Baggett and Andrzejewski, *The Grammar of School Discipline*; Amy J. Anderson and Hannah Carson Baggett, "'I Just Put My Head Down, But They Still Get on to Me': Navigating Silence in an Alternative School in Alabama," *Journal of Critical Thought and Praxis* 9, no. 1

(2020), https://doi.org/10.31274/jctp.9563; Hannah Carson Baggett and Carey E. Andrzejewski, "'Man, Somebody Tell That Kid to Shut Up': YPAR Implementation at a Rural, Alternative School in the Deep South," *Critical Questions in Education* 8, no. 4 (2017): 400–417; Hannah Carson Baggett and Carey E. Andrzejewski, "'I'm Not Good at This Stuff': Using Bravery to Rethink Action in Youth Participatory Action Research," in *Educating for Social Justice: Field Notes from Rural Communities*, ed. Rebekah Cordova et al., 72–85 (Boston: Brill, 2020).

49. David Correia and Tyler Wall, *Police: A Field Guide* (New York: Verso, 2018), 235.
50. Jing Liu, Emily K. Penner, and Wenjing Gao, "Troublemakers? The Role of Frequent Teacher Referrers in Expanding Racial Disciplinary Disproportionalities," *Educational Researcher* 52, no. 8 (2023): 469–81.
51. When I first started writing and conducting research about school discipline and students, I also fell into this trap. It was only after reading abolitionist work about punishment and accountability and reflecting on my experiences as a teacher that I came to understand that language about "disproportionality," although perhaps well intended, actually directs our attention away from the harmful system of discipline and punishment that is in place in public schools.
52. Erica R. Meiners, "Ending the School-to-Prison Pipeline/Building Abolition Futures," *Urban Review* 43, no. 4 (2011): 556.
53. Meiners, "Ending the School-to-Prison Pipeline," 551.
54. US Department of Education, National Center for Education Statistics, "Percentage of Public Schools with Security Staff Present at Least Once a Week, and Percentage with Security Staff Routinely Carrying a Firearm, by Selected School Characteristics: 2005–06 Through 2015–16," *Digest of Education Statistics*, table 233.70 (2019), https://nces.ed.gov/programs/digest/d19/tables/dt19_233.70.asp.
55. Chris Hacker, Aparna Zalani, and Stephen Stock, "New Data: Over 100 Elementary-Aged Children Arrested in U.S. Schools," CBS News, November 16, 2023, https://www.cbsnews.com/news/school-arrest-children-new-data/.
56. Associated Press, "5-Year-Old Cuffed, Arrested in St. Petersburg School," *Herald-Tribune*, March 21, 2005, https://www.heraldtribune.com/story/news/2005/03/21/5-year-old-cuffed-arrested-in-st-petersburg-school/28837733007/; Mihir Zaveri, "Police Body Cam Video Shows Arrest of 6-Year-Old at Florida School," *New York Times*, February 27, 2020, https://www.nytimes.com/2020/02/27/us/orlando-6-year-old-arrested.html; Julie Watts, "Handcuffs in Hallways: Thousands of California Children Are Being Arrested on K–12 Campuses. Why?," Investigations, CBS Sacramento, November 16, 2022, https://www.cbsnews.com/sacramento/news/elementary-school-arrests-thousands-california-children/.
57. Julie Watts, "Cops Called to California K–8 Schools 10,000 Times in a Year. Could State Law Be to Blame?," Investigations: Handcuffs in Hallways, CBS News California, April 10, 2024, https://www.cbsnews.com/sacramento/news/handcuffs-in-hallways-cops-called-to-schools-california-law/; Victor J. St. John, Andrea M. Headley, and Kristen Harper, "Reducing Adverse Police Contact Would Heal Wounds for Children and Their Communities," Trauma & Resilience, *Child Trends*, June 14, 2022, https://www.childtrends.org/publications/reducing-adverse-police-contact-would-heal-wounds-for-children-and-their-communities.
58. Islah Tauheed, "Policing Isn't Just for Cops. Teachers Do It, Too—and They Need to Stop," Chalkbeat, October 1, 2020, https://www.chalkbeat.org/2020/10/1/21496460/breonna-taylor-policing-schools/.

59. Alfie Kohn began writing about the problems with rewards in classrooms as early as the 1990s in his book *Punished by Rewards: The Trouble with Gold Stars, Incentive Plans, A's, Praise, and Other Bribes* (Boston: Houghton Mifflin, 1993).
60. For critiques of ClassDojo, see, for example, Jamie Manolev, Anna Sullivan, and Neil Tippett, "Reshaping School Discipline with Metrics: An Examination of Teachers' Disciplinary Practices with ClassDojo," *British Journal of Sociology of Education* 45, no. 7–8 (2024): 1146–60.
61. Connie Persike, "The Dark Side of Rewards, Part 1: Why Incentives Do More Harm Than Good in the Classroom," Alliance Against Seclusion and Restraint, May 6, 2023, https://endseclusion.org/2023/05/06/the-dark-side-of-rewards-why-incentives-do-more-harm-than-good-in-the-classroom/.
62. These epiphanies are different from Black racial identity epiphanies and encounters that point to possibilities for Black consciousness and liberation, as theorized by foundational scholars like Frantz Fanon, and, more recently, William Cross Jr. and Helen Neville. See, for example, Helen A. Neville and William E. Cross Jr., "Racial Awakening: Epiphanies and Encounters in Black Racial Identity," *Cultural Diversity and Ethnic Minority Psychology* 23, no. 1 (2017): 102.
63. Lauri Johnson reported some similarities in white racial awareness with teachers over twenty years ago in " 'My Eyes Have Been Opened': White Teachers and Racial Awareness," *Journal of Teacher Education* 53, no. 2 (2002): 153–67.
64. Meiners, "Ending the School-to-Prison Pipeline."
65. See the work of scholars like Subini Annamma, Maisha Winn, Monique (Morris) Couvson, Erica Meiners, and Connie Wun, who have documented the experiences of Black girls, girls of Color, girls with disabilities, and queer and trans students with criminalization in schools.
66. Kelly Hayes and Mariame Kaba, *Let This Radicalize You: Organizing and the Revolution of Reciprocal Care* (Chicago: Haymarket, 2023).
67. Interrupting Criminalization and In Our Names Network, *Sexualization Not Safety: Black Girls, Trans, and Gender Nonconforming Youth's Experiences of Police Presence in Schools: Report* (2024), 10, https://www.interruptingcriminalization.com/resources-all/sexualization-not-safety-black-girls-trans-and-gender-nonconforming-youths-experience-of-police-presence-in-schools-report.

Chapter 5

1. Jing Liu, Emily K. Penner, and Wenjing Gao, "Troublemakers? The Role of Frequent Teacher Referrers in Expanding Racial Disciplinary Disproportionalities," *Educational Researcher* 52, no. 8 (2023): 469–81; Advancement Project and Alliance for Educational Justice, *We Came to Learn: A Call to Action for Police-Free Schools*, June 23, 2023, https://policefreeschools.org/resources/we-came-to-learn-a-call-to-action-for-police-free-schools-2/; Ar'Reon A. Watson and Margaret C. Stevenson, "Teachers' and Administrators' Perceptions of Police-to-Student Encounters: The Impact of Student Race, Police Legitimacy, and Legal Authoritarianism," *Race and Justice* 12, no. 4 (2022): 736–54; Libby Nelson and Dara Lind, "The School-to-Prison Pipeline, Explained," *Vox*, October 27, 2015, https://www.vox.com/2015/2/24/8101289/school-discipline-race.
2. Preservice teachers attended classes at universities in Michigan, New York, Connecticut, and Alabama.

3. Carla Shalaby, "Imagining 'Classroom Management' as an Abolitionist Project," in *Lessons in Liberation*, ed. Education for Liberation Network and Critical Resistance Editorial Collective (Chico, CA: AK Press, 2021), 104–12.
4. Amanda Aguilar Shank, "Beyond Firing: How Do We Create Community-Wide Accountability for Sexual Harassment in Our Movements?," in *Beyond Survival: Strategies and Stories from the Transformative Justice Movement*, ed. Ejeris Dixon and Leah Lakshmi Piepzna-Samarasinha (Chico, CA: AK Press, 2020), 27.
5. Three of the vignettes were cowritten with education scholar Alyssa Hadley Dunn, while one is adapted from a textbook by education scholars H. Richard Milner IV et al., *"These Kids Are Out of Control": Why We Must Reimagine "Classroom Management" for Equity* (Thousand Oaks, CA: Corwin, 2018). Preservice teachers made sense of these vignettes via both written group reflections and class discussion, both of which are interwoven throughout the coverage in this chapter.
6. "A Portrait of Reform in Timber County," written with Nanyamka A. Shukura, Sangah Lee, and Jasmine S. Betties, in Hannah Carson Baggett and Carey E. Andrzejewski, *The Grammar of School Discipline: Removal, Resistance, and Reform in Alabama Schools* (Lanham, MD: Rowman & Littlefield, 2021), 129–44.
7. See, for example, this article about Los Angeles Police Department (LAPD) officers in the 1980s "warning parents about kids who, they argued, were 'dressing for death'": Bob Baker, "Dressing for Death: Officers Help Parents Understand What Gangs Are All About," *Los Angeles Times*, May 11, 1988, https://www.latimes.com/archives/la-xpm-1988-05-11-me-2379-story.html.
8. Kristin Henning, *The Rage of Innocence: How America Criminalizes Black Youth* (New York: Vintage, 2021); Dawn Jones, "Flint Community Schools Ban Cell Phones and Hoodies for Students," ABC12 News, December 14, 2023, https://www.abc12.com/news/local/flint-community-schools-ban-cell-phones-and-hoodies-for-students/article_d55a04f4-9ad8-11ee-9c38-636cd72ef530.html.
9. Gene Demby, "Sagging Pants and the Long History of 'Dangerous' Street Fashion," NPR WNYC, September 11, 2014, https://www.npr.org/sections/codeswitch/2014/09/11/347143588/sagging-pants-and-the-long-history-of-dangerous-street-fashion; Rene Lynch, "Saggy Pants Ban Is a Money Maker for Georgia Town," *Los Angeles Times*, September 29, 2011, https://www.latimes.com/archives/blogs/nation-now/story/2011-09-29/saggy-pants-ban-is-a-money-maker-for-georgia-town#:~:text=Violators%20faced%20a%20%2425%20fine,under%20it%20by%20year's%20end.
10. Brentin Mock, "Saggy Pants and 'Respectability Politics' in Dadeville, Alabama," Bloomberg, September 15, 2015, https://www.bloomberg.com/news/articles/2015-09-15/saggy-pants-and-respectability-politics-in-dadeville-alabama.
11. Michelle Zacarias, "Chicago Teens Overturn High School Hoodie Ban," *People's World*, May 28, 2019, https://www.peoplesworld.org/article/chicago-teens-overturn-high-school-hoodie-ban/.
12. We might see these types of mixed messages about things like hoodies as well—for example, teachers might wear a hoodie in a chilly classroom, even as policy prevents students from doing so.
13. A cruel irony is that, although phones are banned in prisons, incarcerated folks often employ "ingenious ways" to access devices. This organizing work is one of the primary ways that the general public has become aware of abysmal prison conditions across the United States. Keri Blakinger, "The Many Ingenious Ways People in Prison Use (Forbidden) Cell Phones,"

Marshall Project, January 19, 2023, https://www.themarshallproject.org/2023/01/19/cell-phones-in-prisons-tiktok-education.

14. Mx. is a prefix used by folks who identify as nonbinary or gender queer. See Julianna Iocovelli, "Existing Outside of the Binary in the Classroom," *Rethinking Schools*, https://rethinkingschools.org/articles/existing-outside-of-the-binary-in-the-classroom/, for an essay on this topic by a nonbinary teacher in Connecticut.
15. For research about school discipline, stereotypes about race, and names, see, for example, Jason A. Okonofua and Jennifer L. Eberhardt, "Two Strikes: Race and the Disciplining of Young Students," *Psychological Science* 26, no. 5 (2015): 617–24; and Watson and Stevenson, "Teachers' and Administrators' Perceptions of Police-to-Student Encounters."
16. He assured us that it was new from the hardware store and had never been used.
17. Erica R. Meiners, "The Problem Child: Provocations Toward Dismantling the Carceral State," *Harvard Educational Review* 87, no. 1 (2017): 122–46. Students in schools across the country have organized to push back on anti-trans legislation, and even to assert their right to period products in schools. Zach Wendling, "Nebraska Students Take Fight Against 'Period Poverty' to Legislature," *Nebraska Examiner*, February 13, 2024, https://nebraskaexaminer.com/briefs/nebraska-students-take-fight-against-period-poverty-to-legislature/.
18. Sheeva Sabati et al., "Dismantle, Change, Build: Lessons for Growing Abolition in Teacher Education," *Teachers College Record* 124, no. 3 (2022): 177–206.
19. Torin Monahan and Rodolfo D. Torres, *Schools Under Surveillance: Cultures of Control in Public Education* (Ithaca, NY: Rutgers University Press, 2009).
20. Baggett and Andrzejewski, *The Grammar of School Discipline*, 96.
21. This vignette is adapted from Milner et al., *"These Kids Are Out of Control"*.
22. Baggett and Andrzejewski, *The Grammar of School Discipline.*
23. Andrea Ball, Dian Zhang, and Mary Claire Molloy, "'She Looks Like a Baby': Why Do Kids as Young as 5 or 6 Still Get Arrested at Schools?," Center for Public Integrity, February 10, 2022, https://publicintegrity.org/education/criminalizing-kids/young-kids-arrested-at-schools/.
24. Shalaby, "Imagining 'Classroom Management' as an Abolitionist Project."
25. Kelly Lagerwerff, "Prizes as Curriculum: How My School Gets Students to 'Behave,'" *Rethinking Schools*, https://rethinkingschools.org/articles/prizes-as-curriculum-how-my-school-gets-students-to-behave/.
26. Hannah Carson Baggett, "Nobody Likes Me, Everybody Hates Me (Worms)," *Qualitative Inquiry* 27, no. 1 (2021): 97–101.
27. Shalaby, "Imagining 'Classroom Management' as an Abolitionist Project."
28. Associated Press, "Judge Threatens to Close Schools," StarNews Online, March 4, 2006, https://www.starnewsonline.com/story/news/2006/03/05/judge-threatens-to-close-schools/30258849007/.
29. Wayne Au and Melissa Bollow Tempel, eds., *Pencils Down: Rethinking High-Stakes Testing and Accountability in Public Schools* (Milwaukee: Rethinking Schools, 2012).
30. Au and Tempel, *Pencils Down.*
31. The district where the school was located had an "open transfer policy" at the time. Many white families transferred away from "low-ranked" schools, resulting in segregated schools with almost exclusively students of Color and high-poverty students; Chris Fitzsimon, "Troubled Schools Miss Mark Set by Judge," NC Newsline, July 20, 2006, https://ncnewsline.com/2006/07/20/troubled-schools-miss-mark-set-by-judge/.

32. American Civil Liberties Union (ACLU), *Bullies in Blue: The Origins and Consequences of School Policing* (New York: ACLU Foundation, 2017), https://www.aclu.org/sites/default/files/field_document/aclu_bullies_in_blue_4_11_17_final.pdf.
33. We learned in chapter 4 about this way of thinking, called "deficit thinking," which is so prevalent in public education.
34. The district that I taught in during the 2000s had one school counselor who was shared among three large high schools.
35. Outside the school context, we blame "bad" people for their "crimes" and punish them via fines and even jail, instead of asking hard questions about if prisons should even exist or looking at what constitutes a "crime" that deserves incarceration.
36. For details, see, for example, Derecka Purnell, "Sex, Love, and Violence," in *Becoming Abolitionists: Police, Protests, and the Pursuit of Freedom* (New York: Astra House: 2021), 169–201.
37. For resources, see Creative Interventions, "Resources for Everyday People to End Violence," https://www.creative-interventions.org/.
38. Mariame Kaba, "So You're Thinking About Becoming an Abolitionist," Medium, October 30, 2020, https://level.medium.com/so-youre-thinking-about-becoming-an-abolitionist-a436f8e31894.
39. Transformative Justice is a "framework for responding to harm and violence that does not rely on the state and does not reinforce or perpetuate violence." For more information, see Colin Kaepernick, ed., *Abolition for the People* (New York: Kaepernick, 2021), 288.
40. Shank, "Beyond Firing," 28.
41. "The Four Parts of Accountability & How to Give a Genuine Apology," Leaving Evidence, December 18, 2019, https://leavingevidence.wordpress.com/2019/12/18/how-to-give-a-good-apology-part-1-the-four-parts-of-accountability/.
42. Keeanga-Yamahtta Taylor, "The Emerging Movement for Police and Prison Abolition," *New Yorker*, May 7, 2021, https://www.newyorker.com/news/our-columnists/the-emerging-movement-for-police-and-prison-abolition.
43. Carla Shalaby's chart about carceral classrooms is a good resource to support this inquiry; Shalaby, "Imagining 'Classroom Management' as an Abolitionist Project," 106–7.
44. Shalaby, "Imagining 'Classroom Management' as an Abolitionist Project," 100.
45. Rachel Herzing, "Abolition Is Practical," Inquest, July 11, 2023, https://inquest.org/abolition-is-practical/.
46. Maureen Mansfield, "Alternatives to Calling the Police," Abolitionist Futures, https://abolitionistfutures.com/latest-news/9m1jx98mayqvorjm7ij8x0zv9g5f85.
47. Kaba, "So You're Thinking About Becoming an Abolitionist."
48. Shank, "Beyond Firing," 39.
49. "The Four Parts of Accountability."
50. Terisa Siagatonu, "Abolitionist Teaching," in *Lessons in Liberation*, ed. Education for Liberation Network and Critical Resistance Editorial Collective (Chico, CA: AK Press, 2021), 126–27.
51. Kristina F. Brezicha and Chandler Patton Miranda, "Actions Speak Louder Than Words: Examining School Practices That Support Immigrant Students' Feelings of Belonging," *Equity & Excellence in Education* 55, no. 1–2 (2022): 133–47.
52. #AssaultAt map, #policefreeschools, Advancement Project, https://policefreeschools.org/map/.
53. It is important to acknowledge here that Mrs. Sue was also a long-standing member of the learning community, and as such had earned trust during her tenure. Preservice and new

practicing teachers, without that kind of shared trust in a shared community, will have to anticipate a power gap when considering these types of risks. For other accounts of adults in schools who have intervened to prevent police-youth contact, see, for example, NIA Dispatches, "Restorative Justice Is Not Enough: A New Essay About School-Based Interventions in the Carceral State," https://niastories.wordpress.com/2013/01/08/restorative-justice-is-not-enough-a-new-essay-about-school-based-interventions-in-the-carceral-state/.

54. This activity is adapted from "Critical Resistance, Abolitionist Exercises: 12 Youth-Friendly Activities to Strengthen Abolitionist Skills and Thinking in Your Lessons, Workshops, and Curricula," Activity 9, Discussing Harm, in *Lessons in Liberation*, ed. Education for Liberation Network and Critical Resistance Editorial Collective (Chico, CA: AK Press, 2021), 312.

Chapter 6

1. Derecka Purnell, *Becoming Abolitionists: Police, Protests, and the Pursuit of Freedom* (New York: Astra, 2022).
2. Kelly Hayes and Mariame Kaba, *Let This Radicalize You: Organizing and the Revolution of Reciprocal Care* (Chicago: Haymarket, 2023); Mariame Kaba and Andrea J. Ritchie, *No More Police: A Case for Abolition* (New York: New Press, 2022).
3. Harper B. Keenan, "Building Classroom Communities: A Pedagogical Reflection and Syllabus Excerpt," in *Lessons in Liberation: An Abolitionist Toolkit for Educators*, ed. Education for Liberation Network & Critical Resistance Editorial Collective (Chico, CA: AK Press, 2021), 156–69.
4. Sheeva Sabati et al., "Dismantle, Change, Build: Lessons for Growing Abolition in Teacher Education," *Teachers College Record* 124, no. 3 (2022): 177–206.
5. Carla Shalaby, "Imagining 'Classroom Management' as an Abolitionist Project," in *Lessons in Liberation: An Abolitionist Toolkit for Educators*, ed. Education for Liberation Network & Critical Resistance Editorial Collective (Chico, CA: AK Press, 2021), 104–12.
6. Erica Meiners, "Abolition: One Genealogy," in *Lessons in Liberation: An Abolitionist Toolkit for Educators*, ed. Education for Liberation Network & Critical Resistance Editorial Collective (Chico, CA: AK Press, 2021), 43–46.
7. Kaba and Ritchie, *No More Police*, 99.
8. Leah Lakshmi Piepzna-Samarasinha and Ejeris Dixon, eds., *Beyond Survival: Strategies and Stories from the Transformative Justice Movement* (Chico, CA: AK Press, 2020), 24.
9. Hannah Carson Baggett and Carey E. Andrzejewski, *The Grammar of School Discipline: Removal, Resistance, and Reform in Alabama Schools* (Lanham, MD: Rowman & Littlefield, 2021), chap. 4.
10. For more about criminalization, adultification, and surveillance as rooted in anti-Blackness, see Baggett and Andrzejewski, *The Grammar of School Discipline*, chap. 2.
11. Maureen Mansfield, "Alternatives to Calling the Police," para. 9, Abolitionist Futures, 2024, https://abolitionistfutures.com/latest-news/9m1jx98mayqvorjm7ij8x0zv9g5f85.
12. Eve Tuck, "Humiliating Ironies and Dangerous Dignities: A Dialectic of School Pushout," *International Journal of Qualitative Studies in Education* 24, no. 7 (2011): 817–27.
13. This teacher pledge can be found online at Black Organizing Project, https://blackorganizingproject.org/wp-content/uploads/2021/07/Black-Sanctuary-Pledge-Final-2.pdf, as well as in *Lessons in Liberation*, 86.
14. Piepzna-Samarasinha and Dixon, *Beyond Survival*.

Chapter 7

1. Denise C. Gottfredson et al., "Effects of School Resource Officers on School Crime and Responses to School Crime," *Criminology of Public Policy* 19, no. 3 (2020), https://neighborsvt.org/wp-content/uploads/2020/09/Gottfredson-et-al_2020.pdf.
2. Moriah Balingit, "How One Preschool Uses PAW Patrol to Teach Democracy," NBC Washington, October 4, 2024, https://www.nbcwashington.com/news/local/how-one-preschool-uses-paw-patrol-to-teach-democracy-2/3730117/. "Copaganda" is, broadly defined, messaging that perpetuates pro-police narratives. Copaganda shows up in popular culture, social media, and even youth-police programming in schools. It socializes us to believe that police are normal and natural parts of our everyday lives, and we cannot live without them.
3. Lewis R. Gordon, *Bad Faith and Antiblack Racism* (Amherst, NY: Humanity, 1995), 8.
4. Antonis Katsiyannis et al., "An Examination of US School Mass Shootings, 2017–2022: Findings and Implications," *Advances in Neurodevelopmental Disorders* 7, no. 1 (2023): 66–76.
5. US Department of Justice, *Critical Incident Review: Active Shooter at Robb Elementary School* (Washington, DC: Office of Community Oriented Policing Services, 2024), https://portal.cops.usdoj.gov/resourcecenter/content.ashx/cops-r1141-pub.pdf.
6. Marjory Stoneman Douglas High School Public Safety Commission, *Initial Report Submitted to the Governor, Speaker of the House of Representatives and Senate President*, January 2, 2019, http://www.fdle.state.fl.us/MSDHS/CommissionReport.pdf.
7. J. Peterson et al., "Presence of Armed School Officials and Fatal and Nonfatal Gunshot Injuries During Mass School Shootings, United States, 1980–2019," *JAMA Network Open* 4, no. 2 (2021), https://www.ojp.gov/ncjrs/virtual-library/abstracts/presence-armed-school-officials-and-fatal-and-nonfatal-gunshot.
8. Melvin D. Livingston, Matthew E. Rossheim, and Kelli Stidham Hall, "A Descriptive Analysis of School and School Shooter Characteristics and the Severity of School Shootings in the United States, 1999–2018," *Journal of Adolescent Health* 64, no. 6 (2019): 797–99.
9. Julie Bosman et al., "Amid a Plague of Shootings, Bystanders Become Heroes," *New York Times*, January 25, 2023, https://www.nytimes.com/2023/01/25/us/shootings-guns-bystanders-civilians.html.
10. "Fast Facts: Firearm Injury and Death," Centers of Disease Control and Prevention (CDC), Firearm Injury and Death Prevention, July 5, 2024, https://www.cdc.gov/firearm-violence/data-research/facts-stats/index.html.
11. Robert Gebeloff et al., "Childhood's Greatest Danger: The Data on Kids and Gun Violence," *New York Times Magazine*, The Lives They Lived: Interactive, https://www.nytimes.com/interactive/2022/12/14/magazine/gun-violence-children-data-statistics.html#:~:text=And%20though%20the%20number%20of,killed%20by%20guns%20this%20year.
12. Dream Defenders, Home page, https://www.dreamdefenders.org/.
13. Decoteau J. Irby and Kylee Coney, "The 1994 Gun-Free Schools Act: Its Effects 25 Years Later and How to Undo Them," *Peabody Journal of Education* 96, no. 5 (2021): 494–507.
14. *Cops in Schools: The COPS Commitment to School Safety*, US Department of Justice, fact sheet, March 2004, https://www.ojp.gov/ncjrs/virtual-library/abstracts/cops-schools-cops-commitment-school-safety.
15. Kathleen Nolan, "Neoliberal Common Sense and Race-Neutral Discourses: A Critique of 'Evidence-Based' Policy-Making in School Policing," *Discourse: Studies in the Cultural Politics of Education* 36, no. 6 (2015): 894–907.

16. Advancement Project National Office Response to Gun Control Bill, Advancement Project, https://advancementproject.org/news/advancement-project-national-office-response-to-gun-control-bill/.
17. Starting after Sandy Hook and continuing after school shootings in states across the nation, politicians have called for arming teachers and administrators. See Addy Bink, "Does Your State Allow Teachers to Cary a Gun?," *The Hill*, April 10, 2023, https://thehill.com/homenews/nexstar_media_wire/3926048-does-your-state-allow-teachers-to-carry-a-gun/, for example. Many of these politicians lean on arguments about "good guys with guns" who ostensibly stop shootings from happening. Data, however, do not support this argument; instead, research tells us that, in states where right-to-carry laws have been passed, violent crime, including gun violence, has actually increased: *States with Right-to-Carry Concealed Handgun Laws Experience Increases in Violent Crime, According to Stanford Scholar*, Stanford Report, June 21, 2017, https://news.stanford.edu/2017/06/21/violent-crime-increases-right-carry-states/.
18. As Jodie Lawston and Erica Meiners write, "Multiple and intersecting state agencies and institutions . . . that have punishing functions" comprise the carceral state, including child and family services, immigration, and public education. Jodie M. Lawston and Erica R. Meiners, "Ending Our Expertise: Feminists, Scholarship, and Prison Abolition," *Feminist Formations* 26, no. 2 (2014): 549.
19. Mariame Kaba and Andrea J. Ritchie, "Reclaiming Safety," para. 10, *Inquest*, August 30, 2022, https://inquest.org/reclaiming-safety/.
20. Terrence Wilson, "At What Cost? A Review of School Police Funding and Accountability Across the U.S. South," *IDRA Newsletter*, February 2020, https://www.idra.org/resource-center/at-what-cost-a-review-of-school-police-funding-and-accountability-across-the-u-s-south/. "Soft policing" happens when we attempt to replace the institution of police with other institutions that govern, and potentially criminalize, our behavior. For example, the "Counselors, not Cops" movement, while well intended, glosses over the reality of having counselors in schools be mandatory reporters. Counselors are compelled to report particular behavior to law enforcement, introducing police to youth in schools just as teachers and administrators do. See resources about "family policing" here: Erin Miles Cloud et al., *Survival Until Revolution: Mandatory Reporting, Anti-Blackness and Education*, Mandatory Reporting Is Not Neutral, recorded from a live event, October 30, 2023, https://www.mandatoryreportingisnotneutral.com/survival-until-revolution?ss_source=sscampaigns&ss_campaign_id=654d3cefb298f33b24c9537e&ss_email_id=6552714e9c1fb83a7edb0c62&ss_campaign_name=New+Resources+and+Recordings&ss_campaign_sent_date=2023-11-13T18%3A56%3A46Z. Other examples of soft policing might include tracking students, especially students of Color and students with disabilities; surveilling students in classrooms and hallways for particular behaviors; and even policymaker and stakeholder efforts to police what's taught in classrooms.
21. Jeff Murray, "Teacher Pay Increases and Their Impacts on Salary Level, Hiring, and Turnover," Thomas Fordham Institute, Ohio, January 16, 2024, https://fordhaminstitute.org/ohio/commentary/teacher-pay-increases-and-their-impacts-salary-level-hiring-and-turnover#:~:text=Overall%2C%20however%2C%20the%20longer%20a,years%20of%20service%20or%20above.
22. Django Paris, "Culturally Sustaining Pedagogy: A Needed Change in Stance, Terminology, and Practice," *Educational Researcher* 41, no. 3 (2012): 93–97.

23. Carla Shalaby, *Troublemakers: Lessons in Freedom from Young Children at School* (New York: New Press, 2017).
24. Our understanding of abolition in school contexts echoes Charles H. F. Davis III's description of the quest for abolitionist education. It "is not exclusively concerned with the removal of school police and severance of carceral relationships in higher education. It is, instead, an abolishing of an educational system that could have policing, that could have food insecurity, that could exploit workers, that could gentrify neighborhoods, and therefore not abolition as elimination but abolition as the creation of life-affirming ways and places in which to teach and learn." Charles H. F. Davis III, "Imagining Abolition and Educational Safety Beyond Policing," *Medium*, November 14, 2023, https://medium.com/national-center-for-institutional-diversity/imagining-abolition-and-educational-safety-beyond-policing-db-d1ea5046c1.
25. Alyssa Hadley Dunn, "Leaving a Profession After It's Left You: Teachers' Public Resignation Letters as Resistance Amidst Neoliberalism," *Teachers College Record* 120, no. 9 (2018): 1–34.
26. Staci Maiers, "New Data Reveals Gains in Educator Pay, but Chronic Problems Persist," National Educational Association, press release, April 30, 2024, https://www.nea.org/about-nea/media-center/press-releases/new-data-reveals-gains-educator-pay-chronic-problems-persist.
27. Mica Pollock et al., *The Conflict Campaign: Exploring Local Experiences of the Campaign to Ban "Critical Race Theory" in Public K–12 Education in the US, 2020–2021*, Institute for Democracy, UCLA IDEA Publications, January 2022, https://idea.gseis.ucla.edu/publications/the-conflict-campaign/.
28. Alyssa Hadley Dunn, "Teacher Self-Care Mandates as Institutional Gaslighting in a Neoliberal System," *Educational Researcher* 52, no. 8 (2023): 491.
29. Emma García and Eunice S. Han, "Teachers' Base Salary and Districts' Academic Performance: Evidence from National Data," *Sage Open* 12, no. 1 (2022), https://doi.org/10.1177/21582440221082138.
30. Tamara K. Lawson, "Teaching Homeplace: How Teachers Can Cultivate Black Joy Through Culturally Responsive Practices in the Classroom," *Theory into Practice* 63, no. 1 (2023): 7–16; "Black Boy Joy, Black Girl Magic, the History of Black Childhoods, Teaching Black History Conference," Center for K–12 History and Racial Literacy Education, July 25–27, 2025, https://ed.buffalo.edu/black-history-ed/programs/conference.html.
31. Gloria Ladson-Billings, "Toward a Theory of Culturally Relevant Pedagogy," *American Educational Research Journal* 32, no. 3 (1995): 465–91; Paris, "Culturally Sustaining Pedagogy"; Allyson Tintiangco-Cubales et al., "Toward an Ethnic Studies Pedagogy: Implications for K–12 Schools from the Research," *Urban Review* 47, no. 1 (2015): 104–25.
32. Beth Sondel, Hannah Carson Baggett, and Alyssa Hadley Dunn, "'For Millions of People, This Is Real Trauma': A Pedagogy of Political Trauma in the Wake of the 2016 US Presidential Election," *Teaching and Teacher Education* 70, no. 1 (2018): 175–85; Alyssa Hadley Dunn. *Teaching on Days After: Educating for Equity in the Wake of Injustice* (New York: Teachers College Press, 2021); Teach Climate Justice Campaign, Zinn Education Project, https://www.zinnedproject.org/campaigns/teach-climate-justice?_ga=2.18052282.2035492599.1709152130-1753950609.1706663825.
33. "Teaching Reparations Won," Curriculum, Chicago Torture Justice Center, https://www.chicagotorturejustice.org/curriculum.

34. Keith C. Lance and Debra Kachel, *Perspectives on School Librarian Employment in the United States, 2009–10 to 2018–19,* SLIDE: The School Librarian Investigation—Decline or Evolution?, July 2021.
35. We use this terminology here consistent with reporting practices of the researchers' use of it, in addition to the language used in the dataset (National Center for Education Statistics). Keith C. Lance, Debra Kachel, and Caitlin Gerrity, "The School Librarian Equity Gap: Inequities Associated with Race and Ethnicity Compounded by Poverty, Locale, and Enrollment," *Peabody Journal of Education* 98, no. 1 (2023): 85–99.
36. Susan P. Cordell, "Is the School Library a Last Safe Place?," Poster Presentation, 28th Annual National Youth Advocacy & Resilience (NYAR) National-Youth-Risk Conference, Savannah, Georgia, March 5–8, 2017, https://digitalcommons.georgiasouthern.edu/nyar_savannah/2017/2017/121; Pam Harvey, "Bibliotherapy Use by Welfare Teams in Secondary Colleges," *Australian Journal of Teacher Education* 35, no. 5 (2010), https://doi.org/10.14221/ajte.2010v35n5.3; Jill Barr-Walker, "Health Literacy and Libraries: A Literature Review," *Reference Services Review* 44, no. 2 (2016): 17.
37. Qi Shi and Margaux H. Brown, "School Counselors' Impact on School-Level Academic Outcomes: Caseload and Use of Time," *Professional School Counseling* 23 (2020), https://doi.org/10.1177/2156759X20904489; Richard T. Lapan et al., "Missouri Professional School Counselors: Ratios Matter, Especially in High-Poverty Schools," *Professional School Counseling* 16, no. 2 (2012), https://doi.org/10.1177/2156759X0001600207; Allison C. Paolini, "Reducing Gun Violence in Schools: A School Counselor's Role," *Journal of School Counseling* 18, no. 12 (2020). We emphasize again the importance of counselors and social workers whose work is also rooted in abolitionist principles such that they refrain from engaging in soft policing. As social worker Caitlyn Passaretti explains, "If we do not analyze the role mandated reporters play in perpetuating abuses of the child welfare and legal systems then removing cops will merely be symbolic, and the harmful system will continue to be upheld by counselors, social workers, and psychiatrists. Simply removing cops will not remove the criminalizing culture that exists for Black and Latino youth unless the new counselors actively work to untangle the lie that safety requires law enforcement." Caitlyn Passaretti, " 'Counselors Not Cops' Is No Panacea for Schools," City Limits, opinion, June 23, 2020, https://citylimits.org/2020/06/23/opinion-counselors-not-cops-is-no-panacea-for-schools/.
38. Brenden Beck, "Local Government Spending: Policing Versus Social Services," *Annual Review of Criminology* 8 (2024), https://doi.org/10.1146/annurev-criminol-111523-122639.
39. "Food Apartheid," para. 1, Regeneration.org, https://regeneration.org/nexus/food-apartheid.
40. Dylan B. Jackson and Alexander Testa, "Household Food Insecurity and Preschool Suspension/Expulsion in the United States," *Preventative Medicine* 141 (2020), https://doi.org/10.1016/j.ypmed.2020.106283.
41. Diane Pien, "Black Panther Party's Free Breakfast Program (1969–1980)," Black Past, February 11, 2010, www.blackpast.org/african-american-history/black-panther-partys-free-breakfast-program-1969-1980.
42. David W. Chen, "15 States Shut Out Food Aid for 8 Million Children," *New York Times*, January 12, 2024, https://www.nytimes.com/2024/01/12/us/school-lunches-assistance-republicans.html#:~:text=Congress%20approved%20a%20Biden%20administration,But%2015%20states%20opted%20out.&text=12%2C%202024-,More%20than%20eight%20million%20children%20in%2015%20states%20will%20be,families%20during%20the%20summer%20months.

43. *YUIR: Youth Undoing Institutional Racism*, American Friends Service Committee, June 12, 2015, https://afsc.org/sites/default/files/documents/YUIR%20St%20Louis%20brochure.pdf.
44. Maya Dukmasova, "Community Gardens Beautify Urban Space, but Some Seek to Transform Urban Society," *Chicago Reader*, March 13, 2019, https://chicagoreader.com/news-politics/community-gardens-beautify-urban-space-but-some-seek-to-transform-urban-society.
45. See organizations such as Soul Fire Farm, https://www.soulfirefarm.org/; SAAFON, https://saafon.org/; and partnerships between universities and community members like Farm to School, NC State Extension, https://farmtoschool.ces.ncsu.edu/farmtoschool-racial-equity/.
46. Amy J. Anderson et al., " 'Why Don't They Just Move Closer?' Adolescent Critical Consciousness Development in YPAR About Food Security," *Journal of Adolescent Research* 39, no. 4 (2024): 861–87.
47. On the relationship between architecture and violence, see Léopold Lambert and Roanne Moodley, "On the Physical Violence of Architecture," e-flux Architecture, November 2020, https://www.e-flux.com/architecture/confinement/359904/on-the-physical-violence-of-architecture/.
48. Critical Exposure, "Our History," https://criticalexposure.org/our-history/.
49. Lisa A. W. Kensler and Cynthia L. Uline, *Leadership for Green Schools: Sustainability for Our Children, Our Communities, and Our Planet* (London: Taylor & Francis, 2016).
50. Rethink Outside, Home page, https://rethinkoutside.org/.
51. These spaces also create an environment for teachers to commit to refraining from the soft policing that comes with mandatory reporting.
52. For resources, see Mia Mingus, "Pods: The Building Blocks of Transformative Justice & Collective Care," SOIL: A Transformative Justice Project, March 16, 2023, https://www.soiltjp.org/our-work/resources/pods; and Mia Mingus, "Pods and Pod Mapping Worksheet," Bay Area Transformative Justice Collective, June 2016, https://batjc.wordpress.com/resources/pods-and-pod-mapping-worksheet/.
53. Black Organizing Project in Oakland, California, #policefreeschools, Advancement Project, July 13, 2021, https://policefreeschools.org/victories/black-organizing-project-bop-in-oakland-ca/.
54. Bettina L. Love, *We Want to Do More Than Survive: Abolitionist Teaching and the Pursuit of Educational Freedom* (Boston: Beacon, 2019).
55. Harley Litzelman, "Cops Don't Keep Kids Safe at School: The Case Against School Police," Rethinking Schools, https://rethinkingschools.org/articles/cops-dont-keep-kids-safe-at-school-the-case-against-school-police/.
56. Hannah Carson Baggett and Carey E. Andrzejewski, *The Grammar of School Discipline: Removal, Resistance, and Reform in Alabama Schools* (Lanham, MD: Rowman & Littlefield, 2021).
57. Sarah Lamble, *Practising Everyday Abolition*, https://abolitionistfutures.com/latest-news/practising-everyday-abolition.
58. Mariame Kaba and Andrea J. Ritchie, *No More Police: A Case for Abolition* (New York: New Press, 2022), 261.
59. Kim Tran, "5 Transformative Justice Experts on What We Should Do with 'Sexual Predators' in Our Communities," Everyday Feminism, November 16, 2017, https://everydayfeminism.com/2017/11/me-too-transformative-justice/.
60. Ejeris Dixon, "Building Community Safety," in *Beyond Survival: Strategies and Stories from the Transformative Justice Movement*, ed. Leah Lakshmi Piepzna-Samarasinha and Ejeris Dixon (Chico, CA: AK Press, 2020), 19.

61. *Miami-Dade County Public Schools: The Hidden Truth*, Power U Center, Advancement Project, October 2017, https://www.poweru.org/?sdm_process_download=1&download_id=1002; David Yusem, "Youth Engagement in Restorative Justice," in *Getting More out of Restorative Practice in Schools: Practical Approaches to Improve School Wellbeing and Strengthen Community Engagement*, ed. Margaret Thorsborne, Nancy Riestenberg, and Gillean McCluskey (London: Jessica Kingsley, 2019), 96.
62. Advanced Trainings, SOIL: A Transformative Justice Project, https://www.soiltjp.org/our-work/201-trainings.
63. For further resources, see the Transformative Justice Help Desk, "Interrupting Criminalization," https://www.interruptingcriminalization.com/transformative-justice-help-desk.
64. Pull Over Prevention and Mutual Aid Fair, the Mutual Aid Network of Ypsilanti (MANY), https://ypsimutualaid.org/programs/pop/.
65. *America's Peacemaker*, 2016 Annual Report, Community Relations Service, US Department of Justice, https://www.justice.gov/crs/page/file/933521/dl.
66. John Klyce, "How These Tennessee Students Fixed the Car of a Memphis Mother in Need," Memphis Commercial Appeal, September 26, 2023, https://www.commercialappeal.com/story/news/local/2023/09/26/cordova-high-school-mscs-auto-shop-students-band-together-to-help-memphis-mom-in-need/70936001007/.
67. Dean Spade and Roberto Sirvent, "BAR Abolition Mutual Aid Spotlight: Ujimaa Medics," *Black Agenda Report*, March 25, 2020, https://www.blackagendareport.com/bar-abolition-mutual-aid-spotlight-ujimaa-medics.
68. Walidah Imarisha, "Introduction," in *Octavia's Brood: Science Fiction Stories from Social Justice Movements*, ed. Walidah Imarisha and adrienne m. brown (Chico, CA: AK Press, 2015), 4.
69. Woke Kindergarten has a series called "Woke Wonderings," which we draw inspiration from here: https://www.wokekindergarten.org/woke-wonderings.
70. Mariame Kaba, "Illusions of Safety," The Baffler, February 13, 2024, https://thebaffler.com/latest/illusions-of-safety-kaba.
71. Jonathan Friedman, "A Mississippi Teacher Was Terminated for Reading a Book. Time to Reverse That Decision," PEN America, April 11, 2024, https://pen.org/a-mississippi-teacher-was-terminated-for-reading-a-book-time-to-reverse-that-decision/; "Black Lives Matter: Teacher Disciplined for Displaying BLM Flag Sues Florida School District for Discriminatory Treatment," Southern Poverty Law Center, April 16, 2021, https://www.splcenter.org/news/2021/04/16/black-lives-matter-teacher-disciplined-displaying-blm-flag-sues-florida-school-district; Mario Vasquez, "After Police Union Pressure, Teacher Fired for Allowing Students to Write Letters to Mumia Abu-Jamal," *In These Times*, May 21, 2015, https://inthesetimes.com/article/teacher-fired-after-police-union-pressure.
72. "Ursula K. Le Guin's Speech at National Book Awards: 'Books Aren't Just Commodities,'" *The Guardian*, November 20, 2014, https://www.theguardian.com/books/2014/nov/20/ursula-k-le-guin-national-book-awards-speech.
73. Eric Blanc, "The Chicago Teacher's Strike Ten Years On: Organizing for the Common Good, Then and Now," New Labor Forum, CUNY Academic Commons, August 15, 2022, https://newlaborforum.cuny.edu/2022/08/15/the-chicago-teachers-strike-ten-years-on-organizing-for-the-common-good-then-and-now/.
74. Nadar Issa, "Board of Education Moves to Pull School Police Officers," *Chicago Sun-Times*, February 20, 2024, https://chicago.suntimes.com/education/2024/02/20/board-education-moves-pull-school-police-officers.

75. Jackson Potter, "School Resource Officers Don't Make School Safer. School Resources Do," Chicago Teachers Union Local 1, February 22, 2024, https://www.ctulocal1.org/posts/school-resource-officers-dont-make-school-safer-school-resources-do/.
76. Liz Schlemmer, "Hundreds of Durham Teachers, School Staff Stage 'Sick-Out' and Rally Against Revoked Raises," WUNC North Carolina Public Radio, January 31, 2024, https://www.wunc.org/education/2024-01-31/durham-teachers-school-staff-sick-out-rally-revoked-raises.
77. Jon N. Hale, "On Race, Teacher Activism, and the Right to Work: Historicizing the 'Red for Ed' Movement in the American South," *West Virginia Law Review* 121 (2019), https://researchrepository.wvu.edu/wvlr/vol121/iss3/.
78. adrienne maree brown, *Emergent Strategy: Shaping Change, Changing Worlds* (Chico, CA: AK Press, 2017), 52.
79. Mingus, "Pods and Pod Mapping Worksheet."

Acknowledgments

I am so grateful to the preservice and practicing teachers featured in this book, who engaged with me as we started—and continue—the hard work of (un)learning about policing, accountability, and safety. Thank you for sharing your classroom spaces, experiences, and stories with me—stories that were at times vulnerable and painful. I hope that our work together has supported your healing process. I am also indebted to the teacher educators who invited me into their classrooms to co-teach and initiate conversations about school discipline, policing, and abolition.

I am also so grateful to Molly Cerrone and the editorial team at Harvard Education Press. Their feedback and guidance were thoughtful and timely. And I am grateful to the coauthors of chapters in this book: (future Dr.) LaKendrick Richardson, Drs. Alyssa Dunn and Crystal Simmons, and Dr. Kaitlyn Selman. They brought joy, ease, community, and levity to the writing process and to content that could be so heavy at times. I had such a blast working with James McGurk for the images inside the book. He took so much care in translating preservice teachers' ideas and words into novel and imaginative art. I am also so appreciative of the graduate students in our weekend writing group over the last several years, who thoughtpartnered with me and listened to me complain about "how much writing I still have to do!" even as we set forth on the business of getting our writing done during those sessions.

This project was supported in part by seed grants from Division 15 of the American Psychological Association, the Office of Inclusion and Diversity at Auburn University, and the Professional Improvement Leave program at Auburn, which I am grateful to have received. To my homies at Auburn, Drs. Sara Demoiny, Martina McGhee, Reggie Blockett, Evelyn Hunter, Mike Cook, and Charlie Lesh, y'all keep me going.

To my mentors, Drs. Jessica DeCuir-Gunby, Patricia Marshall, Heather Davis, and Carey Andrzejewski, thank you for your words of wisdom, guidance, and encouragement over the years. Carey, thank you for our collaboration about school discipline, which provided a foundation for this line of inquiry about school policing. To my hype-man Dr. Leonard Taylor, you always know what to say and do; thank you for speaking this book into being with me. And to my old and new academic besties, Drs. Sarah Bausell, Alyssa Dunn, Crystal Simmons, Jess Weisse, Kamden Strunk, and Kaitlyn Selman, I am so grateful for our friendship and our collaborations. Alyssa, Kaitlyn, and Sarah, thank you for reading and for your invaluable feedback. To my forever besties Lindy, Summer, and Kelsey, thank you for listening to me and supporting me always.

I am so grateful to my parents, who, over the years, have given me quiet places to write, good food, and love and support, even if not always agreement. And I am eternally grateful for my husband and life partner who listened to me talk about this project incessantly on our porch for literal years, encouraging me every step of the way and making me dinners to enjoy on said porch. To 10,000 Hz Records and the customers there, thank you for giving me a much needed outlet on the weekends, even if I made some of you listen to me talk about this book over and over.

Finally, this book would not be possible without the time and labor of countless students—elementary school, high school, undergraduate, and graduate students—who I've had the privilege to teach and be in community with over the last twenty years. They have taught me and continue to teach me how to "do better."

About the Authors

Hannah Carson Baggett is an Associate Professor of Educational Research at Auburn University. She draws on critical theoretical and abolitionist perspectives and her experiences as a public school teacher to interrogate multiple educational contexts and junctures, including K–12 world language education, teacher education, and K–12 school discipline policies and practices. She is coauthor of *The Grammar of School Discipline: Removal, Resistance and Reform* (Rowman & Littlefield, 2021), and her scholarship has appeared in journals like the *American Educational Research Journal, Urban Education, Journal of Adolescent Research,* and *Teaching and Teacher Education.*

LaKendrick Richardson is a doctoral student in Educational Psychology at Auburn University. With experience as a public school educator, he brings a grounded, practice-based lens to his research. His scholarship critically engages abolitionist frameworks, historical analysis, and critical theories to examine how Black teachers support, affirm, and advocate for and with Black students in structurally inequitable systems. His scholarship has been published in *Multicultural Perspectives, Urban Education,* and the *Radical History Review.*

Alyssa Hadley Dunn is a Professor of Curriculum and Instruction and the Director of Teacher Education at the University of Connecticut. She studies how to best support equitable teaching and learning amidst challenging sociopolitical contexts. She is the author of *Teaching on Days After: Educating for Equity in the Wake of Injustice*; *Teachers Without Borders? The Hidden Consequences of International Teachers in U.S. Schools*; and *Urban Teaching in America: Theory, Research, and Practice in K–12 Classrooms.* Her scholarship has also appeared in journals such as the *American Educational Research Journal, Educational Researcher, Teachers College Record, Journal of Teacher Education, Urban Education,* and *Teaching and Teacher Education.*

Crystal Simmons is an Associate Professor of Secondary Social Studies Education at the University of North Carolina, Wilmington. Her teaching and scholarship centers on K–12 Black History education, antiracist, and culturally responsive social studies education. Dr. Simmons's research also explores how teacher candidates engage with issues of race, identity, and power within the social studies curriculum and classroom practice. Her work is published in journals like *Social Education*, *Critical Studies in Education*, and *Journal of Education*.

Kaitlyn J. Selman is an Assistant Professor in Criminal Justice Sciences at Illinois State University. Her work is situated at the intersection of youth justice, critical carceral studies, and abolition geography. Her most recent publications appear in *Crime, Media, Culture*, *Urban Education*, *Social Justice*, and *Contemporary Justice Review*.

Index